Edexcel GCE History

Protest, Crisis and Rebellion in England 1536–88

Angela Anderson   Sarah Moffatt

Series editors: Martin Collier   Rosemary Rees

D0994835

Unit 3 Student Book

A PEARSON COMPANY

Published by Pearson Education Limited, a company incorporated in
England and Wales, having its registered office at Edinburgh Gate,
Harlow, Essex, CM20 2JE. Registered company number: 872828
www.pearsonschoolsandfecolleges.co.uk

Edexcel is a registered trademark of Edexcel Limited

Text © Pearson Education Limited 2011

First published 2011

13 12 11

10 9 8 7 6 5 4 3 2 1

British Library Cataloguing in Publication Data
A catalogue record for this book is available from the British Library

ISBN 978 1 846905070

Edited by Margie Finn and Elina Helenius
Designed by Florence Production Ltd, Stoodleigh, Devon
Typeset by Florence Production Ltd, Stoodleigh, Devon
Cover photo/illustration © Bridgeman Art Library Ltd: National Gallery, London, UK
Printed in Spain by Grafos SA

Acknowledgements

The author and publisher would like to thank the following individuals and organisations for permission to reproduce:

Figures

Figure 007 in unit 5 from *The Reign of Elizabeth England 1558–1603*, published by John Murray (Mervyn, B. 2001) p.211.
Reproduced by permission of Hodder and Stoughton Limited.

Photographs

The publisher would like to thank the following for their kind permission to reproduce their photographs:

(Key: b – bottom; c – centre; l – left; r – right; t – top)

akg-images Ltd: Erich Lessing 90, IAM / World History Archive 61, Musee Cantonal des Beaux-Arts 93; **Alamy Images:** The Art
Gallery Collection 145, Timewatch Images 18, TPM Photostock 37, World History Archive 25, 129; **The Art Archive:** 171;
Bridgeman Art Library Ltd: Burghley House Collection, Lincolnshire, UK 19, 32l, 180, His Grace the Duke of Norfolk, Arundel
Castle 115, © Lambeth Palace Library, London, UK 65, Lambeth Palace, London, UK 26, 63, Mary Queen of Scots House, Jedburgh,
Scotland / Photo © Neil Holmes 48, National Gallery, London, UK 42t, 67, Neue Galerie, Kassel, Germany / © Museumslandschaft
Hessen Kassel 68, Private Collection 71, 89, 95, 102, 162, Private Collection / Photo © Philip Mould 34, Scottish National Portrait
Gallery, Edinburgh, Scotland 86, 156, © The Trustees of the Western Park Foundation, UK 42b; **Corbis:** 6, © Arte & Immagini srl
85, Historical Picture Archive 16; **Mary Evans Picture Library:** 7, 32r, 57, 60, 149, Castle Howard Collection 5, INTERFOTO /
NG Collection / National Portrait Gallery 38, 44; **Lebrecht Music and Arts Photo Library:** Derek Bayes 81, 161; **Penshurst
Place and Gardens © Viscount De L'Isle:** 49; **Photolibrary.com:** Mike Kipling / The Travel Library 10

All other images © Pearson Education

Picture Research by: Chrissie Martin

Every effort has been made to trace the copyright holders and we apologise in advance for any unintentional omissions. We would
be pleased to insert the appropriate acknowledgement in any subsequent edition of this publication.

Contents

Introduction

The impact of the Reformation and the development of Tudor government, 1536–88

Unit 3, Option A1, for which this book is designed, addresses the development of Tudor government in the years 1536–88. However, it is impossible to understand the events of these years without first understanding the impact of the Henrician Reformation, which took place in the years 1529–36. Prompted by his desire for a divorce and a son to secure the continuation of the Tudor dynasty, Henry VIII seized control of the Church in England and established a Church of England – a national Church with himself as its supreme head – to which all his subjects should belong, and whose officials he could appoint. He was able to do this because the Church was already under attack by reformers, many of them influenced by the ideas propagated by Martin Luther in Germany, who were willing to support the change and take on responsibilities under the new regime. Henry's first appointment as head of the Church was to make Thomas Cranmer, a reformer from Cambridge, the new archbishop of Canterbury. In keeping with Henry's expectations, Cranmer declared that Henry's marriage to Catherine of Aragon was invalid. This legalised his marriage to Anne Boleyn, whom he hoped and expected to be able to produce a much-desired male heir.

This simple summary explains what the Henrician Reformation was, but what it involved and encompassed was something far more complex. The Reformation was a religious and political revolution, established in a series of parliamentary acts and administrative changes across the 1530s. It involved dismantling the machinery by which the Pope, as head of the Catholic Church, had exercised power in England, and replacing it with royal officials, as well as new laws to give them authority and to suppress opponents. A strengthened monarchy with new responsibilities sought new powers to create uniformity and secure obedience throughout the kingdom. Religiously it divided the nation and set up conflicting loyalties and factions that would compete for the power to impose their views. Perhaps most importantly, it made religion and politics inseparable, so that acts of religious faith could be considered treason and rebellion justified in the name of God. The practical effects of these changes occupied Tudor monarchs throughout the sixteenth century, in a wider context of religious conflict and social change across Europe. In effect, the Henrician Reformation and its consequences shaped the evolution of the Tudor state.

Themes and issues, 1536–88

This is reflected in the structure of the examination unit in which you will be studying the development of Tudor government in the years 1536–88. Part A of the examination addresses four bullet points, covering the development of the machinery of government, the role of political factions and rivalries, religious changes and the search for a religious settlement, and the interaction of religion and foreign affairs, as demonstrated in the changing relationship between England and Spain. In each of these areas the Reformation affected existing arrangements and assumptions, interacting with changes already taking place, creating new problems and new opportunities. The questions that you will be asked require you *to make and substantiate judgements* about these developments, relating to the concepts *of cause and consequence, change and continuity and the significance of events. No questions will require you to have detailed knowledge of events before 1536*, but the impact of those events shaped the developments that took place from 1536 to 1588. It may therefore be helpful to consider the themes and issues that arise as a result:

1. **The machinery of government**: The establishment of royal supremacy in the Church led to the *Act in Restraint of Appeals* (to Rome) in 1533, the *Act of Supremacy* and the *Treason Act* of 1534. The dismantling of papal influence and the need to suppress opponents encouraged an attack on the monasteries and the extension of royal power in local government, enacted in Parliament. This brought new resources and new powers that required changes in administration, encouraging new institutions to develop and older ones to evolve. Much of this work was undertaken by Thomas Cromwell, who rose to power because of his ability to manage the changes that Henry desired, but whose choice of tools and methods had long-term effects on Tudor government. Your task is to explore the nature, pace and direction of such developments from 1536 to 1553, to assess what factors influenced them, and to evaluate the extent of change as demonstrated in the governments of Mary and Elizabeth.

2. **Faction and court politics**: **Faction** was an integral part of Tudor politics and existed long before the Reformation, but it was redefined and influenced by the political and religious divisions created by the break with Rome. The rise of Cromwell, the fate of Anne Boleyn, the emergence of the Seymours, the reaction of conservatives and the interaction of political and religious loyalties created the context for factional rivalries from 1536 to 1553, and even into the reign of Mary. Your task is to explore the nature of these rivalries, their impact on events in the reigns of Henry and Edward VI, and the extent to which they affected the development of Tudor government up to and beyond the accession of Mary.

3. **Religious changes**: Although the Henrician Reformation has been interpreted as motivated primarily by Henry's political ambition, it was undeniably the source of religious change and conflict. To achieve independence from Rome, Henry employed the services of reformers

> **Definition**
>
> **Faction**
> A like-minded group who work together to advance a cause. Traditionally factions were defined by personal links and political ambition, but in this period they were also shaped by religious conflict.

Definition

Patronage

The granting of help by a patron. Royal patronage included granting land and income, positions at Court or in other powerful roles.

such as Cranmer and Cromwell, whose **patronage** and influence encouraged the development of Protestant ideas. From 1536 both were in a position to introduce changes in the Church and to promote reforming clergy, and while many of these changes were halted or reversed from 1539, they had a lasting effect across the reigns of Henry's three children. Your task is to explore the causes of religious conflict in these reigns, to evaluate the extent of change and the nature of the opposing interests, and to explain how religious attitudes influenced the evolution and effectiveness of Tudor government. You will also need to evaluate the arguments of different historians, whose interpretation of religious developments in 1536–88 is directly influenced by their perceptions of the causes and impact of the Henrician Reformation.

4. **Anglo-Spanish relations**: The same issues affected England's relations with foreign powers, in particular with Spain, a long-time ally. Henry's repudiation of Catherine, his Spanish wife, and treatment of her daughter Mary was damaging, but not fatal, for Anglo-Spanish relations. However, developing religious conflicts in England and Europe and the accession of Elizabeth fostered tensions and finally war. Your task is to explore the impact of religious conflicts, the growth of economic rivalry and the evolution of Anglo-Spanish relations from 1553 to 1588, and to examine the effect on domestic politics and on the development of the Tudor state.

Debates and controversy

Part B of the examination is focused on two historical controversies which require you to evaluate the views of different historians in the light of your own knowledge of the period. You will therefore need to study the rebellions of 1536–69 and the Parliaments of 1566–88 to develop detailed knowledge and understanding of what happened, and to explore the different interpretations offered by historians. This will involve extensive use of sources in order to gain familiarity with different opinions and the reasons for their differences. Part B questions require you to *analyse and interpret sources, evaluate their arguments in the light of the evidence provided and your own knowledge*, and use this to *develop a judgement of your own*. To reach high levels you will need to understand the reasons for debate, including *the nature of historical evidence and the need for interpretation*.

To some extent your study of historical controversy stands alone, but it is important to see the extent of overlap between the two parts of the unit. Part A provides the contextual knowledge with which you can address Part B, but Part B also extends your knowledge and understanding of the period covered in Part A. By examining the conflicts surrounding the development of the Tudor state, you will also gain insight into the problems faced by Tudor governments and the factors that shaped its development. Considering the extent of conflict and co-operation between Elizabeth and her Parliaments will help you understand the issues that shaped her reign. Similarly, although your understanding of historical debates is primarily assessed in Part B, it also develops your understanding of historical debate in general, which, as Part A demonstrates, is an integral part of all historical investigation.

1 How did the Tudor state develop, 1536–53?

What is this unit about?

This unit focuses on the development of the Tudor state in the years 1536–53. The first part examines the structure of government as it emerged from the Reformation of 1529–36. The second part examines the developments that followed to 1553, assessing the extent of the changes and their impact on government and society. In the conclusion you are asked to evaluate the extent and significance of the changes arising from the Reformation and their evolution to 1553.

In this unit you will:

- consider the key features of English government and the changes that were made during the Reformation of 1529–36
- examine the role of Thomas Cromwell in the development of Tudor government
- explore the development of the machinery of government, 1540–53
- consider the political and administrative context in which Elizabethan England developed.

Key questions

- To what extent did royal power increase in the aftermath of the Henrician Reformation?
- In what ways did the machinery of government develop in mid-Tudor England?
- What was the impact of these changes on government and society?

Timeline

1536	*Act for the Dissolution of the Lesser Monasteries*; Court of Augmentations established; Cromwell issues Ten Articles of Faith and Royal Injunctions; Court of General Surveyors set up; Cromwell appointed Principal Secretary and later Lord Privy Seal; *Act for abolishing Liberties and Franchises*; *Act for extending the English legal system to Wales*; Lincolnshire Rising and the Pilgrimage of Grace (October 1536–February 1537)
1537	Bishops' Book issued and English Bible authorised; death of Earl of Northumberland; reorganisation of the Council for the North; birth of Prince Edward
1538	Bible placed in parish churches; trial of John Lambert; execution of Henry Courtenay, Marquis of Exeter, and several associates
1539	*Act for the Dissolution of the Greater Monasteries*; *Act of Six Articles*; *Act of Precedence*; fear of Catholic invasion – establishment of Council for the

	south-western counties and appointment of Lord Lieutenants in Cornwall, Devon and Dorset (both lapsed in 1540)
1540	Court of Wards established; Cromwell becomes Lord Great Chamberlain and Earl of Essex, resigns as Principal Secretary; fall of Cromwell (June) and restructuring of the Privy Council
1541–42	Reorganisation of the Court of First Fruits and Tenths and the Court of General Surveyors; war with Scotland; English victory at Solway Moss (1542)
1543	King's Book issued and act passed restricting Bible reading (1543); *Second Act of Union* with Wales; war with France (1543–46) and debasement of the coinage begun in 1544 to finance it
1545	*Act for the Abolition of the Chantries*
1546–47	Arrest of Earl of Surrey and Duke of Norfolk; execution of Surrey; Norfolk saved by Henry's death in January 1547; accession of Edward VI; Edward Seymour, Lord Hertford, becomes Lord Protector and Duke of Somerset; abolition of Court of Augmentations; second *Chantries Act*; renewal of war with Scotland and France
1548–49	Unrest caused by social and religious problems; Western Rebellion; Kett's Rebellion; fall of Somerset
1550–52	John Dudley, Earl of Warwick becomes Lord President of the Privy Council and Duke of Northumberland; peace made with France and financial reforms begun; Lord Lieutenants appointed in many counties
1552–53	Second Edwardian Prayer Book issued; death of Edward VI and failure of 'Nine Days Queen' plot leads to accession of Mary Tudor in July 1553

The Tudor state in 1536

The diagram on page 3 shows the structure of government in c.1536 with the royal court as its political and administrative centre. Power lay with the King, but to exercise it effectively he relied on the co-operation of the nobility and clergy, who filled the important offices and sat in Parliament. With some representatives of the lesser nobility and wealthier trades they formed a 'political nation' that represented the kingdom as a whole. Hence the King's power was at its strongest when he exercised it as **King-in-Parliament**.

The functions of the various government departments and the royal household overlapped. For example, wills, property and finance were managed by the bureaucratic courts of Chancery and the Exchequer, but both income and expenditure were controlled from within the King's household, under the care of the **Privy Chamber**. The Privy Chamber staff also included a secretary, to whom the King could delegate whatever tasks he chose, and by the 1530s the secretary's duties often covered matters of state as well as the King's personal affairs. The Council included officers of state, leading churchmen, the greater nobility, and the King's personal friends and servants. Power was distributed in a variety of formal and informal ways, as indicated by the arrows.

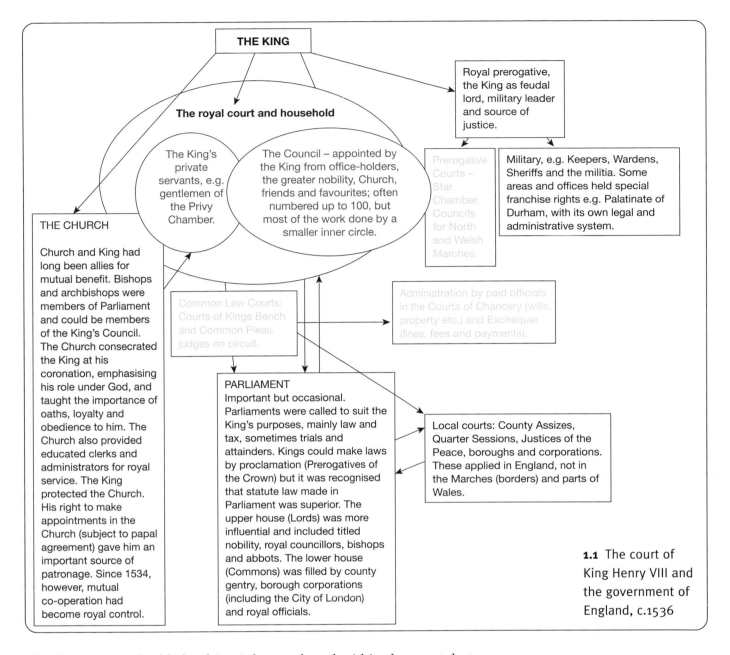

THE KING

The royal court and household

The King's private servants, e.g. gentlemen of the Privy Chamber.

The Council – appointed by the King from office-holders, the greater nobility, Church, friends and favourites; often numbered up to 100, but most of the work done by a smaller inner circle.

Royal prerogative, the King as feudal lord, military leader and source of justice.

Prerogative Courts – Star Chamber, Councils for North and Welsh Marches.

Military, e.g. Keepers, Wardens, Sheriffs and the militia. Some areas and offices held special franchise rights e.g. Palatinate of Durham, with its own legal and administrative system.

THE CHURCH

Church and King had long been allies for mutual benefit. Bishops and archbishops were members of Parliament and could be members of the King's Council. The Church consecrated the King at his coronation, emphasising his role under God, and taught the importance of oaths, loyalty and obedience to him. The Church also provided educated clerks and administrators for royal service. The King protected the Church. His right to make appointments in the Church (subject to papal agreement) gave him an important source of patronage. Since 1534, however, mutual co-operation had become royal control.

Common Law Courts: Courts of Kings Bench and Common Pleas, judges on circuit.

Administration by paid officials in the Courts of Chancery (wills, property etc.) and Exchequer (fines, fees and payments).

PARLIAMENT
Important but occasional. Parliaments were called to suit the King's purposes, mainly law and tax, sometimes trials and attainders. Kings could make laws by proclamation (Prerogatives of the Crown) but it was recognised that statute law made in Parliament was superior. The upper house (Lords) was more influential and included titled nobility, royal councillors, bishops and abbots. The lower house (Commons) was filled by county gentry, borough corporations (including the City of London) and royal officials.

Local courts: County Assizes, Quarter Sessions, Justices of the Peace, boroughs and corporations. These applied in England, not in the Marches (borders) and parts of Wales.

1.1 The court of King Henry VIII and the government of England, c.1536

The departments highlighted in pink were based within the court, but some of the legal and administrative departments, highlighted in yellow, had established a permanent presence in the City of London, and did not travel with the King. The whole arrangement depended on the King's decisions, and was held together by patronage, by which appointments were made and service rewarded. This shaped the working relationships between the different parts of government. The greater nobility expected places at court and on the Council in recognition of their status, but to exercise real influence they took service in the royal household alongside men of more humble origins whose ambition was to join the greater nobility. As the source of power and patronage, the King exercised supremacy over all three of the traditional 'estates': 'knights' who defended the community, 'clerks' (clergy) who prayed for it, and 'labourers' who toiled to provide sustenance for them all.

The position and power of the nobility

By 1530 economic developments were dissolving these social castes into a more general hierarchy of classes. This was hugely accelerated by the Reformation, which transferred wealth from the Church to the Crown and status from the clergy to the **laity**. However, the "knightly" estate of nobility and gentry remained at the heart of government in both court and country. Its members staffed the King's household, formed a significant part of his Council, and increasingly occupied positions in the administrative courts of Chancery and in the Exchequer. There they worked alongside lawyers, who were often themselves the younger sons of gentry and nobility. They provided military support and law enforcement in the localities as Wardens and Governors, Sheriffs and Justices of the Peace. Their ancestors had been granted land by the King in return for taking on these responsibilities within the areas under their control, and this created a territorial nobility who expected to be the King's closest associates, his friends and Councillors, and to occupy the great offices of state. In turn, these positions allowed them to exercise patronage within their localities and to provide access to power and positions at court for their more talented and ambitious supporters. By the early sixteenth century a number of noble families, such as the **Howards** (Dukes of Norfolk), Percys and Nevilles (Earls of Northumberland and Westmorland), and Courtenays (Earls of Devon) possessed regional power bases that gave them some independence, unlike the newer families who were being advanced for recent service to the Crown.

The place of the Church

Alongside those who inherited their lands and titles stood the leaders of the Church, whose path to power lay through education and royal favour. Rewarding talented servants with advancement in the Church cost the King little, but there were dangers in following this approach to the exclusion of the nobility. The type of dominance achieved by Cardinal Wolsey sparked an aristocratic backlash that was primarily directed against the individual minister but could also have repercussions for the King. For medieval monarchs, and for their Tudor successors, the art of kingship lay in managing relations with territorial nobility, to whom a share of power had to be delegated. They were essential for governing the localities, but their rivalries and ambitions could threaten the stability of the kingdom.

By 1530 the power of the territorial magnates had been controlled to some extent. The civil wars of the fifteenth century had pruned their ranks and, as lowland England became a more settled, law-abiding society there was less need for military force. Henry VIII's immediate predecessors had been able to restrict the private armies of the powerful magnates and establish service to the Crown as the way to wealth and power. The steady promotion of royal servants and favourites from the lower ranks of the nobility and gentry went some way towards creating a service nobility who lacked local links and depended on the Crown.

Definition

Laity

All those people who are not in the clergy.

Biographies: The old and new nobility

Thomas Howard, third Duke of Norfolk (1473–1554)

Born in 1473, Thomas Howard inherited his title and the role of Earl-Marshal of England in 1524. The family, which claimed descent from Edward III, lost the dukedom in 1485 because of their Yorkist loyalties during the Wars of the Roses, but it was restored in 1514 in recognition of his father's military service against the Scots. Thomas also distinguished himself in battle. As Duke of Norfolk he was appointed Lord High Treasurer, with a seat on the Royal Council. His political career was characterised by conservative attitudes and factional manipulation. He was the uncle of Anne Boleyn and gained royal favour through this connection, but disliked her radical

1.2 Thomas Howard, Duke of Norfolk

attitudes. Anne thought he was untrustworthy and was proved right when, in 1536, Norfolk was a judge at her trial and condemned both Anne and her brother to death for adultery and incest, when they were almost certainly innocent. Despite his conservative views he played a leading role in suppressing the Pilgrimage of Grace. He persuaded the rebels to disperse by making promises that, he assured the King, could be easily disowned. In 1540 Norfolk was instrumental in the fall of Thomas Cromwell, using another niece, Catherine Howard, to influence the King. When Catherine's behaviour led to her fall and execution in 1542, the family lost favour and several members were imprisoned. Norfolk escaped this, but in 1546 he was arrested as a result of his son's arrogant claims to royal blood and an alleged attempt to install his daughter, Mary, as the King's mistress. He escaped execution for treason because of Henry's death in 1547, but remained imprisoned until the accession of Mary in 1553. Restored to his lands and titles, he helped to suppress Wyatt's Rebellion in 1554 and died shortly after.

Such a man was **Charles Brandon, Duke of Suffolk**, a close friend of Henry VIII who became the leading nobleman in Lincolnshire. In some areas – the principality of Wales and the Duchies of Cornwall and Lancaster – the local magnate was the King himself or his heir. However, in other parts of the Kingdom, such as the north, East Anglia and Devon, law, order and defence were still managed by noble families whose communities 'knew no prince but a Percy' (or a Howard or a Courtenay).

Biographies: The old and new nobility

Charles Brandon, Duke of Suffolk (1484–1545)

1.3 Charles Brandon, Duke of Suffolk

Brandon's father had served Henry VII as standard-bearer and was killed at Bosworth in 1485. He grew up at court as a companion of the princes, and was ennobled as Viscount Lisle and later Duke of Suffolk because of his friendship with Henry. A skilled jouster, he was one of the young King's companions in the early years of the reign, and accompanied him to France in the military campaign of 1513. In 1514 his jousting skills impressed Francis I during the peace negotiations and helped to bring about agreement. He married Mary, Henry's younger sister, in 1515 without the King's permission, but survived Henry's anger through the intervention of Wolsey. Despite this, he helped bring about Wolsey's downfall, playing a significant role alongside the Duke of Norfolk in ensuring that Wolsey was blamed for the fiasco of the Amicable Grant (1525) and helping to convince Henry that Wolsey's failure to obtain a papal divorce in 1529 was the result of negligence and betrayal. Thereafter Suffolk and Norfolk were part of an 'aristocratic faction' hostile to Thomas Cromwell, but there was never any doubt of his obedience to Henry. He served the King in both military and diplomatic functions and was rewarded with grants of land in Lincolnshire, which he extended by marrying his ward Catherine Willoughby when Princess Mary died in 1533. Suffolk was largely responsible for the suppression of the Lincolnshire Rising in October 1536, and was persuaded to exchange some of his lands in Suffolk for others in Lincolnshire to provide a loyal presence in the county. Although he had become the pre-eminent landowner there, his influence was resented by many of the Lincolnshire gentry and he was always the representative of central government rather than the focus of regional loyalties.

SKILLS BUILDER

Compare the lives and careers of Norfolk and Suffolk. In what ways were they similar? How far can the differences between them be explained by their social origins and connections?

The development of the Tudor state, 1530–36

Between 1530 and 1536 the structure of government underwent significant change, occasioned mainly by the establishment of royal supremacy over the Church and carried out mainly by **Thomas Cromwell**. He had travelled widely in Europe and was familiar with humanist and Lutheran ideas. As a lawyer he had both the vision and the skills necessary to carry out reforms through Parliament, creating a powerful state based on law made by King-in-Parliament. In enhancing the power of the Crown in partnership with Parliament he was also imposing limitations on the rule of *Rex Solus* – the King alone. In addition, he set about building up the resources of the Crown and organising a bureaucratic system of administration, based on an inner or 'privy' council, and organised departments of state that could operate, if necessary, without the direct intervention of the monarch.

Biography

Thomas Cromwell (1485–1540)

Thomas had risen from humble beginnings to become a lawyer, and entered service in Wolsey's household. When the cardinal fell from power, Cromwell remained loyal to him. He was elected to Parliament in 1529 and helped to organise activities there to reduce the power and influence of the Church. This and his role in sorting out Wolsey's affairs after the cardinal's death in 1530 brought him to the attention of the King, and by 1531 he had joined the inner ring of royal councillors who were pursuing the King's divorce. In 1532 he

1.4 Thomas Cromwell

was appointed Master of the King's Jewels, a household post that gave him regular access to the King. From that point on he took over the management of the break with Rome and acted as the King's chief adviser, eventually becoming Lord Great Chamberlain and Earl of Essex not long before he was executed in 1540. There has been debate between historians on whether the changes made at this time to the Tudor state were a 'revolution in government' enacted by Cromwell with the Kings' approval. It is now widely accepted that, even if the changes were not the result of Cromwell's far-sighted planning, his political and administrative skills were essential to their success.

In 1536, therefore, Tudor government was in a state of transition. Royal power had been greatly increased by the royal supremacy over the Church. The King was now responsible for the souls of his subjects, as well as their bodies. The new arrangements had been enacted in Parliament, providing clear evidence that they had the support of the political nation but also bringing Parliament into certain areas of government for the first time. This had important implications for the future. By claiming that King-in-Parliament had supreme authority, Henry and his successors could make huge changes in the system of government. As long as they worked with Parliament, there was very little that they could not do. In time, however, it became apparent that the need to work with Parliament could also restrict the monarch's freedom of choice. A start had been made in taking over the property and management of the Church, and in 1535 Cromwell's appointment as Henry's deputy in spiritual matters (Vicegerent in Spirituals) gave him the power to make further changes. In 1536 he also became Principal Secretary and began to develop the machinery necessary for the government to fulfil its new responsibilities and to consolidate royal power across the Kingdom. Between 1536 and 1553 there were major changes in the way that England was governed at both central and local levels.

Religion under the royal supremacy, 1536–47

By 1536 royal supremacy over Church and state was established, and widely accepted. Although the new Archbishop of Canterbury, **Thomas Cranmer**, took the lead in theological debates, it was Cromwell who was given the task of shaping the new Church. In terms of administration there was little need for change. The English Church was divided into two provinces, each headed by an archbishop, with the primacy of Canterbury over York long established. Each was subdivided into a number of dioceses, governed by a bishop with the help of his dean and chapter. They also held Church courts which monitored morals and behaviour as well as enforcing regulations. The King was able to take over the existing machinery, supplemented as necessary by special commissions and, after the monasteries were dissolved, six new bishoprics were established in Gloucester, Peterborough, Oxford, Chester, Bristol and Westminster.
The post of Vicegerent in Spirituals did not continue after Cromwell's fall, and it is likely that its main purpose was overseeing the transfer of Church property and the attack on the monasteries. In January 1535 he had initiated a full survey of Church property, the *Valor Ecclesiasticus,* followed in September by visitations of all the religious houses in the kingdom. By early 1536 he was able to present Parliament with an extensive dossier detailing the 'manifest sin, vicious, carnal and abominable living' that characterised the smaller monasteries and obtain an *Act for the Dissolution of the Lesser Monasteries* and the transfer of their property to the Crown. By the middle of 1536 the process of dissolution, carried out by government commissioners on Cromwell's instructions, was well under way.

Although presented as a process of reform, there is no doubt that the financial benefit involved in the dissolution of the monasteries was a powerful inducement for both Henry and Cromwell. Cromwell may have been aiming to use the wealth of the Church to improve royal finances but he also began to sell off Church lands to the gentry and nobility. It has been suggested that his aim was to give them a stake in the new order and, if this was the case, it proved successful. When Mary restored the power of the papacy in 1554, she was unable to persuade Parliament to restore any significant part of Church lands and property. However, the wider changes enacted by Cromwell during the years 1536–38 suggest that his support for religious reform was sincere.

- In 1536 he issued Ten Articles of Faith, which incorporated distinctly Protestant ideas, for example reducing the necessary **sacraments** from seven to three.

- He followed this with a set of Injunctions in 1536, a Bishops' Book in 1537 and further Injunctions in 1538, all of which attacked superstitious practices and encouraged the dismantling of statues and shrines.

- In 1537 he ordered an English translation of the Bible, and in 1538 a royal proclamation ordered that a copy should be placed in every parish church, accessible for anyone to read.

These measures reflect a distinctly Protestant theology and would, in the long run, significantly change the nature and practice of religion in England. Protestants argued that salvation came only from personal faith and that only the key sacraments of baptism and the Eucharist (communion) could contribute to a soul's salvation, and then only if carried out in the right spirit of faith and repentance. They also emphasised the importance of private prayer and of Bible reading, since the Bible (and not the Pope) was the source of knowledge about God. Hence the Bible must be accessible to all and the role of the clergy was to guide and educate the laity to understand it.

Cromwell, therefore, had many reasons other than finance for dissolving the monasteries. The religious orders were international organisations and encouraged loyalty to authorities outside England. Many had direct links with the papacy. More importantly, their whole purpose conflicted with the Protestant idea of 'Justification by Faith' and the personal nature of salvation. Although monastic orders often fulfilled useful functions – as charities, hospitals, places of safekeeping and hospitality for travellers – their primary purpose was to create a fund of prayer and devotion on behalf of the wider world, for the forgiveness of sins. Protestant ideas were based on the premise that one person's prayers could not atone for another's sins; salvation could only come from personal faith and repentance, so the concept behind monastic life was misleading and spiritually dangerous.

Definition

Sacraments
Rituals given a particularly important place in Catholic practice because they were regarded as capable, in themselves, of contributing to the salvation of all those who were present.

Whatever Cromwell's motives, his introduction of Protestant ideas helped to justify and maintain the break with Rome and extend the attack on Catholic institutions. This was encouraged in 1536 by the outbreak of rebellion in Lincolnshire and the north. While the original causes of the revolt were various, under the leadership of Robert Aske it was given the character of a religious crusade as the 'Pilgrimage of Grace'. It was therefore logical, once the revolt had been crushed, to attack the forces that had lent it support and credibility. The greater monasteries, spared in 1536, were subjected to punishment for any part in the rebellion and to wider pressure to dissolve and transfer their property to the Crown. Cromwell retained some of this to boost royal finances but continued the policy of sales and gifts to supporters to ensure their loyalty. By 1539 the destruction of English monasticism was virtually complete, with both the Crown and its leading subjects benefiting from the process.

The role and influence of the King

At this point, however, Henry himself intervened to slow the process of change and provide clarity about the beliefs that he wanted to define his Church. In response to the growing threat of Catholic invasion, he apparently set out to curb the more extreme Protestants and demonstrate the essential orthodoxy of the English Church by setting out key doctrines and punishments for any deviance from them. In May 1539, he established a committee of bishops to consider a statement of doctrine, from which six questions were derived and debated in the House of Lords. After personal intervention from the King this became the *Act of Six Articles*, which restored Catholic doctrines, such as **transubstantiation**, clerical celibacy and confession to a priest, and set out harsh punishments for heresy.

Definition

Transubstantiation
The belief in the actual presence of Christ in the communion bread and wine rather than a purely commemorative event.

1.5 The ruins of Rievaulx Abbey in Yorkshire, one of the wealthiest abbeys in the country, which was dissolved in 1538

Henry probably had a number of motives. In 1538 he had personally attended the trial of John Lambert for denying the 'real presence' in the Mass, and his distaste for the more extreme Protestant doctrines was clear. On the other hand, his rejection of some conservative demands suggests that he sought unity as well as uniformity. Nevertheless the *Act of Six Articles* was sufficiently shocking for Bishops Latimer and Shaxton to resign, and did mark a change in direction for the Church. This is demonstrated in the so-called 'King's Book', also known as the *Necessary Doctrine and Erudition for Any Christian Man*, licensed in May 1543 and intended to replace the 'Bishops' Book' of 1536. The King's Book interpreted the Creed, the Seven Sacraments, the Lord's Prayer and the Ten Commandments as they had been set out in the *Six Articles*. In the same year the *Act for the Advancement of True Religion* restricted Bible reading to clerics, the nobility, the gentry and the richer merchant class. Women and the lower orders were forbidden to read it, although noble women were permitted to do so in private. This probably reflected the fear that reading and debating scripture could lead to social unrest, as it had in Germany. On the other hand, the act lessened the charges of heresy so that only third-time offenders would be burned.

Historians have been divided on the significance of the *Six Articles* and of the policy that was pursued up to Henry's death. Christopher Haigh argues that 'after Cromwell's fall it seemed that the Reformation was not only stoppable but reversible'. However, the central point of Henry's religious policy was the defence and advancement of royal supremacy, requiring the total rejection of papal authority. It is hard to reconcile this with a return to Catholicism. Moreover, in some areas, reform continued. Some of the *Six Articles* were defined as 'expedient' rather than 'the law of God' as the conservatives had wished, and the dismantling of shrines continued, while **veneration** of saints and pilgrimages were actively discouraged. Similarly the passing of an *Act for the Abolition of the **Chantries*** in 1545 was a continuation from the dissolution of the monasteries and an indication that the Catholic practice of saying masses for the souls of the dead was no longer a key element of faith. Since very few chantries were closed while Henry lived, it is possible to argue that this act was a financial measure and not a religious one. Nevertheless, the act was on the statute books, and under Edward VI another act would be passed that led to the closure of 2,374 chantries. It is difficult to argue that reform was reversed in Henry's last years and it might be fair to argue that policy was eclectic rather than reactionary during these years. Likewise, the royal supremacy was to be taught through an English **primer** and an English litany. The use of the **vernacular**, a key element of reform, was clearly present in the later religious policy of Henry VIII.

In conclusion, therefore, the key features of the Church of England were in place by the time of Henry's death. It was a national Church, led by the King and its key doctrines were defined in Parliament. It was, therefore, subject to secular control. The basic structure of the traditional Church was preserved to fulfil the needs of government in controlling and influencing

Definitions

Veneration

A special act often associated with the honouring of a saint in the Catholic Church.

Chantry

A small religious house that supported one or more priests. It was established by an endowment for the purpose of singing masses for the souls of the dead founders.

Primer

An introductory textbook.

Vernacular

The native language.

the behaviour of the population and securing their obedience to royal authority. However, the institutions that were linked to the authority of Rome had been weakened or destroyed and the doctrines that were their justification had been challenged or repudiated. Doctrinally the Church was already experiencing a 'middle way', although it lacked both coherence and finality. Religious conflicts were by no means resolved, but a decisive shift in government – the subjection of the Church to the state and the redistribution of its wealth – had been consolidated. It would prove difficult to reverse.

The evolution of central government, 1536–53

In the 1560s, scholar Sir Thomas Smith described the essentials of English government in terms that were already recognisable long before 1536: 'The king distributes his authority and power in the fashion of five things: in making of laws and ordinances; in making of battle and peace with foreign nations; in providing of money for the maintenance of himself and defence against his enemies; in choosing and election of the chief officers and magistrates; and fifthly in the administration of justice. The first and third are done by the prince [king] in parliament. The second and fourth by the prince himself. The fifth is [carried out] by the great assize.'

According to Geoffrey Elton these functions were institutionalised in the 1530s by Thomas Cromwell, who enhanced the role and importance of Parliaments; extended royal authority in the localities; and transferred central administration from the King's household to an executive Royal Council supported by bureaucratic 'courts', which could, if necessary, operate without the active participation of the monarch.

The first and second of these claims have been generally accepted by other historians, though with some reservations and differences of emphasis. The third point was, and remains, highly contentious. Debate focused partly on Cromwell's motives and the extent to which he planned the changes that he made. It also related to the pace and direction of development before and after his fall in three key areas: financial administration, the evolution of the Privy Council and the role of the Principal Secretary. By evaluating the extent of change in these three areas it is possible to make a judgement as to how far central government had become 'bureaucratic' (run by professional administrators and officials) by 1553, and how far the machinery of government had developed and strengthened as a result.

How effectively did Tudor governments finance themselves, 1536–53?

As Sir Thomas Smith indicated, financing government was the King's responsibility and he was expected to pay for the costs of administration, maintaining law and order, and external defence. There was no clear distinction between the costs of government and the monarch's personal expenditure. It was recognised that in times of war his private income would not cover all the needs of defence, and in addition to expecting the nobility to provide men and money for his service, he was able to obtain grants of taxation through Parliament. One of these – the right to levy customs duties – was granted to the monarch for life at the beginning of the reign, but the other main form of taxation, the subsidy, was at Parliament's disposal on each occasion that it was requested and was not always forthcoming in peacetime.

The monarch's regular income of about £100,000 a year came from a range of sources – rents from Crown lands, fines from justice, customs duties and feudal payments. The largest of these sources were the royal estates, which had increased under Henry VII and were worth £42,000 a year in 1509. To these could be added the royal franchises, the principality of Wales and the Duchies of Cornwall and Lancaster, which reverted to the King when there was no male heir. Feudal payments were variable, but the system of wardship, by which the Crown gained control of noble estates where the heir was a minor, was very lucrative.

Financial management before 1536

Traditionally, royal income had been paid into the Exchequer but its methods were slow and inefficient. From the late fifteenth century revenues were increasingly paid into the royal household or Chamber. Henry VIII inherited his father's system of chamber finance, under which some 80 per cent of royal revenues were transferred into the Privy Chamber, where income and expenditure were monitored by the King. Lacking his father's interest in administration, Henry tended to delegate many routine tasks to personal servants, such as the Groom of the Stool, who looked after the Privy Purse. Despite Wolsey's efforts to limit their role, the Gentlemen of the Bedchamber wielded considerable influence over the King's distribution of patronage and his management of income and expenditure. Financial management, therefore, depended on the formal but cumbersome Exchequer, supplemented by informal arrangements within the royal household that varied according to the interests and whims of the monarch.

In 1529–32, when Henry was directly in control of government, the Privy Purse was extensively used on matters of state. In 1532, however, Thomas Cromwell seems to have taken over control of government finance, restricting the Privy Purse once more to the King's personal expenditure. As Chancellor of the Exchequer and Master of the Rolls from 1533, he had the clerical staff to oversee the financial arrangements required by the changes in the Church and the seizure of its wealth. In 1534 the *Act for First Fruits and Tenths* transferred clerical taxes from the Pope to the King and set up an administrative court to collect and manage the revenue. Its scope included legal powers similar to those enjoyed by the Exchequer but, unlike the Exchequer, it adopted modern methods of collection and accounting. This court was managed by Cromwell's servant, John Gostwick, and used to finance his policies thereafter.

Changes in the organisation of royal finances from 1536

In 1536 Cromwell established the Court of Augmentations to handle income from the lands of the monasteries, while the Court of General Surveyors (set up by Wolsey) was made a permanent department with its own clerical staff. While Cromwell did not run these departments, he ensured that they followed effective collecting and accounting procedures, so that the Court of Augmentations became a model for further developments. In 1540 the Court of Wards was set up along similar lines to handle income from wardships. After Cromwell's death the Courts of First Fruits and Tenths and General Surveyors were reorganised along similar lines in 1541 and 1542 respectively.

Cromwell reorganised and greatly improved financial administration, as well as finding a vast new source of income in the lands and revenues of the Church. While the Chamber continued to play a significant role in managing the King's personal finances, Cromwell had undoubtedly responded to the needs and opportunities of the 1530s by providing an efficient framework for managing government revenues. According to David Loades: 'The Exchequer remained, processing certain traditional revenues, but effectively moribund, cut off from the financial mainstream. Each of these new Courts had its staff, including regional receivers, and Augmentations in particular constituted a small empire, with nation-wide ramifications. Cromwell did not control any of these courts directly, but he effectively appointed the men who did, and that was sufficient for his purpose.'

Cromwell's 'purpose' was to create financial stability and a firm foundation for government. Although Henry VIII had inherited a financial surplus from his father, he had rapidly spent this (and more) in pursuit of conquests in France. From 1534 the threat of Catholic invasion had mounted as England's rejection of papal authority became clear, and military expenditure had to increase. The likelihood of war led to increased expenditure on the navy, new fortifications along the Channel coast and, in 1539, the appointment of temporary **Lord Lieutenants** to oversee local defence.

Although the Parliaments of the 1530s proved willing to grant subsidies in peacetime, the seizure of Church lands and property offered the best source of revenue to meet the government's financial needs. The ten years following the first closures of the abbeys brought the Crown over a million pounds of new income – some from gold, silver and jewels, but mostly from monastic estates. Some lands were sold or granted for political reasons, some revenue was used to endow new schools, colleges or pay debts, and some was used for defence, but the bulk of it was placed, and could have remained, in the royal coffers.

It did not do so because Henry VIII repeated the mistakes of the past and squandered it in war. His attempts to overawe Scotland, culminating in the battle of Solway Moss in 1542, achieved little except to strengthen the

Definition

Lord Lieutenants
Members of the county nobility who deputised for the King in his military role, and took responsibility for organising local defence against both internal and external threats.

Franco-Scottish alliance. His war against France, in 1543–46, cost over two million pounds and gained only the costly liability of Boulogne, which was returned to France by Northumberland in 1550 as part of his attempt to restore financial stability. To pay for these campaigns Henry received some £650,000 in subsidies from Parliament and took out loans from the banking houses in Antwerp, but was nevertheless forced to sell monastic lands worth over £800,000. In an attempt to strengthen his stocks of bullion he authorised a series of **debasements** of the coinage. This offered some short-term advantage, but making money worth less only increased the problem of inflation, already developing from a rise in population. When he died in 1547, two-thirds of the monastery land had been sold, the gold and silver content of the currency had fallen by nearly 50 per cent – and he still owed over £100,000 to the Antwerp bankers. To make matters worse his effective successor, the **Duke of Somerset**, continued the anti-Scottish policy, incurring more debt, and ordered further debasements that stoked up popular unrest. The attack on the chantries, which gathered pace after the act of 1547, yielded only about £160,000, around 20 per cent of the sum provided by the dissolution of the monasteries. By the time of Somerset's fall in 1549, any chance of financial stability had disappeared.

When the **Earl of Warwick** became Lord President of the Privy Council, serious efforts were made to return to solvency. In 1550 he made peace with France and Scotland and set about clearing some of the government's debts. He also ended the practice of debasement, although the full value of the coinage was not restored until after Elizabeth became Queen. He raised government revenue in many traditional ways, by 'selling Crown lands, confiscating lead, coining bullion from Church plate and seizing episcopal lands – but he was also more vigorous than his predecessor in collecting Crown debts, pruning government expenses and instituting regular audits'. (Towne) In 1552 he appointed a Royal Commission to investigate the work of the revenue courts, in an attempt to cut costs. The Courts of General Surveyors and Augmentations had already merged in 1547. After 1552 others were gradually abolished or absorbed into the Exchequer, so that by 1558 only the Court of Wards and the Duchy of Lancaster remained independent. This did not, however, mean a reversion to traditional methods. Sir William Paulet, Lord Winchester, who oversaw the changes as Northumberland's Lord Treasurer, had previously worked closely with Cromwell. He ensured that the Lord Treasurer had control of the Exchequer, and during Elizabeth's reign the Lord Treasurer became the Queen's most important adviser. Winchester remained in the post during Mary's reign and was Elizabeth's Lord Treasurer until 1572, when he was replaced by William Cecil, Lord Burghley. Rather than indicating a rejection of Cromwell's methods, his decision to merge the courts may simply have been a reflection of the fact that, as treasurer, he could control them all through the Exchequer and that he saw the value of a single financial authority. Most importantly, the methods of administration that were introduced in the new courts were transferred with them.

Biography

Edward Seymour, Duke of Somerset (1506–1552)
The brother of Jane Seymour and uncle of King Edward VI. He played a vital role in diplomacy and fighting in Scotland under Henry. In 1547 he used his links to the young king and his contacts in the royal household to establish himself as Lord Protector and Duke of Somerset. However, his failure to deal effectively with popular unrest in 1549 led to his fall from power, and allowed **John Dudley, Earl of Warwick,** to become Lord President of the Council and take control of affairs.

Somerset's efforts to regain his position brought about his execution in 1550, and Warwick succeeded him as Protector (and Duke of Northumberland) until the king's death in 1553. His attempt to retain power by installing Lady Jane Grey as queen in place of Mary Tudor following Edward's death brought about his own execution in 1553.

SKILLS BUILDER

Cross-referencing

Further detail about the events and policies of the years 1540–53 is included in Unit 2, where it forms part of the explanation of politics and faction in the reigns of Henry VIII and Edward VI. Use the information here to set out a list of key events in the development of financial administration. When you have completed work on Unit 2, write a brief explanation of why each event took place and how it affected the evolution of the Tudor state.

In conclusion, it cannot be claimed that Tudor governments were able to finance themselves effectively in the years 1536–53, but the reasons for this lie in the area of policy rather than administration. Although Cromwell had made a start on finding new sources of revenue and a more efficient system of management by 1540, his work was to some extent undone following his fall. Whether he would have been a restraining influence had he survived longer is doubtful. The impetus for the destructive policies of the 1540s came from Henry himself, on whose goodwill Cromwell always depended. The policies adopted by Northumberland were sensible given the circumstances in which he came to power, and there is no reason to believe that Cromwell would have achieved more. Nevertheless, Cromwell's work was not entirely wasted, nor his policies reversed, and many of the systems and procedures that he had introduced or encouraged were incorporated into the financial administration of the later Tudor monarchs. The work of Northumberland and Winchester drew on experience under Cromwell and, in turn, enabled a new generation including William Cecil and **Walter Mildmay** to develop similar skills. While it cannot be claimed that Cromwell established a permanent bureaucratic system to manage royal finances, the foundations that he laid in the establishment of independent revenue courts had borne some fruit by 1553, and would be of significant value to the Tudor Queens and those who served them.

Biography

Walter Mildmay (1520–1589) provides a good example of the administrators whose careers spanned several reigns and who helped in the development of an effective financial system before and after 1553. He entered royal service in the Court of Augmentations in 1545 as one of its two surveyors-general. He worked closely with Winchester and served on the Royal Commission of 1552. Despite his strongly Protestant convictions he remained in post throughout Mary's reign and was appointed treasurer of the household at Elizabeth's accession in 1558, becoming Chancellor of the Exchequer in 1566.

1.6 Walter Mildmay

To what extent did political administration develop in the years 1536–53?

Alongside the financial departments and revenue courts, there were three main components to government administration:

1. The Court of Chancery

This was a 'writing office', which recorded the King's decisions, sent out his instructions in writing as legal 'writs', and resolved any related disputes. It dealt, in the words of David Loades, 'with every conceivable process leading to the Great or Privy Seal and for the authentication of any judicial process'. It remained largely unchanged and writs 'continued to be essential for what might be termed the transmission of government'.

2. Royal office holders

The second component was made up of royal office-holders, appointed by the King, and in charge of the day-to-day management of various government departments. The main offices in 1536 were those of the Lord Chancellor and Lord Treasurer, who headed the courts of Chancery and the Exchequer, but there were numerous other posts carrying responsibility for financial and legal matters, such as the Chancellor of the Exchequer and the Master of the Rolls, both held by Cromwell from 1533. Others, such as the **Lord Chamberlain** and **Lord Privy Seal**, fulfilled functions that spanned both the royal household and the affairs of state, and there was no clear line drawn between government and household. A number of household officers, such as the Treasurer of the Chamber, the King's secretary and the Groom of the Stool served the King in a personal capacity but could undertake other responsibilities as he directed. (For an example of the power that this could confer, see Unit 2 on the death of Henry VIII and the rise of Somerset.) In addition the King could devise new offices, such as the Vicegerent in Spirituals, to meet new requirements or improve efficiency. As Sir Thomas Smith pointed out in 1583, the 'choosing and election of the chief officers and magistrates' was controlled by 'the prince himself'.

3. The Royal Council

The third component, which overlapped with the others and helped to draw them together, was the Royal Council. Its main role was to advise the King, but Councillors had many other duties. Traditionally the Council consisted of major office-holders, including the higher clergy, some judges, the greater nobility, and the King's choice of associates whom he trusted or chose not to offend. It was not unusual for the Council membership to exceed fifty because an effort was made to include most interests and factions. However, a much smaller number carried out most of the work. Councillors might well be engaged in the work of the Prerogative Courts of Star Chamber, the Court of Requests and the Regional Councils, without attending on the King. According to Peter Servini, 'it appears [that] there were about 25 members who were summoned regularly and frequently, and that a normal meeting consisted of less than ten members.' In that context 'membership' of the Council indicated status, not necessarily power and influence.

Definitions

Lord Chamberlain
The officer in charge of the royal household, responsible for its management and for the public appearances of the King.

Lord Privy Seal
Dealt with private correspondence on behalf of the King, sealing it with the King's private seal, which, like the formal 'Great Seal' of state, showed the validity of a document.

1.7 The front and back of the Great Seal of Henry VIII

These arrangements encouraged personal and factional rivalries, and their effectiveness relied heavily on the character and capacity of the monarch. Until 1529 Henry VIII delegated much of the work to Wolsey, intervening directly in areas that interested him, such as foreign relations. When Wolsey fell from power, the Duke of Norfolk and his associates (who had helped to bring about Wolsey's fall) hoped that his dominance would be replaced by an aristocratic combination of office-holders and territorial nobility. Instead, Henry established an inner ring – the 'Council Attendant' – whose advice he sought on obtaining his divorce. It was Thomas Cromwell's inclusion in this group from about 1531 that marked the beginning of his rise to power.

In many ways Cromwell's career, beginning in the Household and developing through administrative offices, illustrates the way that power was gathered and distributed through both formal and informal channels. At an early stage he was playing a significant role in managing the Council on the King's behalf – drawing up agendas, overseeing attendance and keeping his own records – because the King wished it to be so. In 1536 this was formalised when he became Principal Secretary and, according to Elton, began to overhaul the administrative machinery to make it both more efficient and more institutionally independent. He did this by enhancing the role to include oversight of other departments and by creating a small, executive Privy Council of 19, 13 of whom were leading office-holders. With regular meetings, a defined agenda and its own clerical staff, it was a bureaucratic institution, capable of operating without direct royal intervention.

In 1539 the *Act of Precedence* defined the number and seniority of office-holders in both Parliament and Privy Council. Until Cromwell's fall in 1540 he continued to act as its secretary, thereby keeping much of the management in his own hands, but his demise brought further change. From 1540 the Privy Council ceased to be the inner ring of a larger body, and acquired its own secretary and staff. Appointments to the wider Council ended, and existing members were termed 'Councillors at large'. The Privy Council met regularly and often on its own initiative, with a clerk keeping minutes, and waited on the King when summoned. According to David Loades, '[it] was both more visible and more disciplined than its predecessor, and it also dealt directly with the King, because after Cromwell's fall there was no further chief minister. Politics now found a focus in the Council as never before.'

Nevertheless, the Household remained significant. The Privy Chamber still offered access to the King, and the factional struggles that characterised the period were played out in both arenas. With Henry's death, the new King's uncle (Lord Hertford – soon to be the Duke of Somerset) was able to seize power through his contacts in the Privy Chamber, and tended to bypass the Privy Council, preferring to rely on his relationship with the King and his own household staff. It may be a sign of the Council's significance that this was deeply resented within and beyond the Council itself, and contributed to his fall from power. His successor, the Duke of Northumberland, secured his own power by allying with different Council factions, and increased the number of members in order to accommodate a range of interests. In 1550 he appointed 12 new Councillors, raising the total to 33, and designated a number of them as Lords Lieutenant in their own regions. This enhanced their power, and that of the Council, in the localities while also ensuring that regular attendance at meetings was still limited to a smaller group of members. According to Servini, 'in these ways the administrative machine first expanded by Thomas Cromwell in the 1530s was revitalised and prepared for its role in keeping government going during the ups and downs of the next ten years.'

The importance of the Privy Council increased even more in the reigns of Mary and Elizabeth, partly because they could not use household appointments for political and administrative purposes. Elizabeth appointed Robert Dudley as her Master of Horse, but a Queen's household was, inevitably, staffed mainly by women. Mary enlarged the Council to 43, mainly to make room for her conservative supporters. It continued its administrative role, overseeing, for example, a survey of crown lands and a new Book of Rates that almost trebled Elizabeth's income from customs duties in the first year of her reign. Elizabeth reduced the numbers once more to between 13 and 19, and her relationship with William Cecil enhanced the role of the Principal Secretary to something akin to a managing director. When Cecil became Lord Treasurer, his successor, **Sir Francis Walsingham**, was able to develop the role as the centre of government information and intelligence.

Biography

Sir Francis Walsingham (c.1532–1590)

Studied abroad during the reign of Mary Tudor but returned to England on Elizabeth's succession and was helped into Parliament by William Cecil. His main role in Elizabeth's government was in gathering information, using the contacts he established on the continent.

He played a key role in developing relations with the Huguenots in the Netherlands. He was successful in uncovering the Throckmorton and Babington Plots in which Mary, Queen of Scots was implicated.

1.8 William Cecil, Lord Burghley, the chief advisor to Elizabeth for most of her reign

Definition

Pilgrimage of Grace

A serious rebellion that began in Lincolnshire in October 1536 and spread across the north. It reflected widespread hostility to changes in the Church and the increasing authority exercised by central government over local government, customs and traditions and was probably the most serious challenge to his authority ever faced by Henry VIII. Although the revolt was suppressed in 1537, and the ringleaders executed, there were signs of simmering discontent in the north for some years. (See Unit 5 for more.)

What part did Cromwell play in these developments?

In Elton's view, Cromwell was primarily responsible for the creation of the Privy Council and, by his own example, laid the foundations of the office of Secretary of State, which emerged in the reign of Elizabeth. Further investigation has suggested, however, that while these developments were potentially far-reaching, they were neither as coherently planned nor as attributable to Cromwell as Elton assumed. According to Servini, the Privy Council 'was a long-standing ideal that was helped into being by the events of 1536 [the **Pilgrimage of Grace**] . . . but was then checked by Cromwell's return to prominence for what remained of the 1530s'. He argues that Cromwell's desire to maintain control prevented any further institutional development until after his fall in 1540. This is supported by John Guy, who suggests that 'an executive council taking corporate responsibility for managing the Tudor state under the direction of the Crown' existed from the autumn of 1536. However, it played a lesser role while Cromwell was alive because he still preferred to keep much of the business of government in his own hands. Guy thus states that 'the "permanent" Privy Council was "created" less because he lived than because he died.'

A number of factors helped bring about reform in the 1530s. The political environment encouraged the emergence of an inner ring of advisers, because, unusually in sixteenth-century politics, the government was pursuing a defined objective requiring a programme of legislation. There was every reason, therefore, to develop a council that could act in an executive capacity, managing the passage of legislation, supervising the new arrangements and suppressing opposition. For this purpose a small council of office-holders and managers was far more effective than the larger advisory body. In 1536 this tendency was strengthened when rebellion broke out and Henry needed a small, trustworthy group that could respond rapidly to events as they unfolded. When Cromwell was made Principal Secretary in that year, what had been developing in practice became formally established. On balance it seems that Cromwell did a great deal to create an organised inner council capable of advising the King and helping to implement his decisions. His aim was to make government more effective at dealing with immediate problems, and to enhance his own control of it. For this reason, Guy and Servini are probably right in suggesting that he prevented further institutional development until 1540. Like Wolsey, Cromwell had to deal with the hostility of the King's 'natural' advisers, the greater nobility who held their positions by virtue of birth and status. It was therefore logical to ensure that the Council remained dependent on himself and his staff for its organisation and record keeping. As Servini suggests, '[i]n this way he kept control and it was important for him to do so since the kind of people who were on the Privy Council proved to be his political enemies.'

The same priorities can be seen in Cromwell's management of the various offices that he held, and in particular that of Principal Secretary. According to Loades, 'the secretary's office became the clearing-house for all business, which he and his staff redirected to the appropriate departments. . . .

He ran his own network of spies, both at home and abroad, and their reports came directly to him.' In many ways this foreshadowed the work of a Secretary of State like William Cecil or his successor, Sir Francis Walsingham. However, in Loades' view this was not an attempt to create a new office but 'a completely personal creation, which was associated with the office of secretary because that was where Cromwell was. When he moved on to become Lord Privy Seal, the whole system went with him.'

Throughout his career Cromwell utilised the opportunities provided by the positions he held, but he did not try to institutionalise his power and pass it on to a successor. Like any skilled politician he built up a network of support in all parts of the government machine, including the royal household and Privy Chamber. As Principal Secretary he obtained positions there for his own clients – Peter Mewtas, Ralph Sadler and Anthony Denny – in order to prevent it being used to challenge or undermine him. His later offices included other household positions, such as Chief Noble of the Chamber in 1539 and the office of Lord Great Chamberlain in 1540. When he resigned the post of Principal Secretary in 1540 he made no attempt to preserve it, but divided the duties between two of his supporters, Thomas Wriothesley and Ralph Sadler. If, as Elton suggested, he laid the foundations of later developments, it was by example rather than prescription. According to Loades, '[w]hat Thomas Cromwell did was to create a precedent for a style of organising business. It was not followed up immediately after his fall, when the administration again became fragmented, but after William Cecil, first Francis Walsingham and then Robert Cecil made sure that there was no similar backsliding, and the office of Secretary of State descends directly from them.'

Discussion point

Does the argument that changes in political administration were a response to practical needs rather than part of a coherent plan make them less significant in the development of the Tudor state?

Crown, nobility and people: Government in the localities, 1536–53

Whatever developments took place at court and in the Council, most people's experience of government came through local institutions and the administration of justice in what Sir Thomas Smith termed 'the great assize'. The Common Law Courts of King's Bench and Common Pleas were based in London but extended throughout the kingdom when judges went on circuit to conduct County Assizes, and were supported by local Quarter Sessions conducted by Justices of the Peace (JPs). While the traditional officer of the shire – the Sheriff – was declining in importance, the JPs took on an increasing range of duties. The role was unpaid, but carried considerable status in the local community, and was, therefore, sought after among the ranks of the gentry and even the lesser nobility. JPs dealt with local administration and petty crime, with more serious offences being transferred to the assizes for trial by judge and jury. The laws by which they operated were derived from custom and also from statute law – law made in Parliament – which allowed the system to address new issues, such as vagrancy, when they arose. JPs were supervised by the Council, which compiled lists for each county of those granted the King's commission, and (in theory) removed the names of those found to be inadequate. Their functions were both judicial and administrative, and the

Definition

Liberties and Franchises
Special privileges granted by monarchs to allow individuals or institutions to control the legal system in an area such as Redesdale or Durham. Originally they helped control difficult areas, but they also acted as a barrier to royal authority and consistent application of the law.

number of special commissions appointed to deal with items such as gaol delivery, sewers and commissions of enquiry, contributed to a growing sense among many people that government interference in local affairs was increasing. Whether this was regarded favourably or resentfully depended a great deal on the interests and attitudes of different communities and individuals.

From 1536 to 1553 this system evolved and expanded, but did not require substantive reform. The most significant changes occurred in the extent to which the system, and the royal authority that it represented, operated across the country. Although the King governed the whole Kingdom, in 1536 there was considerable variation in the arrangements that operated in different regions. There were two main reasons for this. The first was the existence of special **Liberties and Franchises**, which allowed private laws and law enforcement to operate alongside, or in place of, royal authority, and the second was the existence of remote border lands where the King's authority and military presence had never been sufficient to maintain the peace and protect the area from foreign invasion. In some cases the two factors overlapped.

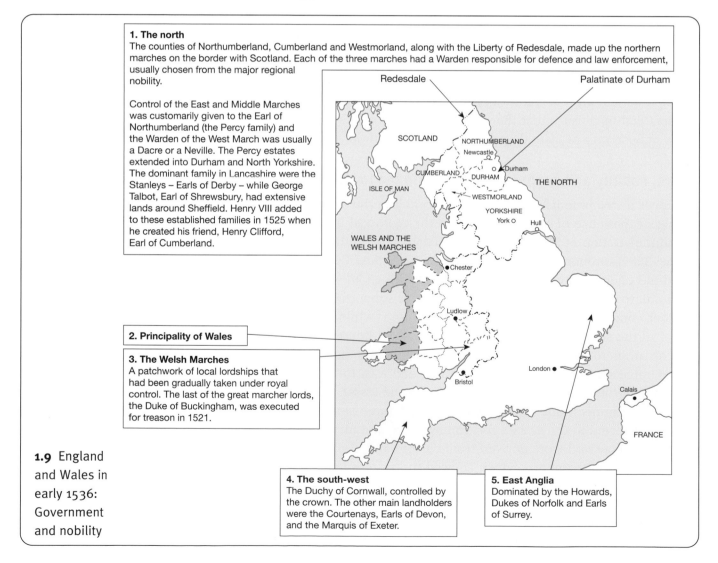

1. The north
The counties of Northumberland, Cumberland and Westmorland, along with the Liberty of Redesdale, made up the northern marches on the border with Scotland. Each of the three marches had a Warden responsible for defence and law enforcement, usually chosen from the major regional nobility.

Control of the East and Middle Marches was customarily given to the Earl of Northumberland (the Percy family) and the Warden of the West March was usually a Dacre or a Neville. The Percy estates extended into Durham and North Yorkshire. The dominant family in Lancashire were the Stanleys – Earls of Derby – while George Talbot, Earl of Shrewsbury, had extensive lands around Sheffield. Henry VIII added to these established families in 1525 when he created his friend, Henry Clifford, Earl of Cumberland.

2. Principality of Wales

3. The Welsh Marches
A patchwork of local lordships that had been gradually taken under royal control. The last of the great marcher lords, the Duke of Buckingham, was executed for treason in 1521.

4. The south-west
The Duchy of Cornwall, controlled by the crown. The other main landholders were the Courtenays, Earls of Devon, and the Marquis of Exeter.

5. East Anglia
Dominated by the Howards, Dukes of Norfolk and Earls of Surrey.

1.9 England and Wales in early 1536: Government and nobility

The extension of royal authority, 1536–53

From early in 1536 Thomas Cromwell began to take steps to remedy this situation and establish a uniform system of law and administration across the kingdom. An act of Parliament allowed the Crown to resume control of Liberties and Franchises, and deprive their Lords of any jurisdiction in criminal cases. In future, only the Crown could appoint judges and justices. Attempts had already been made to strengthen the Regional Councils in Wales and the north, without great success. Henry's efforts to extend control of the northern marches by appointing the Earls of Cumberland and Westmorland to work alongside the Percys and Dacres in 1525 had met such resistance that he was forced to back down, and it was clear that regional loyalties remained strong.

Developments in Wales

Rowland Lee, Bishop of Lichfield and Coventry, was appointed President of the Welsh Council in 1534 and sought to end the lawlessness of the marches by hanging as many felons as he could locate, some 5,000 in his first six years. Recognising that this did not offer a long-term solution, Cromwell ordered the appointment of JPs in the Principality of Wales, and in the Lordships of Pembroke and Glamorgan, held by the Crown. This was followed by an *Act for Laws and Justice, to be Ministered in Wales in like Form as it is in this Realm*, passed by Parliament in 1536, which extended the English legal system into Wales and gave the Welsh a right to send some MPs to Parliament. In 1543 this was followed by a *Second Act of Union* which divided Wales into counties and established Sheriffs and JPs throughout the country. In addition the Regional Council was reorganised to direct and supervise government in Wales and the nearby counties of Cheshire, Shropshire, Herefordshire, Worcestershire, Gloucestershire and Monmouthshire (which had been transferred to England for administrative purposes). The Council was responsible for publishing royal proclamations and transmitting orders, in translation where necessary, and continued to act as a prerogative court of equity (justice) similar to the Star Chamber and Court of Requests in London (see diagram, page 3). The success of these measures can be seen from the lack of unrest and resistance in Wales throughout all the upheavals and changes of the Tudor century.

Developments in the north

Elsewhere the extension of royal authority met greater resistance. The most difficult area by far was the north of England, where a combination of Scottish hostility, conservative communities and magnate power posed serious problems. Defence of the border required a significant military presence and experience had proved that this needed the co-operation of local magnates who were fundamentally opposed to the political and religious changes that Henry had introduced. In 1532–34 Thomas, Lord Dacre and Henry Percy, Earl of Northumberland had successfully dealt with Scottish attempts to seize land in the West March, but neither was regarded as reliable. In 1534 Dacre was accused of treason, and although acquitted, was dismissed and fined because of his Scottish contacts. Henry Percy, the Earl of Northumberland, was childless, ill and in debt. At Cromwell's suggestion, the government took over his debts and used them to force him to name the King as his heir in 1536. The intention was to gain control of the vast Percy estates, which covered large areas of Northumberland, Durham and North Yorkshire, as well as parts of the East and West Ridings. A similar process had already been used to take over the Welsh marcher lordships, but it created fury in the north, and almost certainly contributed to support for the Pilgrimage of Grace. Both of the Earl's brothers participated in the rebellion, as did many of his tenants, agents and dependent gentry. The pilgrims were able to raise an army of 30,000 men and pose a serious threat to Henry's government – but when the rebellion was defeated in 1537 it also created an opportunity to deal with the problem of the north.

In the spring and summer of 1537 the last outbreaks of the revolt were suppressed with considerable loss of life. The main leaders were tried and executed, but many others were executed without trial by Norfolk's forces, and the popular rising in the north-west saw large numbers killed or summarily hanged. The north was being taught a lesson. In addition, the course of the rebellion helped to drive a wedge between the gentry and commons who had participated. Many of the 30,000 men gathered at Pontefract felt betrayed by their leaders' willingness to believe government assurances, while the gentry had been shocked at the independence and lack of respect shown towards them by some of the commons. The dangers of rebellion and the need for social and political authority to be upheld had been clearly demonstrated. In the same year the death of Henry Percy and the reversion of the Percy estates to the Crown provided an opportunity for reorganisation of local government in the north. In the autumn of 1537 Cuthbert Tunstall, Bishop of Durham, was appointed as Lord President of the Council of the North. According to Servini, 'the north was no longer to be governed by a great magnate assisted by a council, but by a permanent bureaucratic council'.

The new Council was made the supreme executive authority for all the counties north of the River Trent, with the exception of the royal Duchy of Lancaster. The Earldom of Northumberland was defunct, and the old Liberties were already being incorporated into the shires (although the Palatinate of Durham retained a few minor privileges). Most importantly, the new Council was responsible for supervising local government in Church and state, and it became very active in doing so. It ensured that the northern bishops implemented the Crown's religious policies, monitored the work of the JPs and acted as an efficient court of equity for the north, based in York. Efforts were also made to address some of the social and economic issues, such as enclosure and rights of tenure that had helped to cause the rebellion. Resentment of change did not vanish and there was a further attempt at rebellion in the so-called **Wakefield Plot** in 1541.

Definition

Wakefield Plot

In 1541 a small group of conservative gentry and clergy in the Wakefield area planned to murder Archbishop Holgate, the President of the Council of the North, and seize Pontefract Castle. However, the conspirators failed to gain popular support and were quickly rounded up. About 15 of them were executed and about 50 others fined or imprisoned. Thereafter the north remained quiet until 1568.

However, the Council proved able to detect and contain it without great difficulty. Perhaps the best evidence of its effectiveness is that, when there was widespread unrest in 1549, the north was remarkably quiet and, when the northern magnates attempted a rebellion against Elizabeth in 1568–69, they found little popular support.

Crown, nobility and gentry – service and reward

Cromwell's desire for a unitary state and his ability to devise appropriate legal and administrative machinery for it played a significant part in these developments. However, they were also enabled and encouraged by changes already taking place in the structure and attitudes of the 'knightly estate' and its relationship with the crown. Without a police force or a standing army, the co-operation of the nobility and gentry was essential in enforcing royal authority across the kingdom, but the Tudors were well aware of the threat that they could pose if they became 'overmighty'. Like his father, Henry VIII was determined to demonstrate that the route to power and privilege lay in service to the King and obedience to his will. Families who showed loyalty did well. The Stanleys, who had supported Henry VII at Bosworth, were created Earls of Derby and became the pre-eminent family in Lancashire and Cheshire. In 1514 the title of Duke of Norfolk was restored to the Howard family because as Earl of Surrey the new duke had shown conspicuous loyalty to Henry in defending the north and defeating the Scots at Flodden. Henry also continued his father's policy of promoting talented servants regardless of their origins, and ennobling men of gentry origins (and below in the case of Cromwell). Although he was far more generous in distributing lands and titles than Henry VII, the vast majority of his creations were 'new men' like Charles Brandon. Some, like Thomas Boleyn, Edward Seymour and William Parr, benefited from the King's marriages, but most were elevated for service given, or expected. Henry Clifford was made Earl of Cumberland; Thomas Cromwell, Earl of Essex; John Dudley, Viscount Lisle and William Paulet, Lord St. John, among a number of similar creations. At the same time, any suspicion of disloyalty led to intimidation and, sometimes, fatal consequences. Both approaches were used to demonstrate that, in any search for advancement, loyalty and service were more important than birth, inheritance and tradition.

1.10 William Paulet

The impact of these policies was seen in the north and elsewhere. In 1536–37 the northern risings were contained and suppressed by the efforts of 'new men' like Henry Clifford and Charles Brandon and the heads of established families who had seen the benefits of loyalty, like the Earls of Derby and Shrewsbury and the Duke of Norfolk. Those who sympathised with the rebels, like Lord Dacre and Henry Percy, found it wise to lie low. What was equally significant was that in 1537 there was no difficulty in finding able men who were willing to serve on the reconstructed Council of the North, and that most of them came from the regional nobility and gentry. As in Wales, the Council was led by a bishop, but its members were drawn from local gentry and lawyers, including some who had actively supported the rebellion, like Sir Thomas Tempest and the lawyer Robert Bowes. The demise of their patron, the Earl of Northumberland, concerns about the dangers of popular unrest, and the benefits of royal service seem to have converted them into loyal administrators.

The crushing of magnate power in the regions

These changes played a crucial role in strengthening royal authority and enabling the machinery of government to work effectively. At the same time, Henry set about the reduction, if not the destruction, of magnate power elsewhere. In 1538 Cromwell mounted an attack on the leading magnate family in the south-west, the Courtenays, culminating in the execution of Henry Courtenay, Marquis of Exeter. Two members of the Privy Chamber, Sir Edward Neville and Sir Nicholas Carew, who, like Exeter, held estates in Devon and Cornwall, were also tried and executed. They had supported Catherine of Aragon, but had remained loyal to the King when fellow members of the Aragonese faction had rebelled in 1536. Despite this the arrests were probably ordered by Henry himself, because of their association and family links with Reginald Pole, whose brother, Lord Montague, was also tried and executed. The Poles were Yorkists, with a claim to the throne, and Reginald was also a Catholic who had fled to Rome and organised a propaganda campaign against Henry and all his works. Such associations were too dangerous for Henry to overlook in a man who, like Exeter, had a territorial base from which a challenge could be mounted.

1.11 Reginald Pole, who became a Cardinal in 1536

In 1547 the same fate befell the Howards of Norfolk. Despite the Duke's loyal service, and his willingness to condemn two nieces to death in order to maintain his position with the King, the behaviour of his son, the Earl of Surrey, brought about their joint downfall. After a poor showing in the war with France, the Earl had made rash claims that when the King died it was the right of the Howards, as the premier nobility of England, to take control of Prince Edward and act as regents. Failure and arrogance were a dangerous combination, especially when the King already suspected that Norfolk had tricked him into sacrificing Cromwell in 1540, and both the Duke and the Earl were sent to the Tower of London in December 1546. In 1547 Surrey was tried and executed, while Norfolk escaped the same fate only because Henry died before signing the death warrant. He was nevertheless stripped of his lands and titles, and remained in prison until released and restored by Mary in 1553.

Crown, nobility and people – changes in the balance of power

By 1547, therefore, Henry had altered the balance between Crown, nobility and people in favour of the Crown. Noble rivalries and factional manoeuvrings did not cease, but they increasingly operated within the boundaries set by the King, and the prize for which they competed was royal favour. According to David Loades, '[by] the end of Henry's reign, although some ancient families were still represented, the majority of peers were of the King's own creation, and constituted a service nobility . . .

[When they took on office in any part of the Kingdom] the King's authority was a sufficient warrant in all circumstances, and needed no endorsement from the personal resources of the officer concerned.'

Nevertheless, it remained easier and more effective to govern with rather than against local noble influence. While much of local administration was carried out by the gentry and lawyers, with some help from the Church, there were still benefits in the existence of a local leader with an oversight and the capacity to bring different offices and sections together. In the north and the Welsh marches there were Regional Councils to fulfil this role, but elsewhere there was a lack of formal arrangements and a powerful local figurehead could do much to fill the gap.

This was particularly the case with arrangements for local defence and for law and order in times of emergency – both aspects of government in which a military caste had an important role to play. In Henry's reign a variety of measures were used. In 1539, when fears of French invasion were rife, Henry ordered the establishment of a Council for the West, on similar lines to those in Wales and the north. The counties of Devon and Cornwall were particularly vulnerable to a French (or Spanish) attack, and Cornwall also had a reputation for unrest and rebellion. At the same time he appointed a number of Lord Lieutenants in the West and elsewhere, with particular responsibility for raising local forces, while the post of Vice-Admiral with jurisdiction over private shipping in the area had been created in 1536. The Council was allowed to lapse in 1540, as was the post of Lord Lieutenant, but the Vice-Admirals continued. Most of those appointed were of gentry status rather than greater nobility, but Henry also sought to establish a reliable nobleman in the area to strengthen royal authority. Lord John Russell, later to become Earl of Bedford, was appointed President of the Council in 1539, and from this time the family's influence in the south-western counties began to develop, replacing the Courtenay connection. In 1545 Russell was given a special commission of array to manage defence in the four south-western counties of Cornwall, Devon, Dorset and Somerset and after he had managed the suppression of the Western Rebellion in 1549, he was appointed Lord Lieutenant of all four counties in 1551.

Similar arrangements were adopted throughout southern England in 1549 when the government was faced with widespread unrest and the establishment of protest 'camps', culminating in the Western Rising and Kett's Rebellion. A series of appointments were made in 1549 and 1550, and although some of them lapsed thereafter, a more systematic approach was gradually adopted. It was from this time that the system of Lord Lieutenants, usually noblemen with regional connections, began to become established across the country. The system did not develop fully until the 1580s, but by 1553 a start had been made in the creation of an effective national system of civil and military administration, staffed by the political and social elite under the close supervision of the monarch and Privy Council. In the words of David Loades:

'An important corner was turned during Henry's reign: this was the process that turned the provincial magnate of the fifteenth century into the court-based politician of the Elizabethan period and eventually into the political patron and party manager of the eighteenth century.'

SKILLS BUILDER

The role and influence of the nobility in Tudor government and their relations with the King are discussed in several different parts of this unit. Reference is made to a number of examples, which you can use to explore the key features of the relationship in the years 1536–53, and trace the changes that took place. Use this information to compile brief biographies of some of them (there are two examples on pages 5–6) and then consider:

1. Who gained and who lost between 1536 and 1553?

2. What features seem to define the winners and losers?

3. How did this affect the authority of the Crown and the development of the Tudor state?

Unit summary

What have you learned in this unit?

- Between the establishment of royal supremacy in the Church and the accession of Mary in 1553, the machinery by which the Tudor state was managed and the political and social relationships that made it work changed considerably.

- The Church was under secular control and the nature and functions of the political nation evolved.

- Royal finances had been overhauled and the Privy Council had emerged as a permanent body of office-holders and advisers, capable of overseeing government on behalf of the monarch.

- The authority of central government and the application of the law had been extended across the localities.

- Perhaps most importantly, a new partnership had been established between the monarch, the nobility and the gentry, based on service to the crown at both local and central government level as the source of social status and economic advancement.

- The relationship was further cemented and given legal authority by regular meetings of the monarch and the political nation in Parliament. Although there would be further development in the reigns of Mary and Elizabeth, by 1553 the essential components of effective national government were in place.

What skills have you used in this unit?

You have analysed events in order to explain their causes and impact, and you have assessed the role of key individuals. The main conceptual focus, however, has been on change and development. You have explored changes in different areas and utilised a thematic analysis to trace developments over a period of time and consider the significance of events as turning points, accelerators or obstacles to change. To develop further understanding of the nature and extent of change, you now need to cross-reference between the key areas to establish an overall judgement. You will also be able to develop a greater appreciation of the impact of the changes as you work through the period and see how government functioned under Mary and Elizabeth – it may well be worth revisiting these issues then.

Exam style question

This is the sort of question you will find appearing in the examination paper as a Section A question:

'To what extent did royal power increase in the years 1536–53?'

Exam tips

This is a Part A question, and it asks you to weigh up the changes made in the system of government and take different aspects of power into account in making an overall judgement. There is no doubt that the system of government changed – your judgement should be about how far the changes *strengthened the power of the monarch*. What does this mean? What made a monarch powerful – or weak? To help you address this you could look at the different aspects of government as Sir Thomas Smith did – see page 12. For example, a strong monarch needed to make laws and be able to enforce them, to maintain law and order, and to defend the country if it was attacked. All that had to be paid for. He also needed reliable partners to do it. This would give you four themes that you can use to trace changes in the machinery of government and how they would affect the monarch's power.

- The royal supremacy and control of the Church.
- The making of laws and the role of King-in-Parliament.
- Law enforcement: central administration and local government.
- Resources: finance and taxation, the role of patronage.

These themes are a starting point. You need to address the question, not describe the nature of government, so your focus should be on the benefits and problems that any changes brought. Take each theme and make a brief list of evidence that you might use to argue for and against the view that royal power increased. Remember that you must span the full time period and not focus on only one king. You should also remember that government operated as a whole, so that changes in one area might well affect others. This is where your conclusion comes in – when you have explained the effects of change in all four areas, take the time to look at how they worked together and weigh up the extent to which royal power increased.

2 Government and faction, 1539–53

What is this unit about?

This unit focuses on the last years of Henry VIII and the short reign of Edward VI, which were marked by factional struggles over religion and access to power. It considers the rivalry between the conservative and reformist factions and the extent to which the struggle undermined the stability of the government in a period of religious conflict, financial weakness and popular unrest. It assesses the effectiveness of Henry VIII's kingship and problems that he left for his successors, and evaluates the extent to which they threatened the monarchy and the state.

In this unit you will:

- examine the extent to which Henry VIII was in control in the last years of his reign
- consider the problems that he left for his successors
- assess the effectiveness of government under Edward VI
- evaluate the impact of faction and court politics on the stability of mid-Tudor government.

Key questions

- What role did faction play in Thomas Cromwell's fall from power?
- How far was Henry VIII in control in the last years of his reign?
- What problems did Henry leave for his successors?
- How far did faction undermine the stability of government in the years 1539–53?

Timeline

1539		*Act of Six Articles*
1540	January	Henry VIII marries Anne of Cleves; marriage annulled in July
	July	Execution of Thomas Cromwell; marriage to Catherine Howard
1542	February	Execution of Catherine Howard
1543		Marriage to Catherine Parr; plot against Cranmer defeated
1543–46		War with Scotland and France
1546		Plot against Catherine Parr defeated
1547	January	Execution of Earl of Surrey
		Death of Henry VIII; accession of Edward VI
	February	Hertford/Somerset becomes Lord Protector; war renewed

1549	June–August	Western Rebellion; Kett's Rebellion
	October	Fall of Somerset – executed 1552
1550	February	Northumberland becomes Lord President of the Council
1553	July	Death of Edward; Jane Grey proclaimed Queen; accession of Mary Tudor; Northumberland executed in August

An ageing King: What was Henry's condition in the last years of his reign?

Henry VIII had acceded to the throne in 1509 with great acclaim. Thomas More had declared at his coronation: 'This day is the end of our slavery, the fount of our liberty, the end of our sadness, the beginning of joy.' By 1540, it would have been hard to recognise the monarch for whom these words were written. More had been executed as a traitor in July 1535 over his objections to the royal supremacy and his successor as Chief Minister, Thomas Cromwell, had followed him in July 1540. In the last years of his reign Henry has been characterised as a vindictive, bloated old man. A recent biographer, Robert Hutchinson, has described him as 'a hideously obese, black-humoured old man . . . [a] bloody-handed tyrant', not at all the 'extremely handsome' young man with 'fair skin glowing' that the Venetian Ambassador Giustiniani reported on in 1521. Age and injury had taken its toll on Henry. His inability to indulge in the sports of his youth combined with his huge appetite had led to his weight ballooning. His disappointments in his marriages, and with his ministers, along with his limited successes in achieving foreign glory had turned him into an embittered character.

Some historians have argued that by 1540 Henry's control over government and policy had waned, that ill-health prevented him from leading in the way that he had in the first three decades of his reign. It is certainly true that Henry suffered from ill health; a jousting accident had led to a wound in his leg that had never healed and varicose ulcers swelled with pus. This condition brought on fevers that were temporarily abated when the pus was drained from his leg (or legs, the evidence is unclear as to the extent of the problem), but the cure was not permanent and so Henry was frequently incapacitated. It has sometimes been written that Henry suffered from syphilis; however, there is no evidence that his doctors treated him with mercury, which was known to relieve the condition, and there were no traces in his children, so this diagnosis is unlikely to be correct. Nevertheless, it is quite clear that there were periods when Henry was physically unable to dominate government as he had earlier. However, it is a matter for considerable debate as to how far Henry's condition meant that he was not in control. A key focus in this unit is the development of factional struggles in government and the extent to which Henry was a victim or a manipulator of them. One event that illustrates the problem was the fall of Thomas Cromwell in 1540.

2.1 Henry as a young man

2.2 An anonymous portrait of Henry in old age

Why did Cromwell fall from power?

The key event that marks the onset of a new era in Henry's reign was the execution of his chief minister, the Vicegerent in Spirituals and newly-ennobled Earl of Essex, Thomas Cromwell. Cromwell's fall represents the victory of the conservative faction over the reformists.

The role of faction: Religion and politics

Faction was not new to government but the events of the 1530s had made factional rivalries more intense as personal ambition and the struggle for patronage and power became interwoven with religious loyalties. The conservative faction was led by the Duke of Norfolk and **Stephen Gardiner**, Bishop of Winchester. In politics the conservatives opposed the rise of the '**new man**' and believed that the nobility should take the lead in advising the Crown. They accepted the royal supremacy and the break from Rome, but they were orthodox in religion and believed that Cromwell's reforms had gone too far. Their role in Cromwell's fall is outlined on pages 34–5. On the other hand, the reformist faction, at this time led by Cromwell and Thomas Cranmer, Archbishop of Canterbury, regarded the royal supremacy as the starting point for reform. They wanted, in particular, to develop the English Church practices so that there was a greater emphasis on both the authority of scripture and the need for preaching than there had been before the break with Rome. As long as Cromwell remained the King's chief adviser, the reformist faction was able to advance their cause, but in 1538–40 a number of events combined to weaken his position.

The trial and execution of John Lambert, 1538

In the mid 1530s, Cromwell had steered the Reformation along reformist lines. The emphasis on the essential role of scripture, the lesser role of the sacraments in the Bishops' Book (1537) and the discouragement of pilgrimages in the Royal Injunctions (1538) were all innovations that were associated with the continental Reformation. Henry had accepted these changes in so far as his minister was not prevented from implementing them, but by 1538 there were clear signs of his preference for orthodox religious beliefs. The first signal was the trial and execution of John Lambert. Lambert was accused of denying the real presence of Christ in the Eucharist in a sermon he delivered to a congregation that included Bishop Gardiner. He was duly arrested and charged with heresy. Henry himself presided over the trial at Whitehall. The trial exposed the weaknesses of the reformist faction. Cranmer's defence of Lambert was weak, while Cromwell was not prepared to intervene and Henry pronounced Lambert condemned by his own words. Lambert was burnt to death at the stake on 22 November 1538. This was then followed by a royal proclamation confirming transubstantiation and clerical celibacy. The reformist faction was now significantly threatened. Cranmer felt obliged to despatch his wife to Germany to safeguard his own position.

The importance of the Act of Six Articles, 1539

The conservative faction was now able to take the initiative. Although Gardiner was temporarily excluded from the Council at the time, conservatives such as the Earl of Surrey and Sir John Russell were able to promote the fortunes of their faction at the expense of Cromwell and Cranmer, who found themselves isolated in the Council. They were delighted by the announcement that Henry intended to pass a bill through Parliament that would establish uniformity in religion and bring an end to experimentation. Although Cromwell was made chairman of the committee to draw up the bill, his position was too weak to temper Henry's desires and, in any case, Norfolk and Gardiner were there to ensure that orthodoxy was restored to the Church. The *Act of Six Articles* reasserted the royal supremacy – the reform that the conservatives accepted – and went on to confirm transubstantiation, enforce communion in both kinds for the clergy alone and outlaw clerical marriage. The punishment for denying the real presence of Christ in the Eucharist was now automatic burning with no leniency for retraction. The act, which was steered through the House of Lords by Norfolk, demonstrated that Henry had returned to more traditional Catholic doctrine and raised the conservatives' hopes that the time was ripe to launch an attack on Cromwell.

At first, Cromwell appeared to have regained some of his lost influence by the passing of the *Act of Precedence*. As Vicegerent in Spirituals he was given precedence over all the peers of the realm, but the act also elevated the holders of the great offices of state and many of these were held by hereditary peers who were then given positions in the Privy Council. This tilted the balance in favour of the conservative faction.

Biography

Stephen Gardiner (1483–1555)

Stephen Gardiner became Bishop of Winchester in the reign of Henry VIII and was restored to office (known as a see) by Mary Tudor. He opposed the Reformation and was removed from office during the reign of Edward VI. He spent the latter years of Edward's reign in the Tower. He became Mary's most valued adviser and served on her Privy Council as Lord Chancellor.

Although Cromwell sought to redress this weakness by taking the leading position in the Council and by his successful pressure on the King to ennoble him as Earl of Essex, he was unable to prevent events conspiring against him. In 1540, it was foreign affairs that gave his enemies the opportunity to strike.

The Cleves marriage and the rise of Catherine Howard

Cromwell's management of Henry's foreign affairs in the latter years of the 1530s had been focused on a Protestant alliance with the Duke of **Cleves** to counteract the threat of a Catholic crusade against England by Francis I of France and Charles V, Holy Roman Emperor. This was achieved by Henry's marriage to the Duke's sister Anne on 6 January 1540. However, the marriage was spectacularly unsuccessful. Henry was gravely disappointed with his fourth wife's appearance and refused to consummate the marriage. Henry believed that his chief minister had duped him into the marriage by means of a flattering portrait combined with warnings of dire consequences if the marriage did not go ahead. By mid-1540, however, the marriage was no longer necessary because of developments in the ongoing wars involving Francis I and Charles V (the **Hapsburg–Valois conflict**). The Duke of Norfolk, acting as Henry's envoy, had entered into discussion with the French king concerning the circumstances in which the French would be prepared to break the peace established with the Emperor at Nice the previous year, and indeed by April 1540 the renewal of the Hapsburg–Valois conflict seemed certain. What was now most threatening to Cromwell was that his removal from office appeared to be one factor that would enhance Henry's chances of reaching an accord with Francis I.

The Duke of Norfolk was not slow to act. He had long desired to exercise the same degree of influence that he had done when his niece, Anne Boleyn, was Queen. The circumstances were all propitious and the final ingredient presented itself in the figure of Catherine Howard, the daughter of his impoverished younger brother, Edmund Howard. Catherine was attractive and flirtatious, and soon caught the eye of the King when she was introduced at court. It was not long before she was the King's mistress. Henry was flattered that a young girl (Catherine was aged between 17 and 19 years) could be attracted to him. He described her as his 'rose without a thorn' and was desperate to end his marriage with Anne in order to wed Catherine. Cromwell was quick to oblige and set about securing an annulment, but the tide was already moving against him.

The arrest and execution of Thomas Cromwell

Norfolk took advantage of Cromwell's weakness to drive home accusations that the King's chief minister was a heretic and supported **sacramentarians** in Calais, who had been charged with heresy by Lord Lisle. This accusation was given greater validity when Robert Barnes, a reformer who subscribed to some Lutheran ideas and a friend of Cromwell,

2.3 Catherine Howard

Definitions

Cleves

A duchy in the Holy Roman Empire, located on the northern Rhineland.

Hapsburg–Valois conflict

The series of wars between the imperial house of Charles V (Hapsburg) and the royal house of Francis I (Valois) between 1521 and 1559.

Sacramentarian

Christians who denied the real presence of Christ in the Eucharist.

reverted to the reformist views that he had previously recanted under pressure from Gardiner. Barnes and two others – William Jerome and Thomas Garret – were arrested, tried in secret and then burned at Smithfield two days after Cromwell's execution.

Cromwell's association with reformers proved to be the final nail in his coffin. He was arrested at a Council meeting on 10 June 1540 and charged with heresy and treason. The King's former chief minister was denied the right of a full trial. Instead he was convicted by means of an *Act of Attainder* that was steered through the Lords by Norfolk, and which gave Cromwell no chance of putting up a defence. He was beheaded on Tower Hill on 28 July, after he had provided the necessary evidence that allowed Henry to obtain his annulment from Anne of Cleves. His manner of execution was the final act of revenge by his master. The executioner, a man called Guerra, was – it has been claimed – selected for his inexperience and the execution was a botched affair with several axe strokes swung into Cromwell's body before the final decapitation.

The victory of the conservative faction

The execution of Cromwell marked the high point of the conservatives' fortunes, and it was followed by Henry's immediate marriage to Catherine Howard. This would give greater access to Henry and they had high hopes that the new Queen could be used as a means of influence over the King. The reformist faction appeared to be much weaker in 1540; Cromwell, its leader, had been executed and there was no one of sufficient ability to take his place. Archbishop Cranmer may well have played that role, but he did not have political ambitions and deferred to Henry. Cromwell's most loyal supporters had been purged at the time of his fall, so the leadership of the reformist faction fell to Edward Seymour. He was the brother of Jane (Henry's third wife, who died soon after childbirth) and uncle to Prince Edward, Henry's son by her. The victory of the conservatives was not, however, to be permanent. As Henry aged, the factional strife around the throne intensified and struggle was to be a constant feature of government for the next seven years.

SKILLS BUILDER

How far was factional struggle responsible for the execution of Thomas Cromwell?

This is a causation question which requires you to identify the reasons for Cromwell's fall and execution. You need to make a list of the reasons. Then look at each reason in more depth. Which reasons are caused by factional struggle? Which reasons were independent of the factions? Can you identify any ways in which the factions were able to exploit these reasons? Now, weigh up the relative importance of the reasons. Consider whether the outcome would have been different if faction had not played any role. Is it possible to distinguish between Cromwell's fall and his execution?

Victory squandered: The fall of Catherine Howard, 1542

The victory of the conservatives was short-lived. Catherine Howard had been a key player in Norfolk's scheme to lure Henry away from Cromwell and to ensure the rise of his family and the conservative faction. Henry had married her on 28 July 1540, the same day as Cromwell was executed. However, Norfolk was to be greatly disappointed in the value of his niece after the marriage. Catherine was no Anne Boleyn; she possessed no political skills to manage or manipulate the King, and had very little personal interest in him either. Henry was more than 30 years older than Catherine, obese and with pustulating sores on his legs that no doubt stank. Catherine was young, fond of dancing and inclined to flirtation. Catherine's indiscretions, which appear to have been known and encouraged by the women of her household, soon became her undoing. The anti-Howard faction gathered the evidence and Cranmer presented it to Henry in a sealed document at Mass. Initially Henry was furious with the 'messengers' whom he believed had been duped by Catherine's enemies, but as the investigation progressed, it became evident that it was Henry who had been made the fool. Catherine, it emerged, had been caught with lute player, Henry Manox, at the home of her aunt, the Dowager Duchess of Norfolk, at the age of 15, and at the age of 17 may well have contracted herself in marriage with Francis Dereham. If vows were exchanged then the union would have been regarded as legally binding by the Church. Even more indiscreetly, Catherine had appointed Dereham as her private secretary and usher of her chamber when she became Queen. Under interrogation, Dereham confessed and implicated Thomas Culpeper, one of Henry's favourites in the Privy Chamber. Full details of the affair were extracted and a trial was held. Dereham was hanged, drawn and quartered at Tyburn on 10 December 1541. Culpeper was executed the same day by beheading – his sentence reduced because of his past service to the King. Catherine and her 'minder', Lady Jane Rochford, followed him on 13 February 1542.

The entire affair was disastrous for Norfolk and could have had more serious consequences than it did. Norfolk disowned his niece; he declared himself to be outraged by her behaviour. However, although his family suffered – his step-mother Agnes, the Dowager Duchess of Norfolk, and Lord William Howard were both imprisoned and their property seized – Norfolk himself managed to escape the worst punishment, though he and his son removed themselves from court for a period until Henry's wrath had been quelled. Most importantly, the conservative faction was significantly weakened, leaving the Privy Council divided under the erratic control of an ageing monarch.

The ageing tyrant: The struggle for control, 1543–46

The picture of Henry VIII in his final years is that of a vindictive bully, conducting a reign of terror in which fear was the main method of control. Raphael Holinshead, the English chronicler who died in 1580, claimed that Henry executed 78,000 people. More recently, Robert Hutchinson has put

Discussion point

What do you think was the most important effect of faction on Tudor government?

the figure at 150,000 by using evidence from reports of executions from the county assizes compiled throughout the reign together with those killed for treason, heresy and insurrection. This is an astonishingly high figure for a country with a population of approximately two million in 1520. It certainly supports the view of Henry as a tyrannical leader and there are few historians who would dispute this depiction. At best, the more sympathetic historian points to mitigating circumstances: disappointment in marriage, debilitating illness and factional struggle that affected the stability of the government. The plotting by those around Henry who vied for power intensified in the last three years of his reign and serves to illustrate the extent to which Henry can be regarded as a bully – unpredictable, dangerous and taking pleasure in watching others squirm as he encouraged the plots before turning on the instigators.

How far did Henry direct policy during this period?

There is little doubt that this period was dominated by factional struggle and most historians agree that it had a significant impact on the development of government, in particular on the extent to which the King could exercise authority. Henry was certainly weakened by illness and embittered by a series of failed marriages, and it is thus difficult to challenge A.G.R. Smith's conclusion that Henry was 'at best only in partial control of the court intrigues'. However, it is important not to exaggerate Henry's weakness. After the execution of Catherine Howard, he sought solace in adventurous foreign affairs that would restore his manhood and his honour, and enable him to taste the glory that had eluded him in his earlier years. The results were unimpressive and could not justify the cost, but Henry's own objectives were fulfilled. In spite of increasingly frequent bouts of illness, Henry led his own army of 48,000 men into battle against the French in June 1544. This action clearly refutes the claim that Henry had little or no control over policy in the final years of his reign. It is also certain that it was his decision not to honour the agreement made with Charles V in 1543 and, instead of participating in a joint attack on Paris, Henry laid siege to Boulogne and captured the port. The total cost of his foreign affairs in the 1540s exceeded two million pounds. This was the equivalent of the total expenditure for a decade in peacetime.

2.4 The English land at Boulogne

Cromwell's plans to make the Crown financially independent by the dissolution of the monasteries were swept away within a matter of years. Henry was obliged to fund his military campaign with increased borrowing and the sale of ex-religious lands, as well as by taxation and forced loans. Finally, he resorted to debasement of the coinage, which left a disastrous legacy for his children and ultimately weakened the English monarchy. However, at the time, the decision of the King was paramount and it is clear that this was his policy.

There is further evidence that Henry directed policy if one considers the development of the Reformation during the period. It was Henry's decision to end religious experimentation by the *Act of Six Articles* in 1539, and this position was reinforced in the so-called 'King's Book' and the *Act for the Advancement of True Religion* in 1543. Indeed, in his last speech to Parliament at Christmas 1545, Henry emphasised that he wanted an end to the struggle between the two extreme positions on religion and that his decision to steer a middle way in religion was the only policy. According to David Starkey, he was serving a clear warning to both sides that they were 'flouting royal spiritual authority' and this would not be tolerated. This attitude is clearly demonstrated in Henry's response to the factional struggles in which both sides were embroiled in the last four years of his reign, as the conservatives sought to restore their position by accusing the reformist leaders of heresy.

Discussion point

What is the evidence that Henry had control over policy during this period? With a partner make a list with three points in favour and three against.

The rise of the reformist faction: Marriage to Catherine Parr

Henry had at last learned something from his marriages. In his final marriage, he did not seek to boost his ego, but instead chose a wife who could best attend to his needs. **Catherine Parr**, who had been widowed twice and whose previous husband had been much older than her, proved to be an ideal choice. She married Henry on 12 July 1543, much to the alarm of the conservative faction for Catherine held reformist views. Catherine was close to the Seymour family and she introduced reformist scholars to court and, perhaps more significantly, into the education of the royal children, Edward and Elizabeth. Catherine's presence and influence with the King gave the reformist faction a definite advantage in Henry's final years. It was this influence that drove the conservatives to instigate plots against both Cranmer and the new Queen in an attempt to wrest control from the reformers.

Biography

Catherine Parr (1512–1548)

Catherine was born around 1512. She was the eldest child of Sir Thomas Parr, a descendant of Edward III. She played a very influential role in the education of Edward and Elizabeth, and encouraged the appointment of reformist humanist tutors. After Henry's death, she married Sir Thomas Seymour, brother of the Lord Protector and uncle of the King. She died six days after childbirth in 1548.

SKILLS BUILDER

Use the Internet to find out more about Catherine's reformist views and her associates. Use this research to develop your notes on the influence Catherine had at court and her importance to the reformist faction.

2.5 Catherine Parr

The plot against Cranmer, 1543

The conservatives greatly desired to remove Cranmer as archbishop. The development of religion along more traditional lines provided them with their long-desired chance to denounce Cranmer as a heretic and a traitor. Gardiner collected evidence from the clerics in Canterbury that Cranmer continued to promote reformers and encouraged preaching. The evidence was presented to Henry, who agreed that Cranmer should be seized at the Council table and sent to the Tower. However, when the Council turned upon Cranmer, he produced a ring given to him by the King and indicating that Cranmer had Henry's full support.

It was the turn of the conservatives to panic. Henry put Cranmer in charge of the very investigation that was supposed to unseat him! In the meantime, Henry savagely reprimanded Gardiner and his supporters. It is possible to argue from this event that Henry had learned not to allow another faithful servant to fall victim to factional intrigue, or that he wanted to show both sides that he would not tolerate division when he was preparing for war against France. Whatever the reason, it is impossible to ignore the spiteful attitude he adopted by allowing the conservatives to proceed with the plot in the knowledge that he intended to turn the tables upon them. He demonstrated the same characteristic in handling the plot against Catherine Parr in 1546.

The plot against Catherine Parr, 1546

Having failed to remove Cranmer, the conservatives turned their attention to Catherine Parr. Norfolk believed that Catherine was a dangerous influence on the King and that she pressurised him to accept her reformist views. Gardiner was sent to the King to alert him to Catherine's heretical views and to offer to gather the evidence against her. Henry agreed and put **Thomas Wriothesley** in charge of the investigation. However, in the meantime, he contrived to make sure that Catherine was alerted to the danger. She threw herself on the King's mercy and promised to be guided by him in religious matters. When Wriothesley arrived with 40 men to arrest the Queen he was subjected to a dressing down and thrown out of the chamber as a 'knave'. Again, all the evidence of this incident points to the relish with which the King played off the two sides against each other rather than bringing the struggle to an end.

Victory of the reformists: The collapse of the conservative faction

The failure of the plots against Cranmer and Catherine spelled disaster for the conservatives. Although they must have gained some satisfaction from the traditional religious policy that had achieved pre-eminence, there was no doubt that they had lost the struggle for control of the King. Hertford's success in Scotland, the influence of Catherine Parr and the rise of Sir Anthony Denny all put the ball firmly in the reformist court. In October 1546 Denny, a key supporter in the reformist faction, was made Chief Gentleman of the King's Privy Chambers, a position that had increasing significance since the King's illness meant he spent a greater amount of time in his private apartments and Denny was able to control access to him. Most importantly, Denny was one of those authorised to witness the use of the **dry stamp**. This was used in the latter years of Henry's reign, as failing eyesight and ill health reduced the number of official documents he handled himself.

While the reformist faction grew in strength, the power of the conservatives collapsed. The first to fall was Stephen Gardiner.

Biography

Thomas Wriothesley, 1st Earl of Southampton (1505–1550)

Wriothesley came into government in the service of Wolsey and Cromwell. He was richly rewarded for his work with extensive ex-religious lands in Southampton and Winchester. In 1540 he became one of the King's Principal Secretaries and in 1544 was made Lord Chancellor. He was created Earl of Southampton in February 1547 according to the dead King's wishes.

Definition

Dry stamp

A copy of Henry's signature that was stamped onto documents and inked in to provide a perfect 'signature'.

In late 1546, he refused a request to hand over certain ecclesiastical lands to enable Henry to define more explicitly the boundaries of his royal estates. Gardiner found himself excluded from court. Unable to bring himself to leave the centre of power, he spent the King's last month skulking around in the outer chambers hoping in vain for readmittance.

Gardiner would survive to serve once more under Mary Tudor; the Howard family were not so lucky. Norfolk's son, the Earl of Surrey, had initially distinguished himself in the French campaign, but in January 1546 he lost 205 men in a skirmish with a French force at St Etienne. Surrey was blamed for the defeat, the consequence of his incompetent leadership, and he immediately fell out of Henry's favour. Hertford was elevated to the supreme military role. Worse was to come: Surrey was indiscreet, not only in voicing his family's royal heritage and particularly his Plantagenet blood through his mother's line (the Plantagenets had been the ruling dynasty before the Tudors), but also in bearing the royal arms of Edward the Confessor. This was particularly dangerous as Henry's health declined and it became increasingly evident that he would be leaving a minor to succeed him. Hertford, who had ambitions to rule as protector for his nephew, struck. On 2 December, he brought evidence to the Privy Council that Surrey had committed treason. Henry was seized with a great desire to destroy Surrey. He was arrested and taken to the Tower, where he was interrogated. He was executed for treason on 19 January 1547. Norfolk was lucky to escape with his life. He, too, was arrested and sent to the Tower. An act of attainder declared both Surrey and Norfolk guilty of treason – of plotting to control Edward after Henry's death. However, Norfolk escaped death because Henry died before signing the order for his execution. The conservative faction was finished.

The death of Henry VIII

Henry died on 28 January 1547, probably of kidney and liver failure aggravated by his obesity. His death was kept secret for three days while the victors in the factional struggle manipulated the contents of his will. Henry had left instructions for a Regency Council of 16 men to rule equally until Edward reached the age of 18. In fact, Edward Seymour, Earl of Hertford and uncle to the new King, would rule as Lord Protector until his fall in 1549. Therefore, even before Henry was buried, his orders had been disregarded and his legacy was in tatters. He left behind a minority government and an economy that had been devastated by his costly wars. He also bequeathed to his heir a Church free from papal interference, but with the fluidity to follow a traditional or reformist religious policy.

Discussion point

Why did Surrey's Plantagenet blood represent a threat to the Tudor dynasty?

Discussion point

What were the achievements of Henry VIII?

Working in a small group, make a list of Henry's achievements and failures. What is your opinion of Henry's kingship?

SKILLS BUILDER

One of the main issues relating to Henry's achievements is how far he maintained control of his government, and how far he allowed factional rivalries to weaken his authority. To develop a judgement on this, consider the following statement: 'Henry retained the reins of power to the very end.' How far do you agree with this? Make a list of points to support the statement and then a list of points to challenge it. Then use the lists to develop an argument for or against the statement. Which do you find more convincing? Do you have to choose between them, or can you bring them together into an overall judgement? Write a conclusion to explain your judgement.

SKILLS BUILDER

Why did the reformist faction succeed in gaining the upper hand by the end of Henry's reign?

This question requires you to identify a range of reasons to account for:

- the rise of the reformist faction
- the decline of the conservative faction.

Study the narrative in this chapter and make a list of the reasons. Consider which reason(s) are most significant. In doing this you could consider using a counter-factual argument; try eliminating each reason and then ask: 'How would the outcome have differed if this had not happened?' In this way you will be able to determine the reasons of overwhelming importance.

The accession of Edward VI

Henry VIII's will

Henry's health had deteriorated rapidly in the last years of his reign, and it had become obvious that he would be passing his throne to a minor. His will was therefore written and revised in order to prevent any disputes about the succession and to provide for the care of his son during his minority. Edward would succeed him as King and, if he died without heirs, the throne would pass first to Mary and then to Elizabeth, in spite of the fact that they had both been made illegitimate by the acts of 1534 and 1536. The claims of Mary, Queen of Scots, the infant daughter of the late King James V of Scotland, Henry's nephew, were excluded from the succession.

2.6 Henry on his death bed pointing to Edward

Henry wished to preserve the royal supremacy and so excluded the Howard faction from any role in the anticipated regency, fearing that they would guide the country back to Catholicism. Consequently the balance of power swung towards the Seymours, uncles to the prince and moderate in religion. Henry's will provided that a Regency Council of 16 men, Edward Seymour and his supporters, would share power and run the government until Edward reached the age of 18. They would be rewarded with titles and lands from the dissolved monasteries, as well as lands confiscated from the Howards.

2.7 Edward Seymour, Duke of Somerset (see p.15)

The rise of Edward Seymour, Duke of Somerset

Henry's death was not even announced before key provisions in his will were disregarded. England's government was based on rule by a single person (the monarch), together with the Council and Parliament, not by a committee and it is likely that the Regency Council would have proved unworkable. Furthermore, Edward Seymour was a man of great ambition and was determined to stamp his authority on the government. Therefore, Seymour and his close ally and secretary, William Paget, who had custody of the will, kept Henry's death a secret while they gathered support for Seymour as leader of the Council. They did not reveal that Henry had died until 1 February when they summoned members of the nobility and higher clergy to the Tower of London and announced at the same time that Edward Seymour had been made leader of the Council and was to be called the Lord Protector. He was invested as Duke of Somerset and rewarded with lands to support his new position.

The choice of Somerset was not unwelcome; he had proved himself to be an accomplished military leader in the campaigns in Scotland in the last years of Henry's reign, and he rallied support to his new position. This is not to suggest that he faced no opposition; factionalism remained rife in the ruling classes. A warning for the future was signalled when his own brother, **Sir Thomas Seymour**, who was disappointed that he had not been appointed to the Regency Council, demanded that he should have the powerful role of governorship of the King's person. Thomas was encouraged in this claim by John Dudley, Earl of Warwick, who was later to emerge as Somerset's greatest rival on the Council and eventual replacement as leader. On this occasion, Somerset was able to placate Thomas with a place on the Council and an appointment as Lord Admiral, but the rivalry between the two brothers was not over. Thomas continued scheming to win the favour of his nephew, King Edward, and thus enhance his own power – until he overreached himself by plotting to marry Princess Elizabeth in 1548, which resulted in his arrest and execution in March 1549.

King and protector: How did the government function?

The influence of Edward VI on government

G.R. Elton took a very uncompromising view of Edward's role in government: 'In fact as one might suppose, Edward played no part in his reign; his so-called opinions were those of his advisers, and his so-called acts were his endorsements of accomplished facts.' This opinion is not fully supported by historians today. Although it is clear that Edward could not rule like a mature monarch, his influence cannot be entirely discounted. As an anointed King, Edward could not be ignored and it was expected that he would grow up and take the reigns of power; therefore Councillors could not afford to contradict or disregard him. The fate of Somerset is evidence of this. When Edward withdrew his support from his uncle, Somerset's fall was guaranteed. Furthermore, the evidence of Edward's 'chronicle', the diary he kept from the age of 12, shows he had a keen interest in the government, particularly in foreign affairs, and as he grew older he began cultivating contacts among ambassadors and making use of his own secretaries, so that his appraisal of situations was not entirely based upon that provided by his Council.

During Somerset's rule, Edward's time was mostly preoccupied with education and he had no direct involvement in politics, but as he matured his role became more significant. By August 1551, after the Duke of Northumberland had taken control of the Council, Edward began attending its meetings. He impressed the Council with his level of maturity so much that, in early 1552, it was announced that Edward would reach his majority at the age of 16 rather than 18, as stipulated by Henry's will. However, it is important not to exaggerate Edward's influence. He had no say in foreign affairs, which was regarded as the preserve of adults, and the Council remained under the control of Northumberland's supporters and allies.

Biography

Sir Thomas Seymour (1508–1549)

Sir Thomas Seymour was the second surviving brother of Jane Seymour, and uncle to Edward VI. He married Henry's widow, Catherine Parr, in secret but with Edward's approval. He was popular with Edward, but was executed in March 1549, after Catherine Parr had died in childbirth and he was suspected of plotting to enhance his power by marrying Elizabeth.

Discussion points

Working with a partner, discuss the following questions:

- What changes were made to the government compared to the provisions left in Henry's will?
- Why did Somerset become the leader of the government? Give at least four reasons.
- In what way do the events surrounding the accession suggest that faction played a key role in the establishment of the system for government during Edward VI's minority?

2.8 King Edward VI

However, it is also true that the enthusiasm with which Northumberland pursued Protestant reforms in the Church stemmed from Edward's keen desire to complete the Reformation. Overall, it must be concluded that Elton's opinion does not take account of the development of Edward from a child to a confident youth on the verge of adulthood by the time he died at the age of 15.

The role of the Lord Protector

The role played by the Duke of Somerset in Edward's government was affected not only by the position he held but also by his personality. He was determined to exercise full authority. Somerset's powers did not come from Parliament but from **letters of patent**, issued in March 1547 by Edward, which granted him **quasi-royal** power. Essentially this meant that he could rule almost independently and it was not long before other members of the Council complained that he ruled in an **authoritarian** manner. Although Parliament was called and was in session every year during Edward's reign except 1551, Somerset ruled mostly by proclamation. Kings had ruled by proclamation when Parliament was not sitting, with the expectation that Parliament would examine and ratify laws made by the monarch when it was called. What distinguished Somerset from previous rulers was the extent to which he used proclamations. He issued more than 70 in the three years that he led the government. This has led John Guy to characterise his rule as **autocratic**. Furthermore, Somerset took sole control of the dry stamp. Originally, the use of the dry stamp had to be supervised by four men, but Somerset used it alone, and also insisted that the King's own signature had to be countersigned by him. Somerset bypassed the Privy Council by using his own servants for consultation. Ultimately these methods led to considerable opposition by ambitious men, like the Earl of Warwick, and his mishandling of both foreign and domestic policy paved the way for his removal in 1550. Somerset's decision to rule alone, without reference to the Privy Council and landed elite, who were vital in the management of local government, left him exposed to charges of arrogance and incompetence. At his trial in 1552, members of the Council accused him of 'evil government'.

How effectively did Somerset govern?

Key problems facing Somerset's government

Somerset inherited a difficult situation:

- England was still involved in a war against France and Scotland that had begun in the latter years of Henry's reign.

- England's financial position was precarious: in spite of the enormous wealth that came from the dissolution of the monasteries, Henry's foreign affairs had left the government on the verge of bankruptcy.

- The rapid growth in population had led to inflation and poverty, which was made worse by financial problems.
- Henry's *Act of Six Articles* had proved an imperfect settlement of religious issues, and clamour for reform was building up among the Protestant clergy.

The success or failure of Somerset's rule would depend upon how effectively he solved these key problems.

The Treason Act, 1547

It was common practice for a new reign to begin with some signal that the ills of the previous regime had ended and a new and bright future beckoned. The early legislation passed by Edward's government was very much in this tradition. The new *Treason Act* abolished many of the harshest features of Henry VIII's rule – the heresy, treason and censorship laws. It repealed the *Act of Six Articles* that had restored Catholic practices and sacraments into the Church, and it also revoked the *Proclamation Act* of 1539 that had been very unpopular because it suggested that the King could rule without Parliament. As discussed earlier, this had little effect on Somerset who largely ruled through proclamation. The new act would punish the following incidences of treason:

- saying that the King was not supreme head of the Church for a third time
- writing that the King was not supreme head of the Church for the first time
- attempting to deprive the King or his successors from the title
- saying someone else was King
- interrupting the succession to the throne as laid down in the *Succession Act* of 1543.

The new act was much less exacting than the *Treason Act* of 1534 and the population certainly would have felt the lifting of a great burden. It was an important move towards religious reform since the lifting of the heresy laws enabled Protestants to practice their faith more freely, while the removal of the censorship laws led to a rapid increase in the circulation of Lutheran and **Calvinist** pamphlets and books. It also encouraged outbreaks of **iconoclasm** in churches and so led to more cases of public disorder, all of which encouraged difficult situations that the Protector struggled to control.

The Chantries Act, 1547

This act was a logical extension of the dissolution of the monasteries. Chantries were small religious houses set up by rich benefactors, who left money to pay for masses to be sung for their souls after their death.

SKILLS BUILDER

In groups, prioritise these problems in terms of their potential to threaten royal power. You will need to give reasons for your decisions. Then compare your decisions with those of another group.

Definitions

Calvinist
Follower of the Protestant doctrines taught by John Calvin in Switzerland: the sovereignty of God, the authority of the scriptures and predestination (the belief that God pre-selected that certain souls were to be saved).

Iconoclasm
The practice of destroying religious images associated with the Catholic Church and believed by Protestants to encourage superstition and false worship.

They were an entirely Catholic institution that had no place in Edward's religious beliefs, but the motivation to close them in 1547 had far more to do with finance than religion. The commissioners sent to visit them seized their land and property and melted down their gold and silver to replenish the treasury that was in dire need of money to pay for the war in Scotland.

Financial policy under Somerset

The financial problems that England faced were severe and it is possible to argue that Somerset's failure to solve them played a key role in his downfall. Guy has described Somerset's economic policy as 'his worst'. The war against Scotland that had begun in 1544, and was waged at a cost of £2,100,000, had depleted the treasury by 1546. Henry had resorted to raising loans from continental bankers and selling crown lands, but this had merely added to the debt and further reduced the Crown's income. From subsidies and forced loans he raised £656,245 and £270,000 respectively, which meant he was £1,173,755 short of meeting his debt. This was passed on to his son.

In order to restore the financial position, it was necessary for Somerset to introduce taxation and customs reforms. However, these would not have been popular with the nobility and gentry, and so he continued with a disastrous policy of debasement of the coinage that had begun under Henry VIII. This lead to spiralling inflation. Debased coins caused prices to rise because those selling goods demanded more coins for the same amount of goods to compensate for the fact that the coins had a lower value. However, wages did not rise in line with the new prices. This left the poorer classes considerably worse off. Meanwhile, richer people saw the value of their wealth being eaten away.

The royal mints were ordered to reissue the coinage with a greater percentage of copper in silver coins. By 1551 silver coins were 75 per cent copper. The policy of debasement therefore did nothing to tackle the underlying financial and economic problems, but instead fuelled discontent across all classes, including the poor. Only an end to the war could bring about a real difference and this was one policy that Somerset would not countenance.

Social policy and care for the poor

The traditional opinion of Somerset is that he was motivated by a keen desire to help the poor. Historian A.F. Pollard for example described Somerset as driven not by 'selfish motives but by the desire to achieve aims that were essentially noble'. There is evidence that he was genuinely interested in the plight of the poor: he established a court of requests at Somerset House to hear the cases of the poor and he criticised the wealthy (although, given the riches that he amassed as Lord Protector, this criticism was not exactly convincing).

However, his failure to tackle inflation and his slavish insistence that the war in Scotland must be pursued undermined the measures that he did take. Somerset introduced two policies that were aimed at alleviating the plight of the poor.

The Vagrancy Act, 1547

The *Vagrancy Act* moved closer towards a proper poor relief provision that would emerge under Elizabeth I. It ordered local officials to provide housing and collections for the 'deserving poor', those described as 'idle, impotent and aged' who were not **vagabonds**. However, the other provisions of the act dominated and have led some to describe it as the 'Slavery Act'. It ordered that able-bodied persons who were unemployed for more than three days were to be branded with a V and sold into slavery for two years for the first offence, and punished with permanent slavery for a further offence. Their children could be removed from their care and forced into apprenticeships.

The act was extremely unpopular with JPs and so, in fact, it was never put into effect, but its provisions have caused historians to revise the opinion that Somerset was the champion of the poor.

Enclosures

Somerset opposed the practice of **enclosure** that reduced the land for growing crops and increased rural unemployment. He set up a commission under John Hale to investigate cases of enclosure in the Midlands and in June 1548 he issued proclamations enforcing all previous statutes against enclosures established for grazing sheep. This policy was further enhanced by the introduction of a five per cent tax on personal property and a tax on sheep.

The policy was a failure. It raised great hopes among the labouring classes that significant reforms would be introduced, and this – coupled with the rising price of grain after poor harvests in 1549 – increased unrest in the countryside. This, in turn, kindled fears in the gentry and, more importantly, in the nobility that rebellion was brewing, threatening their position and financial security. For this they blamed Somerset.

Why did Somerset fall from power?

Somerset's fall from power was the result of a combination of factors. The considerable problems he faced at home were exacerbated by the foreign affairs he pursued. Somerset inherited a country at war with Scotland and France, and Henry VIII's binding wish that Edward should be married to Mary, Queen of Scots – a move that would bring about the political unity of England and Scotland – and secure the northern border forever. However, he failed to achieve victory and secure the marriage.

Definitions

Vagabond
A wanderer who has no fixed home, usually because he is driven from place to place looking for work.

Enclosure
Refers to the fencing of fields by individual owners. If communal land and wastes were enclosed, the poorest people lost grazing and gathering rights.

SKILLS BUILDER

How far do you agree that Somerset was the champion of the poor?

Examine the evidence in this section and make two lists:

- Evidence in favour
- Evidence against

Use the details in your lists to help you reach a conclusion.

2.9 Mary, Queen of Scots

Definitions

Garrisoning

Stationing troops in a place.

Comptroller

An ancient spelling of controller that refers to a position in the royal household.

- Although Somerset defeated the Scots at Pinkie Cleugh in September 1547, King Henry II of France had Mary removed to France and arranged her betrothal to the French dauphin.

- Somerset's policy of **garrisoning** Scotland failed to subdue the Scots and the garrisons were ruinously expensive to maintain, costing £351,000 in wages compared to the £235,383 that Henry VIII spent on raids.

- When rebellions broke out in England in 1549 Somerset prevaricated for some time before recalling the troops in August. The consequence of this was that both foreign and domestic policies were left in tatters.

The events of these rebellions are covered in detail in Unit 5, pages 117–28.

The consequences of the rebellions for Somerset's government

Somerset had already been concerned about public disorder when the rebellions broke out. In 1548 his government issued proclamations against spreading rumours, as well as banning football on the grounds that games were liable to end in riots. However, the rebellions went beyond the capacity of local officials to control them and so had a significant and indeed fatal impact on Somerset's government. Although the demands of the rebels made it clear that they did not intend to threaten the established order, but merely redress grievances, the nobility and especially the members of the Council were convinced that Somerset was to blame. Moderate Catholics blamed him for the religious changes (see pages 117–120) that sparked the Western Rebellion, while his social policy, especially with regard to enclosures, was seen to be the root cause of Kett's Rebellion (see pages 121–128). Above all, Somerset was seen to have demonstrated poor leadership in his slow and prevaricating response to the rebellions. His desire not to disturb his Scottish campaign meant that he released the troops too late and allowed rebellion to take hold. Sir William Paget, the **comptroller** of the King's household and Chancellor of the Duchy of Lancaster, accused Somerset of showing 'softness' and of failing to take the advice of the Council. The jealousies that had reverberated around the halls of power now all came to the surface and the leading nobility began manoeuvring to remove Somerset.

Somerset's fall from power

While Somerset's star was waning, that of the Earl of Warwick was in the ascendancy. In September, Somerset attempted to create a new Council, but he was opposed by the Earls of Arundel, Southampton and Warwick. He then proceeded to take the King under his care at Windsor Castle, but Edward complained of the cold and accused his uncle of keeping him prisoner. Somerset had not been careful enough to keep the good opinion of the King. Edward had long complained that he kept him short of pocket money, which embarrassed him because he could not reward his courtiers in a manner befitting a king.

Before his execution, Thomas Seymour had done much to undermine Edward's relationship with Somerset by supplying him with ready funds. At this crucial moment, Edward abandoned his uncle, saying Somerset had threatened that there would be riots on the streets should the King deprive him of his position. Although Somerset denied the charge, he could not contradict the King and his fate was sealed. In October 1549 he was sent to the Tower and, although he was later released and restored to court, the Council was reformed under the leadership of the Earl of Warwick, who was made Duke of Northumberland in 1551 and who took the title Lord President of the Council. Somerset was executed in January 1552 on trumped up charges brought about by Northumberland.

The rule of Northumberland

Why did Northumberland replace Somerset?

Northumberland, like Somerset before him, had risen to prominence in the last years of the reign of Henry VIII and he too had shown himself as an able military leader in the French and Scottish wars. He was named as a member of the Council in Henry's will and had played that role under Somerset. However, Northumberland was ambitious for more power and, in common with the other members of the Council, he had been greatly aggrieved by Somerset's arrogant control and his bypassing of the Council in decision-making. Furthermore, Northumberland's handling of the rebellion in Norfolk meant that he returned to London in September 1549 as the commander of an army and this put him in a position of considerable strength. He was clearly the leading contender in the power struggle and it was he who engineered Somerset's arrest in October.

Elton describes Northumberland as 'exceedingly ambitious of power and very greedy'. Indeed Elton very much represents the opinion that Northumberland was the 'evil duke' who made gains at the expense of King and country. This opinion has been revised in more recent times. Northumberland is recognised as being driven by ambition but also as very politically astute, and more inclined to implement the will of the King than his predecessor. This was clearly demonstrated in the manner in which he took control of the Council. Initially Northumberland allied himself with its conservative members, appearing to support their desires for a halt to religious change and return to the Catholic worship established under the *Act of Six Articles* of 1539. However, once in position, Northumberland rapidly disassociated himself with their position and instead aligned himself with Cranmer and the reformers. In doing this he also gained the favour of the King, which enabled him to eject the conservatives from the Council and take the position of Lord President. This title reflected Edward's growing maturity and a recognition that he would play an increasingly influential role. Northumberland had certainly learned from Somerset's fate that cultivating the approval of the King was essential, even though he was a minor.

2.10 John Dudley, Duke of Northumberland

Northumberland's changes in government

Northumberland restored the Council to its prime position in decision making and expanded its membership to 33. He packed it with his own supporters, but was still sensible enough to include the supporters of Somerset who demonstrated significant ability, such as **William Cecil** and William Paget. Northumberland also established inner committees in the Council in order that business might be carried out more efficiently. In all other respects the government functioned much as it had done under Somerset, with a little less reliance on proclamation and more focus on Parliament.

Financial policy under Northumberland

The resolution of expensive foreign affairs was a vital step in the achievement of what Guy has described as 'the duke's prime administrative task' – the restoration of the Crown's finances. According to Nigel Heard, Somerset had spent £1,356,000 on war and had financed this by selling Crown lands, raising loans and debasing the coinage. The excessive costs of Somerset's foreign affairs had led to spiralling inflation and virtual bankruptcy. The inflationary situation was the greatest challenge facing England and had played its part in the rebellions of 1549.

Northumberland gave first priority to ending the unaffordable expense of aggressive foreign affairs by agreeing the Treaty of Boulogne with France in March 1550, which returned Boulogne to France and enabled him to withdraw English troops from Scotland. This reduced expenditure and so enabled him to focus on the restoration of finances at home.

Northumberland identified his priorities in financial policy in June 1551:

- the debasement of the coinage must end
- the King's regular income must match his regular expenditure
- the King's debts must be paid so that once again he would be solvent.

Northumberland appointed William Paulet, later Lord Winchester (see page 15), as Lord Treasurer and placed William Cecil in charge of financial planning. He also sent **Sir Thomas Gresham** to the Netherlands to manipulate the stock market and between them they were able to bring about a series of changes that, according to Elton, 'provided the basis for sound finance' by the reign of Elizabeth.

An end to debasement of the coinage

The last debasement of the coinage took place in May 1551. Although it gave a further boost to inflation, it also provided the government with a profit of £114,000 that it used to pay off the immediately pressing loans and expenses. The value of the coinage was not restored after this point; it was not until 1560 that the debased coinage was recalled and reissued, although the silver content of coins was restored to the 1527 level in 1552. However, the measure did suffice to slow down inflationary pressures.

Reductions in expenditure

Northumberland ordered radical cuts in royal expenditure. This was made possible by the ending of the wars with France and Scotland and supported by the reports returned from the commissions he set up to investigate the state of royal finances and particularly the methods of collection. Northumberland set up an emergency fund known as the 'Privy Coffer' to cope with contingencies. Gresham's efforts in crossing to Antwerp more than 40 times to manipulate the exchange rates in **sterling's** favour, and to renegotiate loans on better terms, helped to pay off much of the Crown's debts. Northumberland also attempted to restructure the system of collecting and accounting for revenues by reducing the number of revenue courts to two, but this policy had not been implemented by the time of Edward's death. It was, however, completed by Winchester during Mary's reign.

How successful was Northumberland's financial policy?

Northumberland's measures went a considerable way to restoring the Crown to solvency. He halted the debasement of the coinage and removed the heavy burden of debt from the Crown. The end of the wars allowed him to make significant cuts in expenditure. However, his own position was dependent on his supporters and the need to reward them reduced his room for manoeuvre. Elton claims that Northumberland was 'hampered by his own and his party's greed'. It is certainly true that financial necessities, coupled with his need to give patronage, meant that he continued to sell Crown lands, as well as using the profits from the dissolution of the chantries and the plate seized from the churches in the second round of reforms after 1550. This meant that the deep-seated problems were not solved but were to be inherited by Edward's sisters in their turn.

Social and economic policy under Northumberland

Somerset's government had raised the expectations of the poor while delivering very little. In the process, he lost the support of the nobility and gentry who blamed him for sparking the rebellions. Northumberland was careful to avoid the pitfalls of his predecessor's policies. In 1550 he introduced a new *Treason Act*, which restored censorship and enabled JPs to restore law and order in their localities. In that same year he oversaw the repeal of the *Vagrancy Act* and the hated Sheep Tax, and this played an important role in dampening discontent among the masses as well as landowners. He also attempted to do something for the poor by vigorously enforcing the existing anti-enclosure legislation and introducing a poor law to enable parishes to provide for the aged and infirm. Furthermore, while his financial reforms did not solve the underlying problems, they did help by reducing inflation, and the controls introduced on the distribution of grain after poor harvests in 1551 did alleviate the greatest pressures on the poor. Therefore, although Somerset has traditionally been seen as the champion of the poor, in fact the poor were likely to have fared somewhat better under Northumberland's rule.

Definition

Sterling
English currency that took its name from the sterling silver content.

Discussion point

Why was Northumberland unable to solve the country's financial problems completely?

In your groups, identify four reasons why it was so difficult for him to achieve his financial aims.

SKILLS BUILDER

Who was more effective in managing the government, Somerset or Northumberland? Compare the two rulers by constructing a table, as shown below, and entering the key features of their policies in it.

A comparison of Somerset and Northumberland as rulers

	Somerset	Northumberland
Aims		
Management of government		
Financial policy		
Social policy		
Success or failure?		

Rebellion and conspiracy: Edward's death and the tragedy of Lady Jane Grey

Edward's 'devise for the succession' and his death

The traditional picture painted of Edward is of a sickly boy who was never going to survive into adulthood. This is an image that has arisen largely as a result of hindsight. Although Edward had suffered from measles and smallpox at the age of 14, he was otherwise healthy and his more frequent attendance at the Council meetings and the announcement, in 1552, that he would reach his majority at the age of 16, confirms that his advisers expected him to rule as an adult King. However, in early 1553 he contracted tuberculosis and by the summer it was clear that he was not going to recover. This placed both the King and Northumberland in a dilemma. His heir, according to the terms of Henry VIII's will, was his Catholic sister Mary. If she took the throne, the strides towards Protestantism would be undone and it was likely that Mary would renounce the royal supremacy.

There has been considerable historical debate about the events that unfolded at this time, particularly regarding who was the motivating force behind the changes that were made to the succession. Elton claims that the changes were a desperate and doomed attempt by Northumberland to pervert the succession in favour of his family. However, although Guy claims that Northumberland intended to usurp power, he also acknowledges that Edward did not want Mary to succeed, and this is borne out by the 'devise' that Edward himself drafted in January. In this document, Edward passed over his sisters, who according to the *Succession Acts* of 1534 and 1536 were illegitimate, and passed the throne onto the Suffolk branch of the family, to 'Lady Jane Grey's heirs male'. In May, Lady Jane was married to Northumberland's eldest son, Guildford Dudley.

Lady Jane Grey was chosen because she was a committed Protestant. It does appear that when the devise was originally drafted, Edward was expected to recover from his illness. However, as his health declined in the summer of 1553, the devise was changed to leave the throne to 'Lady Jane Grey and her heirs male'. It had become obvious that there was no time for Lady Jane to produce sons before Edward's death.

Edward died on 6 July 1553. Before his death, Northumberland ordered that a new will be drawn up incorporating Edward's devise. This caused great concern among the lawyers because, as a minor, it was not legal for Edward to write a will that overthrew the succession as laid down by the previous king. Northumberland was obliged to exert considerable pressure and in the end 'Letters Patent for the Limitation of the Crown' were drawn up incorporating Edward's wishes. Edward died before this could be put before Parliament.

Northumberland's conspiracy and the victory of Mary Tudor

Northumberland kept Edward's death secret for two days while he made arrangements. He bullied members of the Council and the Mayor of London into agreeing to the devise, and then declared Lady Jane as Queen. However, he had little support for his position. Mary, who was at Framlington Castle in Suffolk, also proclaimed herself Queen and began mustering troops. Northumberland was obliged to move to Suffolk with 2,000 troops to meet the challenge, but his troops deserted him and in his absence the Council changed sides. Mary was acknowledged as Queen on 20 July and entered London on 3 August. Northumberland, who had been arrested on 17 July, was executed for treason on 22 August. The unfortunate pawn in these proceedings, Lady Jane Grey, who had been Queen for just nine days, was arrested and imprisoned in the Tower. Mary recognised that she had not been a conspirator, but she was executed, together with her husband, in February 1554 after Wyatt's Rebellion – when Mary decided she was simply too dangerous to keep alive (see page 130). Mary succeeded because of the strength of her legitimate claim to the throne and because she had not hesitated to fight to save her inheritance. The issue was finally put to rest by the passing of two acts, one in 1553 which declared the Queen to be legitimate and in 1554 the *Act Concerning Regal Power*, in which the rights of female monarchs in England were asserted.

Discussion point

Study the section above. Was Edward or Northumberland the driving force behind the change to the succession?

SKILLS BUILDER

Look back at the material that you have collected about government by Somerset and Northumberland and list their strengths and weaknesses. How justified have historians been in stylising the Duke of Northumberland as the 'evil duke' compared to the 'noble' Duke of Somerset?

Unit summary

What have you learned in this unit?

- Government in the last years of Henry VIII was dominated by struggles between two competing factions. At the end of the reign, the conservatives were defeated and the reformist faction led by the Duke of Somerset seized control of the new King.

- Somerset's arrogance and style of government that ignored the Council made him very unpopular. He failed to respond to the rebellions of 1549 effectively and he was replaced by the Duke of Northumberland.

- Northumberland was careful to court popularity in the Council and with the King and retained his position until Edward's death.

- Edward's government was virtually bankrupt when he came to the throne and Somerset's war with Scotland and France merely accelerated inflation. Northumberland took measures to restore the financial position of the Crown but, while reducing the immediate problems, they reduced the overall income of the monarch in the long run.

- Northumberland tried and failed to ensure a Protestant succession on Edward's death by declaring Lady Jane Grey as Queen in July 1553, in accordance with Edward's wishes. He was defeated by Mary Tudor and executed.

What skills have you used in this unit?

You have analysed what happened in order to define and explain the causes of key events. You have explored a number of issues in order to make developed judgements supported by your understanding of the key events. You have developed skills in comparing different people and policies and drawn conclusions about successes and failures.

Exam style question

Section A questions require you to make and sustain a balanced judgement about important issues. These can include causation, the significance of events and developments, the role of key individuals and their success or failure. They may refer to a single reign, or to developments over a longer period of time. For example:

'How far do you agree with the opinion that in the years 1538–53 the power and authority of the monarch were undermined by court factions and rivalry?'

Exam tips

This question spans the reigns of both Henry VIII and Edward VI. It invites a thematic approach to addressing the question and you should work towards this in your planning. It is unwise to try to deal with this chronologically since there is a tendency to lapse into a narrative and it would also be difficult to achieve in the limited time (50 minutes) under exam conditions. You therefore need to identify a range of themes related to the power and authority of the monarchy and consider the impact they had upon the monarch's ability to rule, for example:

- the power and authority held by the monarch
- the age of the monarch and his ability to exercise control
- the role of faction in decision-making and the exercise of power
- the role of the chief minister/leader of government.

These themes are a starting point. You need to address the question, not describe the nature of government. Develop your plan to consider 'how far' the monarch's power and authority were undermined. Take each theme and make a brief list of evidence that you might use to argue for and against the interpretation in the question. You must span the full time period and not focus on only one king. What differences were there between them and the ways in which they exercised control? You need to develop judgements and so as part of your plan you should write a brief sentence summing up your argument for each section – was the power of the monarch undermined? If so, was this because of factional rivalry or other reasons? When you have looked at each theme, you will be in a position to make an overall judgement. Now you are ready to write your answer.

RESEARCH TOPIC

A mid-Tudor crisis?

This is a view put forward by historians writing before the 1980s. They argued that the legacy of Henry's last years and the accession of a minor weakened the monarchy and threatened the state. Research these views using the Internet. Identify and investigate the views of the 'revisionist' historians, who have criticised this opinion. Consider how the events you have studied might be used to support and refute this opinion.

3 Reformation, conflict and settlement in religion, 1547–66

What is this unit about?

This unit focuses on the contrasting religious policies implemented by the Tudor monarchs, Edward VI, Mary I and Elizabeth I. It examines in detail the differences between the monarchs' religious aims and it explores the methods they used to implement their preferred religious settlements. It assesses the level of opposition to their religious policies and evaluates the degree to which their settlements succeeded in terms of public support and adherence.

In this unit you will:

- compare and contrast the aims, policies and achievements of the three monarchs' religious policies
- discuss the extent to which the policies succeeded and consider the limitations of the achievements
- examine the nature of opposition to the religious settlements.

Key questions

- What were the intentions of Edward VI, Mary Tudor and Elizabeth I in their religious settlements and what methods did they employ to achieve their aims?
- How far did Edward VI, Mary Tudor and Elizabeth I succeed in their religious settlements?

Timeline

1547	January	Accession of Edward VI
1549		*Act of Uniformity*; First Prayer Book
1552		*Act of Uniformity*; Second Prayer Book
1553	July	Accession of Mary I
	October	First Statute of Repeal
1555		Second Statute of Repeal (revival of the heresy laws)
	February	Execution of Bishop Hooper
	October	Execution of Bishops Latimer and Ridley
1556	March	Execution of Archbishop Cranmer
1558	November	Accession of Elizabeth I
1559	February	Introduction of religious bills into Parliament

	April	*Acts of Supremacy and Uniformity*
		Passing of the Royal Injunctions
1563		*The Thirty-Nine Articles*
1566		*The Vestiarian Controversy*

The Edwardian Reformation: Religious change under Somerset and Northumberland

The Church that Edward inherited was one that was decidedly Roman Catholic in doctrine and in its rites. The Protestant experimentation of the mid-1530s had been brought to an end by the more orthodox ideology promoted by the *Act of Six Articles*. However, this had not turned the tide of Protestantism. A number of Protestant innovations were there to stay; the Ten Commandments and the Lord's Prayer were being taught in English and large numbers of the elite were reading the Bible in English. Under Edward, significant moves were made towards establishing a fully Protestant Church; the doctrine shifted much closer to that of Calvinism and the fabric of the churches, and the church services, were cleansed of what were regarded as superstitious and devilish practices.

Edward's influence in the Reformation

Edward's influence should not be underestimated. The people closest to him, including his step-mother Catherine Parr and his tutor Sir Richard Coxe, were all Protestants and he delighted in surrounding himself with reforming preachers whose views, it would seem, he shared. By the time he reached the age of 13, he made it quite clear that he did not believe the First Prayer Book went far enough and the evidence shows that he was involved in the legislation for the *Second Act of Uniformity*. Furthermore, Edward was the driving force behind efforts to force his sister Mary to submit to the new religion and he was greatly frustrated when she invoked the support of her cousin, the Hapsburg Emperor Charles V, to maintain her Catholic practices in her own household. Edward's keen interest and his growing involvement in the affairs of state probably go a long way to explaining why the Reformation entered a more radical phase on the accession of Northumberland, who was certainly more aware of the need to satisfy the King than Somerset had been.

3.1 Henry VIII with his children, Edward, Mary and Elizabeth

Religious reforms under Somerset's protectorate

Somerset's religious views

Somerset was undoubtedly an avid Protestant. He kept a Protestant household and became a correspondent of Calvin. Under his influence, the tone of the Court changed as Protestant preachers began to make their presence felt there. However, the progress towards Protestantism was not swift under Somerset. According to Haigh, religious change under Somerset was spasmodic and uncertain because he feared the dangers associated with reform. Somerset was probably more astute than Haigh credits. The reforms introduced under Henry VIII are associated with the Pilgrimage of Grace and Somerset wanted to avoid a repetition while he was engaged in hostilities in Scotland. The events of the Western Rebellion bear out his reticence; the desire to halt the Reformation was one motivating factor behind the revolt. Somerset, therefore, proceeded with caution and, on occasions, it is possible to see that the movement from below pushed reforms further than he intended.

Initial reforms

Some important legislation was enacted by Edward's first Parliament and put England on the road to Protestantism. The *Act of Six Articles* and the heresy laws were repealed while the moderation of the *Treason Act* lifted censorship. This resulted in an upsurge in the publication of Protestant literature, as well as an increase in the number of clergy preaching openly Protestant ideas in their parishes. The closure of the chantries from 1547 onwards may well have been motivated by financial necessities, but it was a logical continuation from the dissolution of the monasteries and effectively demonstrated that the new government rejected the Catholic doctrine of **purgatory**.

Iconoclasm

A more decidedly Protestant change was brought about by Archbishop Cranmer's preaching against the images of saints that adorned churches. A Royal Injunction of 1547 had forbidden the veneration of images, but Visitation commissioners took the instructions much more strictly and began removing images from churches. In September 1547, images were torn down from St Paul's in London. In a clear sign of confusion, the Council ordered their restoration. Across the country, communities were split over the issue. In the end Somerset sided with the radicals and in February 1548 the order to ban images was extended to the whole realm. The incident suggests that Somerset was pushed into reform by pressures from below. Although there had been opposition to the initial order, it seems that most churches complied without complaint and removed the offending images – many hiding them away in case of a later change of policy.

Definition

Purgatory

The Catholic Church taught that the souls of the dead went to purgatory to atone for sins committed during life. When their time had been served, the souls were released into heaven. Families of the dead could speed their journey by making offerings to monks and priests to pray for them. This doctrine was rejected by Protestants as having no biblical foundation.

Cranmer's Homilies

Another step in a Protestant direction was taken when Stephen Gardiner, Bishop of Winchester and Edmund Bonner, Bishop of London, were imprisoned for complaints about the 'Book of **Homilies**', issued in July 1547, and which included preaching on *sola fide*. The purpose of the book was to provide model sermons for members of the clergy who were unable to preach for themselves. It was ordered that a copy should be placed in every church. According to Haigh, some churches did not use the book. However, the imprisonment of the conservative bishops is clear evidence that reformation was intended and that the clergy was expected to conform.

The *First Act of Uniformity* and the First Prayer Book, 1549

Somerset was mindful of the dangers of rapid religious change and tried to follow a moderate path. He approved of the inclusion of English prayers in the communion service and asked the people to be content with these changes while Cranmer worked on a new prayer book. The *Act of Uniformity* passed by Parliament in January 1549 enforced the Book of Common Prayer, or First Prayer Book as it is more usually known. Although the bill had little trouble in the House of Commons, in the more conservative and Catholic House of Lords it faced opposition from eight bishops and three lay peers. The First Prayer Book outlined the form of worship to be used in services. It retained transubstantiation in the communion service but emphasised that there was no sacrifice involved. In this way it hoped to achieve compliance from the Catholic population. From prison, Gardiner gave his assent to the changes, which also included the use of English in services instead of Latin. The purpose of the *Act of Uniformity* was to ensure that services across the country conformed to the new teaching and brought an end to the wide variety of services that were being used in parishes across the nation. Nevertheless, in spite of Somerset's cautious approach, and the approval given by conservatives, the introduction of the prayer book was one of the grievances voiced by the western rebels (see pages 118–20). However, we should not exaggerate the extent or depth of resistance by Catholics. Beyond the Western Rebellion, there is no evidence of organised resistance and most parishes appear to have complied. However, Colin Pendrill does claim that many priests mumbled the words so that they might as well have been in Latin and used alternative gestures to compensate for the fact that they were forbidden to **elevate the Host**. It should also be noted that some of the most vociferous complaints came not from Catholics, but from Protestants who thought the prayer book did not go far enough. John Hooper, Bishop of Gloucester, complained that the book was full of popish errors and demanded a completely Protestant prayer book.

Henry VIII's orders forbidding clerical marriage were overturned in the same Parliament. This move was probably more significant in highlighting the pathway to fully-fledged Protestantism. However, it would be under the stewardship of Northumberland that this journey would be completed.

Definitions

Homily
A sermon, usually a reflection upon scripture or doctrine.

Sola fide
The Protestant doctrine of justification by faith alone, first taught by Martin Luther, and which contradicted orthodox Catholic teaching that it was necessary to perform good works in order to achieve salvation.

Discussion point

What was the reaction to Somerset's religious reforms?

Working with a partner, make a list of the reforms and note down the reaction to each. On balance were they popular or not?

Definition

Elevation of the Host
The Catholic ritual of raising the consecrated bread and wine during the celebration of the Eucharist in the Mass, indicating that transubstantiation has taken place.

The achievement of Protestantism: Religious reforms under Northumberland

Northumberland's religious views

The religious views of the Duke of Northumberland present the historian with something of a dilemma. He rose to power with the support of the Catholic members of the Council in revolt against what they saw as the dangerous path towards Protestantism that Somerset was pursuing. Furthermore, he died a Catholic, affirming his beliefs shortly before his execution. However, it was under his stewardship that England embraced Protestant doctrine and practices. It is certain that he was more responsive to the wishes of the King than Somerset had been. Haigh claims that Northumberland did not care about formal religious allegiance; instead, he says, Northumberland treated religion as a useful policy in attracting allies and he concurs with Elton's view that Northumberland was primarily motivated by the gains that could be made from seizing Church property.

Cranmer's Ordinal, 1550

The first step towards full Protestantism under Northumberland was the adoption of a new Ordinal, a code for the ordination of priests. It was written by Archbishop Cranmer and marked a clear move away from Catholic priest to Protestant minister. The rites of ordination were simplified, although the ceremony remained traditional. The key change was in the emphasis on the role of the cleric as a preacher. The service would later be incorporated into the Second Prayer Book.

The issue of communion tables

One of the most contentious issues was the move from Catholic altars to Protestant communion tables. This was one of the most visual signs of a break with the past and emphasised that the communion service was a memorial and not a sacrifice. In fact, when communion tables were placed in the nave, there was a clear implication that there was no presence of Christ in the mass. The removal of altars had tended to be the result of local initiatives where reforming clergy took it upon themselves to do so. Nicholas Ridley, Bishop of London, who ordered their removal in his diocese, accelerated the process, as did Bishop Hooper of Gloucester through his Lenten sermons. Although many dioceses followed their lead, there was some dissent in Sussex and Carmarthen. In the end, in November 1550, the Council stepped in and ordered their removal in order to ensure uniformity. In some churches the altars were dismantled and stored in the hope that they might one day be restored.

The removal of the conservative clergy

By 1551, the dominance of the conservative bishops that had prevented a full-blown reformation had come to an end. Gardiner and Bonner were already in prison because of their objections to the Book of Homilies and their complaints that Cranmer had abandoned the key Catholic doctrine of transubstantiation. Now reformers replaced them.

3.2 Archbishop Thomas Cranmer

Definitions

Episcopacy

The body of bishops that presided over the dioceses of the Anglican Church.

Surplice

A white gown that reached down to the ground, with wide sleeves.

Nicholas Ridley took Bonner's see in London, while the energetic reformer, John Hooper, used his role as Bishop of Gloucester to examine the credentials of his clergy and found them wanting. According to Haigh, his discovery that over half of the clergy in his diocese could not recite the Ten Commandments was a motivating factor towards the production of a new, more Protestant prayer book.

The removal of the conservative **episcopacy** provided Northumberland with the opportunity to seize more ecclesiastical property. The sees of London and Winchester were combined, for example, and this allowed the state to take possession of lands and manors that had previously been Church property. In this way Northumberland was able to obtain valuable lands that he could use to cement alliances in the Council. It is evidence of this nature that has led some historians to claim that he was motivated primarily by the wealth of the Church rather than any devotion to doctrinal change.

The *Second Act of Uniformity* and the Second Prayer Book, 1552

The poor educational state of the clergy, from a reformist point of view, and the development of a more radical episcopacy were behind the production of a new prayer book. Many reformers had complained that the First Prayer Book was dominated by Catholic superstition and was an unsatisfactory compromise between tradition and reform. By 1551, there had been a definite shift towards a Protestant doctrine and the Privy Council moved to silence those who sought to oppose further reform. The *Second Act of Uniformity* imposed the Second Prayer Book. It was presented as a clarification of the first, but in fact its adoption marked the culmination of the reformation in Edward's reign. It abandoned the structure of the Mass and removed any suggestion of transubstantiation from the communion service, which was now to be called 'the Lord's Supper'. Although it provided for kneeling at communion, there was such an outcry from radical reformers such as **John Knox** that the Council inserted what has become known as the 'Black Rubric', a statement that kneeling did not imply an adoration of the Host or a belief in the bodily presence of Christ. The Second Prayer Book also removed the wearing of Catholic vestments; these were to be replaced by a **surplice**.

The Forty-Two Articles, 1553

The Forty-Two Articles, written by Archbishop Cranmer, defined the reformed theology that was now at the heart of religious belief and practice in England. It was intended that its publication would protect the Church of England from both Catholic falsehoods and **Anabaptist** zeal. The articles were a mixture of Lutheran and Calvinist teaching and emphasised the centrality of scriptures in determining doctrine, ceremony and the path to salvation. The attaining of salvation was to be achieved, as Luther taught, 'by faith only in Jesus Christ' while Article 14 introduced into the English Church – for the first time – the doctrine of **predestination**.

Biography

John Knox (c.1510–1572)
John Knox was a Scottish clergyman who is considered to be the founder of the Presbyterian version of the Protestant religion. He was exiled in England in 1549 and rose to be chaplain to Edward VI. He played a key role in drawing up the Book of Common Prayer. He went into exile during the reign of Mary Tudor but returned to Scotland in 1559 to become a leader in the Scottish Reformation.

3.3 John Knox

Definition

Anabaptist
A Protestant who believed in the primacy of the Bible, baptism only for adult believers not infants, and the complete separation of Church and state.

The Forty-Two Articles underscored **lay** control of the Church, the Supremacy of the Monarch, and that the clergy were not raised above their congregation. This was clearly demonstrated in the emphasis that the laity would take **communion in both kinds**.

The success of the Reformation in Edward's reign

By the time of Edward's death in July 1553, England was clearly a Protestant country, at least in as far as its head of state, Church hierarchy, doctrine and services were concerned. Although the implementation of changes was patchier across the nation, there was little sign of real resistance beyond the Western Rebellion, which had been crushed in 1549. The English people had been schooled over the decades to obey the leadership of their monarch in religious matters. Although Duffy claims that the English people 'breathed easier' when the ultra-Catholic Mary acceded to the throne, David Loades notes that the events of Mary's reign show that Protestant preachers, who flourished under Edward, had accomplished more than was first thought. Stamping out Protestantism proved to be much more difficult than Mary anticipated. If Edward had survived there is a real chance that the roots that had been laid by his legislation would have taken a firm hold and Protestantism would have developed and blossomed. What cut the Reformation short was the untimely death of its keenest advocate.

SKILLS BUILDER

How far was England a Protestant country by 1553?

In order to address this question, you will need to identify key Catholic and Protestant doctrines, rites and practices. Compare each of these against the changes that were introduced in 1547 to 1553.

Consider how far the changes were accepted.

You will then be in a position to judge the extent to which England was a Protestant country by the time of Edward's death.

The Marian settlement

Mary's aims

Of all the Tudor monarchs, Mary's religious beliefs and aims are the easiest to pinpoint. Mary had been brought up as a strict Catholic and she had maintained her position against all attempts to quash her stance during Edward's reign. She was determined to restore Catholicism to England, to return to the supremacy of Rome and to enforce Catholic doctrine, including transubstantiation. Indeed she interpreted her accession, in the face of Northumberland's plot to prevent her taking the throne, as divinely ordained and that its purpose was to defeat the Protestant heresy, and so save England.

Mary believed that the outburst of popular support that accompanied her accession was a confirmation that the people were eager for a return to the 'true religion'. In this she was probably mistaken; the adulation that greeted her was more likely to have been the consequence of support for a true Tudor against Northumberland's attempt to usurp power. However, it is also fair to state that all her subjects, from the greatest nobles to the lowest classes, were in no doubt that she would halt the progress towards Protestantism and reintroduce Catholicism and that in July 1553 there was no obvious opposition to this.

The restoration of Catholicism

The *First Statute of Repeal*, 1553

Parliament met in October 1553 and immediately began the task of dismantling the Protestant Reformation in England. The *First Statute* of *Repeal* reversed all the religious legislation passed in Edward's reign and restored the Church of England to the position that it had been in the last year of Henry's reign, with doctrine governed by the *Act of Six Articles* of 1539. The approach taken emphasises the essentially Catholic nature of religion under Henry and also demonstrates that Mary was prepared to act cautiously in implementing her aims. At this stage there was no move to restore papal supremacy and the medieval heresy laws were not revived. Indeed, the first attempt to reintroduce these laws was not made by Mary but by Gardiner in the spring of 1554 in an effort to ingratiate himself with the Queen, whom he had offended by his vociferous objections to her marriage to Philip of Spain. This attempt failed, but Mary experienced no difficulty in the passage of the *Act of Six Articles*. The support shown by Parliament was aided by the fact that Bishops Hooper and Ridley and Archbishop Cranmer had been arrested and imprisoned before the session and therefore the House of Lords was quieter than usual. Overall, it appeared that Parliament was at the very least prepared to accept that religious policy was to be led by the preferences of the monarch of the day.

The *Second Statute of Repeal*, 1555: The restoration of papal headship

The reintroduction of Catholicism continued apace. In March 1554 the bishops were instructed to enforce the *First Statute of Repeal*, the Mass in Latin was restored and married clergy were made to give up their wives and families or lose their livings. However, the next great stage in the Marian settlement had to wait for the arrival of **Cardinal Pole**, the papal legate (messenger) whose task it was to restore the English Church to Rome. Cardinal Pole arrived in England in November 1554. He pronounced a solemn absolution (forgiveness) on England and so prepared the ground for the restoration of papal authority over the English Church. Parliament duly met and passed the *Second Statute of Repeal,* which repealed all religious legislation passed in the reign of Henry VIII after 1529. By this act the monarch ceased to be Supreme Head of the Church and thus the headship of the papacy was restored. As a consequence of the repeal, the medieval heresy laws were also revived.

Biography

Cardinal Reginald Pole (1500–1558)
Cardinal Pole was the grandson of George Plantagenet, First Duke of Clarence. He therefore had a claim to the throne in his own right. He had refused to support Henry's divorce and went into exile from 1532. In 1536 Pope Paul III made him a cardinal and in 1542 he was appointed papal legate. In 1554 Pole returned to England to spearhead Mary's restoration of Catholicism. As Archbishop of Canterbury he bears a responsibility with Mary for the persecution and execution of Protestants. He died on 17 November 1558, just 12 hours after Mary's death.

3.4 Cardinal Pole

The limitations to the restoration of Catholicism

Although the *Second Statute of Repeal* swept away all religious innovations since 1529, the clock could never really be turned back. Mary achieved support in Parliament for her policy principally because she did not threaten the position of the gentry and nobility. She was obliged to accept that the price of support for the return to Catholicism was to sacrifice her ambition to restore the monasteries. Monastic lands had been sold by Henry VIII to the laity and many of the beneficiaries were sitting in Parliament. She realised that she would not gain support for a restoration of the monasteries from laymen who currently held the lands and who would oppose any move to return them to the Church. In what appears to be an uncharacteristic move, Mary compromised on this demand, only restoring the monastic lands still held by the Crown, valued at £60,000 a year. Furthermore, it is possible to speak of papal headship after 1554, but not of papal supremacy. The English monarch and Parliament continued to exercise great control over the Church. The Pope's leadership was spiritual but distant and the type of interference in internal affairs that was seen before 1529 would not be tolerated. This was demonstrated when in 1555 Pole was stripped of his position as legate and summoned to Rome to face charges of heresy. Mary refused to allow the new legate entry to England and argued that Pole, as an Englishman, could not be made to face charges in Rome. She continued to support Pole and he remained the Archbishop of Canterbury until his death in 1558.

Therefore, the English Counter-Reformation (the reversal of the Reformation) did not return England to the same religious position as it had been in 1529. The influence of the monarch and laity in religion would not be halted. Lay control was exercised at both national and local level and the success of the Marian settlement depended to a great extent on the fact that it was backed by the nobility and gentry represented in Parliament.

Cardinal Pole's reforms

The history of the Marian settlement is overwhelmingly dominated by Mary's policy of persecuting Protestants; however, the restitution of Catholicism was achieved not only through fear, but through a programme of education modelled on that adopted on the continent. Pole appointed a dedicated team of Catholic bishops who were instructed to visit the parishes of their diocese to supervise the work of their priests. Pole intended to revitalise the education of the clergy by setting up **seminaries** in every diocese. However, this was only achieved in the diocese of York because considerable funds were needed to set up a system that embraced the whole country, and Pole's attempts to restore Church finances had not succeeded by the time of his death in 1558. Consequently the majority of the clergy remained poorly educated. This may account for why very few of the clergy objected to the Elizabethan settlement after 1559. They were not fired with the same zeal as the Marian bishops.

Definition

Seminary

A theological college primarily aimed at educating the priesthood.

Discussion point

Mary was a strict Catholic but she was prepared to compromise on the speed and extent of the restoration of the Catholic Church in England. Why?

Case study: The religious persecution of 'Bloody Mary'

Mary Tudor's historical reputation is that of 'Bloody Mary', the motivating force behind the brutal persecution of Protestants that resulted in the death of 284 men and women burned at the stake as heretics in the period 1555–58. Although Duffy has more recently attempted to rehabilitate Mary's reputation, arguing that her actions were neither extreme nor disproportionate for the time, the traditional view has stuck. The revival of the medieval heresy laws provided the legal justification for this action. Her moral justification was her belief that the removal of persistent promoters of lewd and seditious ideas was essential for the wellbeing of the country, and to demonstrate to the population at large the folly of pursuing heretical practices. Although Mary was clearly a force behind the executions, she was not alone in advocating the policy; she was supported by Pole, who advised her not to be afraid to take up the sword in defence of the Catholic faith, and by Bishop Bonner of London, as well as by zealous magistrates who organised nocturnal raids on the homes of suspected heretics.

The accounts of the executions have been immortalised in John Foxe's 'Act and Monuments', more commonly known as the 'Book of Martyrs', which was first printed in 1560 and rapidly became a best-seller. The majority of those executed were from the lower orders and most came from London, the south east and East Anglia. The most notorious executions were those of the Edwardian bishops: Hooper of Gloucester, in February 1555; Latimer of Worcester and Ridley of London, in October 1555; and of Archbishop Cranmer, in March 1556, after he had retracted his recantation of the Protestant faith. Although the executions did not lead to an outbreak of rebellion and were by and large accepted by the population, there were individual protests in crowds where Protestants had gathered. Even the Spanish Ambassador, Renard, suggested in February 1555 that another approach might be taken, perhaps imprisonment or secret executions that would not attract the same attention.

The scale of the burnings sanctioned by Mary and her Councillors is limited if they are compared to the executions on the continent during the Counter-Reformation of the sixteenth century. However, during the period February 1555 to November 1558 they averaged six a month, which in that time-frame was considerably higher than on the continent and, thus, it is difficult to claim that Mary's policy was moderate. There is evidence to suggest that they were effective: the number of deaths peaked in June 1557 and began to decline thereafter. Furthermore, because Protestants were executed in their own districts, many people in the country would never have experienced the policy of persecution first-hand, and their perception of Mary's reign would have been very different from those in communities where Protestantism had taken hold during Henry's and Edward's reigns.

In the case of committed Protestants, Mary's policy had a limited impact. The scale of persecutions led to some more wealthy Protestants leaving England to join colonies of Protestants on the continent. In time this would strengthen the Protestant faith and imbue people with Calvinist ideas that ultimately resulted in a more radical form of Protestantism being introduced into England in the reign of Elizabeth. In England the burnings did not lead to an increase in the number of Protestants, in fact, it would be fair to conclude that the majority of the population was Catholic in November 1558. However, it did lead to a more committed resistance to Catholicism in the now underground Protestant communities, and this did seriously undermine Mary's popularity in those areas.

3.5 The burning of Archbishop Thomas Cranmer as shown in Foxe's 'Book of Martyres'

SKILLS BUILDER

1. Work with a partner to research the evidence for 'Bloody Mary'.
2. Make a list of the reasons why Mary executed Protestants.
3. Use textbooks and the Internet to explain the executions of:
   - Latimer, Ridley and Hooper
   - Cranmer.
4. Consider what alternative methods she could have used to enforce Catholicism.
5. Compile your results as a PowerPoint® presentation for class discussion.

How successful was the Marian settlement?

Traditionally historians have tended to see the Marian settlement as a failure, an aberration in the march towards Protestantism that began in 1529 and was completed by the Elizabethan settlement. This argument, promoted by Elton and Dickens, claims that the triumph of Protestantism was inevitable because Protestantism was already so established that it would be impossible for Catholicism to be restored to England. There has been recent criticism of this position, particularly by revisionist historians Haigh and Duffy. They argue that, far from being well established, Protestantism had only a loose hold on the population, particularly outside of the south east, and that in many places the revival of Catholicism was genuinely popular. They offer the response of the Edwardian bishops to the Marian settlement as evidence that there was limited genuine adherence to Protestant ideas and a clear willingness to embrace Catholicism once more. Only seven of Edward's bishops were deprived of their livings by 1554 as a result of their refusal to accept the restoration of Catholicism. This compares favourably to the response of the Marian bishops to the Elizabethan settlement where all but one of them refused to take the Oath of Supremacy. Furthermore, only 800 members of the lower clergy were deprived or their livings, the majority because they were married men and not because they opposed the religious change. The majority retrieved their livings by ending their marriages. Consequently, Haigh argues that the Marian settlement was a success. Although all Protestants could not be crushed and enthusiasm was patchy in places, there is evidence from the parishes that there was considerable and continuing support for traditional services and celebrations, and recruitment to the clergy was the strongest it had been for 30 years.

The research of Haigh and Duffy has helped to provide greater balance to an argument that has been driven by the hindsight of the triumph of Protestantism. However, it is important not to exaggerate the success. Mary reigned for only five years and died without leaving a Catholic heir.

Pole's reforms had been only partially implemented, considerably hampered by the lack of finances required to restore the churches to their pre-Reformation condition and to provide an effective education for the clergy. Although it is possible that if Mary had lived longer England may have been fully restored to Catholicism, the inescapable fact is that she did not and the Elizabethan settlement of 1559 put England firmly on the path to embracing Protestantism. In the long run, Mary's policy of persecution, coupled with her unpopular marriage to Philip of Spain, would help ensure that Catholicism was associated with intolerance and was considered to be alien. Therefore, the success that Mary did enjoy was short-lived.

The Elizabethan settlement, 1558–66

The accession of Elizabeth I, November 1558

Mary fell ill in August 1558, a victim of the seasonal influenza that exacerbated an underlying medical condition. By the end of October she was growing weaker and her chances of recovery seemed slim. On 28 October she added a **codicil** to her will that she would be succeeded by 'my next heir and successor by the laws of this realm'. Although she could not bring herself to name Elizabeth, she had accepted that she would not produce an heir and so bowed to the inevitability that her Protestant half-sister would succeed her. In early November, Mary despatched her lady, Jane Dormer, to inform Elizabeth and to ask Elizabeth to pay her debts and keep the re-established Catholic religion. Elizabeth's response to this is unclear. Jane Dormer reported that Elizabeth had declared herself a 'true Catholic' while Protestant accounts state that she agreed not to change anything that could be 'proved by the word of God'. Elizabeth would, in time, prove herself to be a pragmatic politician and it is quite likely that she sent back to Mary the assurances that she needed then circulated a different account to her Protestant supporters, whom she would call upon after her accession.

According to David Starkey's account, however, Elizabeth was leaving nothing to chance. Her servants were positioned around the country in country houses and even at court. They had stockpiled weapons and laid plans for raising troops in the event of Mary diverting the succession away from Elizabeth. This, Starkey suggests, raises questions over Elizabeth's proclaimed innocence in the various plots in which she was implicated during Mary's reign. However, in the event, Elizabeth's succession was one of the smoothest since that of Henry VI. Parliament was already assembled and on 17 November, when they were informed of Mary's death, Lords and Commons proclaimed Elizabeth as Queen.

Discussion point

Examine the attitudes and the responses of the Catholic and Protestant bishops and clergy to both the Marian and Elizabethan settlements.

To what extent do they reveal support and/or opposition to the religious changes? Explain the reasons why.

Definition

Codicil
A document that amends a will.

3.6 The coronation of Elizabeth I

Matthew Parker (1504–1575)

Parker was educated in Cambridge where he came under the influence of the Cambridge reformers. He was chaplain to Anne Boleyn and Henry VIII. Under Edward, he was made Dean of Lincoln. He was deprived of his living under Mary Tudor but became Archbishop of Canterbury after the passing of the Elizabethan settlement. He was a moderate reformer and an influential theologian. He was one of the authors of the Thirty-Nine Articles.

Elizabeth's religious beliefs

An understanding of the English Church settlement of 1558–66 cannot be achieved without an appreciation of Elizabeth's religious inheritance and beliefs. Elizabeth's upbringing had been decidedly Protestant. Her mother, Anne Boleyn, had left her religious welfare in the care of her chaplain, **Matthew Parker**, later to be appointed Elizabeth's first Archbishop of Canterbury. Furthermore, she had been cared for by Catherine Parr, an enthusiastic Protestant, in her formative years and had been educated alongside her brother Edward by tutor Roger Ascham from Cambridge, a hotbed of Protestantism. The evidence that we have from Elizabeth's personal translations, her book of private devotions and her attitude to what she considered popish influences – candles, images of saints and the elevation of the Host at Mass, which she refused to permit – all point to her Protestant beliefs. However, Elizabeth was a more astute politician than her sister Mary. She was not about to foment religious strife in England without taking due consideration of both national and international concerns.

Key issues affecting Elizabeth's decision in 1558

National considerations

Elizabeth was aware that the majority of the population, especially outside of London and the south east, were conservative in religion, and preferred the ceremonies and celebrations that were an integral part of the Catholic Church. She wanted to avoid the mistakes of Edward's and Mary's reigns;

3.7 Elizabeth I and her Privy Chamber

Edward's attempt to introduce Protestantism led to the Western Rebellion in 1549, while Mary's persecution of Protestants had given the victims the status of martyrs and hardened attitudes against her. Elizabeth did not want to spark a similar response from England's Catholics. Furthermore, although she could expect support for legislation reforming the Church in England along Protestant lines from the largely Protestant House of Commons and Privy Council, she knew that the response from the House of Lords, dominated by Catholics including the Marian bishops, was likely to be hostile.

Diplomatic considerations

It was not only the impact of religious change at home that Elizabeth had to consider. Spain and France were both Catholic countries, and unlikely to support a Protestant reformation in England. However, Spain needed its alliance with England to maintain its diplomatic position in Europe, and this offered the opportunity for Elizabeth to pursue moderate reform without fearing Spanish intervention. On the other hand, Elizabeth did not want to antagonise France during the peace negotiations that were to bring the recent war to an end. She was hopeful of regaining Calais and did not want to provide further reasons for French resistance. She also worried about the power of the papacy. The Pope could use the ultimate weapon of **excommunication** against Elizabeth. This would not only encourage the European powers, principally Spain, to launch a religious crusade against England, but also release her own subjects from their duty of obedience to her.

Elizabeth could not even be certain of support from the Protestant states in Europe. In the Netherlands Protestant sympathies were growing, but it was under Spanish control and since it offered Philip II the possibility of launching an invasion of England from its ports, Elizabeth had to tread cautiously in her relations there. Furthermore, although the Scottish population and its Lords were **Presbyterian** Protestants and would not oppose Elizabeth in reforming the English Church on Protestant lines, its regent, Mary of Guise, and its absent Queen Mary were both Catholic.

Mary, Queen of Scots was married to Francis II of France and, on their accession to the French throne in July 1559, Mary claimed the title of Queen of England. England's Catholics might well regard Mary as the rightful Queen rather than Elizabeth since they did not recognise the legality of Henry VIII's marriage to Anne Boleyn. Elizabeth was aware of the dangers present on her northern border and had to take them into consideration when proposing religious change. Therefore, when Elizabeth made her choice, she could not decide purely on the basis of personal preference, she had to take into account the likely domestic and foreign reactions.

Definitions

Excommunication

The censure pronounced by the Pope on an individual who has committed an act that requires him or her to be separated from the Church and to be forbidden to take any of the sacraments. It is necessary that other Catholics should not associate with the excommunicated person.

Presbyterian

The Presbyterian Church is a Christian Church that has no hierarchy but instead has a structure in which power is vested in ministers and lay elders. Its doctrine is based largely on the sovereignty of God and the authority of the Bible.

SKILLS BUILDER

In groups discuss the pros and cons for Elizabeth in making an alliance with Spain.

What were Elizabeth's aims for the religious settlement?

Elizabeth's religious settlement reveals that she was a pragmatic politician. Her own preferences were for a Protestant Church, but she was aware that the introduction of radical Protestantism in England would spark discontent at home and threats from abroad. Consequently she steered a middle way. Her religious bills sought to introduce a Protestant doctrine, including the rejection of transubstantiation, but to keep a traditional structure to the Church, as well as familiar rituals. She believed that this would be acceptable to the majority of the population. She would avoid the persecution that had characterised Mary Tudor's reign and made her so unpopular in the south and east, as well as reassuring the Catholic European powers that the Church in England had changed very little. Above all, Elizabeth sought two outcomes from her religious settlement.

- Uniformity: Elizabeth wanted to establish a national Church that would be acceptable to all.
- Conformity: Elizabeth was determined that her subjects would conform to the demands of her religious settlement regardless of their personal religious beliefs.

These two aims were central to the successful establishment of a religious settlement that would avoid the type of religious war that was present on the continent. In time, Elizabeth hoped that her subjects would know no other type of Church. Catholicism would die out with the older generations.

The Church settlement, 1559

The introduction of the religious bills

It was necessary for Parliament to be called to enact religious legislation and it was duly summoned. In early February 1559, three religious bills were introduced into the House of Commons. One was to establish the monarch as the head of the Church and the other two were to establish a Protestant form of worship. On 21 February they were combined into a single bill and passed by the Commons, whose MPs favoured Protestantism. However, the House of Lords forced the bill into a committee dominated by Catholic sympathisers and they stunned Elizabeth by rejecting the restoration of Protestantism, refusing to repeal Mary Tudor's heresy laws and questioning Elizabeth's right to supremacy over the Church. It seemed as if Elizabeth had stumbled at the first hurdle.

The Easter disputation

It was at this point that Elizabeth's political ability came to the fore. She did not want to lose the support of the Commons, and while fresh elections might well return a similarly favourable house, this could not be guaranteed. Dissolving Parliament was, therefore, a risky venture with an uncertain outcome, so Elizabeth chose a different path: at Easter, Elizabeth **prorogued** Parliament.

Definitions

Prorogue

To suspend a parliamentary session or to discontinue it without formally ending the session.

Disputation

A formalised method of debate that was designed to uncover truths in theology. It had developed from the scholastic tradition of the Middle Ages.

During Holy Week a **disputation** was held at Westminster Abbey. The debate – a set piece – was to be held between four Catholic bishops and doctors and an equivalent number of Protestants. There were three propositions for debate:

- 'It is contrary to the word of God to use a tongue unknown to the people in worship' (i.e. Latin).
- 'Every Church has authority to change its ceremonies'.
- 'It cannot be proved by the word of God that there is in the Mass offered up a sacrifice propitiatory for the quick and the dead'.

Elizabeth's ministers left nothing to chance. The Catholics were barely able to state their case. **Sir Nicholas Bacon** intervened as soon as they suggested that the debate take place in Latin, as was traditional, and stopped them in their tracks. On the following day, he stonewalled the bishops (by using delaying tactics) and forced them into an act of defiance that justified the arrest of the Bishops of Winchester and Lincoln, who were sent to the Tower for contempt. The rest of the bishops were bound over. By these means, Elizabeth won the disputation.

The Act of Supremacy and Act of Uniformity

Elizabeth reconvened Parliament after Easter. Two new bills were introduced into the Commons, so that if one failed the other might pass.

The Act of Supremacy

- Elizabeth was made Supreme Governor of the Church of England. This was a lesser claim than Head of the Church and eased the worries of both Catholics and Protestants who had doubts as to whether a female could be head of the Church. In reality, Elizabeth would be able to exercise as much power over the Church as her father had done.
- The clergy and royal officials were obliged to swear acceptance of Elizabeth's title on oath.
- Papal supremacy was revoked.
- The heresy laws were to be repealed.
- An ecclesiastical high commission was established to ensure that the changes were implemented at parish level, and those whose loyalty was suspect could be prosecuted.

There were no other changes to the structure of the Church in England. The Archbishop of Canterbury remained the **primate**, presiding over the Archbishop of York and the bishops who governed their dioceses. In this respect the English Church was unique. The Protestant Churches in Europe did not have a hierarchical structure that had its origins in the Roman Catholic Church, but instead the congregations organised themselves. However, the presence of a familiar structure was a great comfort to the traditionalist sympathies of the English population.

3.8 Sir Nicholas Bacon

The *Act of Supremacy* passed easily in both Commons and Lords but the passage of the second act, the *Act of Uniformity*, proved much more difficult.

The *Act of Uniformity*

The *Act of Uniformity* focused on the appearance of the churches and the acts of worship that took place in them.

- A new Book of Common Prayer was issued based on those of 1549 and 1552.
- All churches were obliged to use the new prayer book and there were punishments for those who failed to use it or publicly raised objections to it.
- The priest was instructed to use the wording of both the 1549 and 1552 prayer books in the communion service when offering communion in both kinds. The words were sufficiently ambiguous for Catholics to perceive the presence of the living Christ in the Eucharist, while Protestants could regard it as a commemorative act.
- Everyone was to attend church on Sunday and holy days.
- A fine of one shilling for every absence was imposed on those who failed to attend church services. These people were known as recusants.
- The ornaments in church and clerical dress were to be the same as in the second year of Edward VI's reign. This discouraged enthusiastic Protestants from attacking what they considered to be popish idolatry in the churches.
- The taxes known as First Fruit and Tenths were to be paid to the Crown.
- The monasteries and chantries that Mary Tudor had founded were to be dissolved and their assets transferred to the Crown.

Although the *Act of Uniformity* passed through the Commons without incident, it faced a considerable struggle in the Lords, where all the bishops were united in their opposition and nine temporal peers joined them. In the end the act passed by the narrowest of margins: 21 to 18. This victory was only possible because the bishops of Winchester and Lincoln were still detained in the Tower and the Abbot of Westminster and the Bishop of St Asaph were both absent.

To what extent was the Elizabethan settlement a Puritan settlement?

In the 1950s historian John Neale argued that Elizabeth had intended to establish an Anglo-Catholic Church modelled on that of Henry VIII's, but that she was thwarted in her plans by a vociferous **Puritan** opposition in the House of Commons, which forced her into a more radical settlement. He termed this opposition a 'Puritan choir' and regarded it as holding significant influence in the Commons. Neale's thesis has been questioned in more recent years. Although there were Puritan challenges in the Commons in the 1570s and 1580s, there is scant evidence that the Commons was a hotbed of radicalism in 1559. Only 19 of the **Marian exiles** were elected in 1559 and they were not sufficiently organised to exert any concerted pressure on the Commons as a whole.

Discussion point

Why was Elizabeth able to pass her religious bills?

Work with a partner to make a list of at least three reasons.

Definitions

Puritanism

The beliefs and practices of more extreme Protestants who were influenced by John Calvin. Puritans aspired to introduce some key features into the Church of England: an emphasis on preaching and private prayer rather than ceremonies and rituals; the removal of all traces of Catholic practice; and the reduction of central control exercised by the Crown and the bishops.

Marian exiles

The English Calvinist Protestants who fled to the continent during Mary's reign.

According to Norman Jones, in total only 25 MPs could be labelled as Calvinist or radical Protestants and, since there were 400 MPs in the Commons, their impact was extremely limited. Although it may have been expedient for Elizabeth to push a conservative line when negotiating with the French and the Spanish, her religious beliefs and her choice of Protestant ministers – Cecil, Bacon and the Earl of Bedford – do not support the notion that she favoured an essentially Catholic settlement. In fact, as the previous narrative has demonstrated, the greater challenges to Elizabeth's proposals came from the conservative House of Lords not from the Commons.

SKILLS BUILDER

1. How Protestant was the settlement of 1559?

2. 'Both Catholic and reformed.' Is this a true reflection of the Church settlement of 1559?

Study the narrative on the passing of the *Acts of Supremacy* and *Uniformity* and complete a two-column table under the headings 'Protestant elements' and 'Catholic elements'.

In drawing up this table, you have categorised the key features of the acts and the circumstances in which they were passed. In order to address the question you now need to reach a judgement as to 'how far' the settlement was Protestant. Consider the weight of each side. Which factors are of overriding significance? How acceptable would the settlement be to Catholics? How acceptable would it be to Protestants?

The development of the English Church settlement, 1559–66

Additions to the settlement

The Royal Injunctions, 1559

The *Acts of Supremacy* and *Uniformity* were a starting point but they required enforcement. The Royal Injunctions of 1559 were issued to perform this task. They were drafted by Elizabeth's Chief Minister, William Cecil, and contained direct instructions to the clergy, covering a wide range of practices, to establish a uniformity of worship and behaviour. They confirm Elizabeth's desire to establish a moderate but distinctly Protestant Church:

- the clergy were instructed to observe and teach the royal supremacy and to denounce papal supremacy
- Catholic practices including processions, pilgrimages and monuments to 'fake' miracles were banned

- recusants were to be denounced and reported to the Privy Council or to JPs
- recusants were to pay a shilling fine for every time they failed to attend church on Sundays or holy days
- unlicensed preaching was forbidden. This attacked radical Puritanism and was based on Elizabeth's fear that it could lead to civil disorder, as well as undermining her authority and that of her bishops
- each parish was to possess an English Bible (the Geneva Bible with Calvinist notes was printed in 1560)
- the congregation was to bow at the name of Jesus and kneel in prayer
- the clergy were to wear distinctive clerical dress, including the surplice
- clerical marriage was only permitted where the priest had permission from his bishop and two JPs.

In order to ensure that the acts and the injunctions were enforced, 125 commissioners were appointed to visit churches across the country and to require clergy to take the Oath of Supremacy.

The Thirty-Nine Articles, 1563

The Canterbury Convocation drew up the Thirty-Nine Articles when it met in 1563. They were a statement of the doctrinal beliefs of the Church of England, based on Archbishop Thomas Cranmer's Forty-Two Articles of 1552. The articles repudiated key Catholic doctrine, such as the miracle of transubstantiation, the sacrifice of the Mass and the sinlessness of Mary, the mother of Christ, while confirming key elements of Protestant belief: the authority of the scriptures, that Adam's fall compromised human free will, the necessity of communion in both kinds and that ministers may marry. They were finally approved in 1571 and all the ordained clergy had to swear to them.

The English Church settlement and the bishops

The reasons for establishing a Protestant episcopacy

Elizabeth, as supreme governor, needed to be represented by a body that would supervise the Church and its clergy and enforce her decisions. It was clear to her that the bishops could perform this function and that their presence would also calm Catholic fears both at home and abroad. Her bishops were perhaps more distinctly Protestant than she might have desired. This was because all but one of the Marian bishops refused to take the Oath of Supremacy. Consequently, Elizabeth turned to men who had been exiles during Mary's reign. Elizabeth chose her mother's chaplain, Matthew Parker, as Archbishop of Canterbury. He was a moderate Protestant who used his influence to keep the spread of Puritanism in check. **Edmund Grindal** was appointed Bishop of London, **John Jewell** to Salisbury and **Edwin Sandys** to Worcester.

Biographies

Edmund Grindal (1519–1583)

Grindal succeeded Matthew Parker as Archbishop of Canterbury in 1575. He had qualms about vestments and other popish elements that he perceived in the Elizabethan Church. He came into conflict with Elizabeth over prophesyings (Puritan gatherings to practise preaching skills) and was placed under virtual house arrest in 1577 until his death in 1583.

John Jewell (1522–1571)

Jewell supported Cranmer and Ridley and consequently fled to Frankfurt to avoid Mary's persecution. He returned to England after Elizabeth's accession to the throne and was appointed Bishop of Salisbury. He defended the Elizabethan Church against its critics. He died in 1571.

Their enthusiasm for the more stripped-down version of Protestantism that they experienced on the continent during their exile is reflected in their actions in the Visitations (see below), in which they approved the removal and destruction of church ornaments. Many bishops regarded the settlement of 1559 as the starting point for reform, thus conflicting with Elizabeth's view that the acts and the Royal Injunctions were a complete settlement.

The role of the bishops

Elizabeth regarded her bishops first and foremost as loyal administrators, civil servants who could be relied upon to enforce the royal will. Her attitude is demonstrated in action to curtail their power and influence in the *Act of Exchange*, 1559. Under this act, Crown lands that had once belonged to the Church were returned in exchange for valuable diocesan properties of a non-spiritual nature. In practice this meant swapping rectories and church buildings for castles and manor houses. Elizabeth used this newly-acquired wealth to reward courtiers. She also put pressure on bishops to grant favourable leases to laymen. The practice overcame some of the difficulties Elizabeth faced with her shortage of income, but it did not sit well with the bishops, who perceived that they were being used as tools of the Crown, especially as it was more often used as a means of punishment than for economic gain.

How significant were the challenges to the Church settlement to 1566?

The Visitations

The Visitations were essentially inspections of parishes by bishops to ensure that the acts and the Royal Injunctions were being properly enforced. As previously mentioned, the visiting bishops often went further in their enforcement of a Protestant Church than Elizabeth had intended. In many cases, images, Catholic clothing, relics and altars were deliberately destroyed and, although Elizabeth demanded that crucifixes were to be replaced, she was obliged to back down and content herself with the display of a crucifix in the royal chapel where it would be seen by foreign ambassadors and reassure them that Elizabeth's faith differed very little from their own Catholic faith.

The clergy

Those making the Visitations were empowered to examine the beliefs of the clergy and to ensure that they took the Oath of Supremacy and subscribed to the Book of Common Prayer and the Royal Injunctions. Four hundred of the clergy, divided almost equally between Catholics and Protestants, refused to take the oath and were obliged to resign their livings as a result. There were 8,000–9,000 parishes in England at that time, so the number of dissenters was, in fact, remarkably low.

Biography

Edwin Sandys (1519–1588)

Sandys was arrested for his part in the rebellion in favour of Lady Jane Grey in 1553 and imprisoned in the Tower. He was later moved to the Marshalsea, from which he escaped and then fled to the continent. He returned on Elizabeth's accession and became Bishop of Worcester, Bishop of London and Archbishop of York successively.

Discussion point

How far did the bishops accept the Elizabethan settlement?

The Vestiarian Controversy, 1566

In January 1565, Elizabeth wrote to Archbishop Parker expressing her concern that members of the clergy were not abiding by the injunction about the correct clerical dress. Elizabeth had required full vestments for church services. Parker reprimanded the clergy involved and then went further. In his effort to clarify the settlement in terms of clerical dress, doctrine, prayer and the sacraments, he issued the 'Book of Advertisements'. Although Parker reinforced the Queen's insistence on issues such as communicants kneeling to receive the sacraments in both kinds, he showed himself very willing to compromise on clerical dress, allowing the clergy in parishes to wear the surplice and only insisting on full vestments in cathedral services. Consequently, Elizabeth refused to give the Advertisements an official endorsement. Parker also faced opposition from the Puritan clergy. In a display of the correct clerical clothing held at his palace at Lambeth, 37 of the 110 clergy present refused to wear clothing that they deemed to be Catholic. They were removed from office.

How far had Elizabeth secured religious peace by 1566?

By 1566, Elizabeth's desire for a Protestant settlement that retained a traditional Catholic appearance had been largely successful.

> **Definition**
>
> **Church papists**
>
> A disparaging term for those English Catholics who outwardly conformed to the established Protestant Church and yet inwardly remained Roman Catholics.

- The majority of the largely Catholic population had accepted the settlement. Most Catholics fell into the category known as '**Church papists**'. They attended church services regularly. It is true that many parishes were slow to introduce all the reforms outlined in the injunctions and consequently for some there was very little evidence of change initially. This, however, suited Elizabeth's desire that no radical change should lead to rebellion. Through the process of Visitations, these changes would eventually be implemented and in such a way as to be imperceptible to the population. There were very few fines levied for recusancy. This is a difficult area to assess. The levying of fines depended upon the church wardens and they would be less inclined to report offences if they were Catholic sympathisers themselves. Furthermore, Elizabeth did not want to pursue the matter with vigour, lest such a move result in open opposition. In spite of these difficulties, it is reasonable to conclude that up to 1566 the population did conform to the settlement. It was not until the arrival of Mary, Queen of Scots that the Catholics felt their loyalties divided and even then the response of the great majority was to support Elizabeth.
- Foreign ambassadors reported that the Queen might be led back into the Catholic Church and this allowed Elizabeth to maintain cordial relations with France and Spain. Hence the settlement had performed its role in this respect.
- The lower clergy had for the most part accepted the settlement. Over 8,000 took the Oath of Supremacy. This, in turn, would facilitate the gradual demise of Catholicism in England without rebellion, as the population grew to accept the new services.

- The idea that that settlement was merely a starting point still held sway with more radical reformers who wanted to see a purer form of Protestantism introduced into England. They were, perhaps, more threatening at this point because they had the sympathy and, in some cases, support of the Elizabethan bishops. As long as Parker was at the helm such ambitions could be kept in check, but Puritan challenges would increase under Archbishop Grindal in the 1570s.

- Elizabeth's position as Supreme Governor of the Church was secure and she was able to enforce her wishes through her bishops with only limited challenge.

Unit summary

What have you learned in this unit?

- Moderate Protestant reforms were implemented by Somerset. With the enthusiastic support of the King, Northumberland pushed England firmly on the path towards Protestantism.

- The religious policies of the two Tudor Queens were driven firstly by their beliefs, but while Mary was less prepared to compromise in those beliefs and so adopted a policy of persecution to restore Catholicism, Elizabeth learned from Mary's mistakes. She adopted a more pragmatic approach to the achievement of her settlement, focusing on the need for uniformity and conformity as the essential factors.

- The majority of English subjects were prepared to conform, at least outwardly, to the form of religion imposed by the monarch. Therefore, although in 1558 the majority of the population was Catholic, by 1566, most had accepted the Anglican Church.

What skills have you used in this unit?

You have discussed a number of issues and weighed up a range of alternatives to enable you to provide explanations and reach informed judgements.

Exam style question

This is the sort of question you will find appearing on the examination paper as a Section A question:

'At the time, the Church settlement of 1559–66 was an arrangement acceptable to most of Elizabeth's subjects.'

How far do you agree with this judgement?

Exam tips

In order to answer this question successfully, you will need to plan and prepare your answer with care:

- use the material in this chapter to identify the different religious priorities of Elizabeth's Catholic and Protestant subjects
- examine the Elizabethan settlement of 1559 and consider how far those priorities were met for both Catholics and Protestants
- study the reactions of Catholics and Protestants in the years 1559–66 to weigh up how far they found the settlement acceptable and what issues they were prepared to oppose
- make your judgement as to how far, on balance, the settlement was acceptable to most subjects.

RESEARCH TOPIC

What challenges were there to the Elizabethan settlement in the period 1566–88?

Work with a partner to research the following challenges:

1 The Puritan challenge:
- Thomas Cartwright and the 'Spring Lectures'
- Grindal and prophesying
- Whitgift and the attack on the Puritans
- the Puritan challenge in Parliament.

2 The Catholic challenge:
- the Northern Rebellion
- the papacy and the excommunication of Elizabeth
- the seminary priests and the Jesuits.

SKILLS BUILDER

Do you agree that Elizabeth achieved most of what she wanted in the period 1559–66?

1. Draw up a table to record her achievements and possible failures. Remember you will need to refer back to her aims in order to make the assessment.

2. How far do you agree that subjects were prepared to accept the religious preference of the monarch?

Compare the key features and differences of the religious settlements of Edward, Mary and Elizabeth, including the nature of opposition to the settlements.

4 Anglo-Spanish relations (1): The era of alliance and diplomacy, 1553–72

What is this unit about?

This unit focuses on Mary's and Elizabeth's aims in their relations with Spain and the extent to which they fulfilled them in the period to 1572. It explores Mary's decision to contract a marriage to Philip of Spain – the great-nephew of her mother, Catherine of Aragon – and the implications that had for England's foreign affairs. It examines Elizabeth's attempts to guarantee English security and independence in the face of the developing wars of religion in continental Europe. In particular, it considers the significance of the role of religion in foreign affairs and the pressures from members of Elizabeth's Privy Council to intervene in conflicts for religious reasons. It also considers the extent to which her relations with Spain had reached crisis point by 1572.

In this unit you will:

- explore the reasons why Mary was determined to marry Philip of Spain
- examine the impact Mary's marriage had on her conduct of foreign affairs
- make judgements on the importance of religion in the development of foreign affairs
- identify Elizabeth's aims in diplomacy and compare them with the policies pursued
- discuss the extent to which her policies succeeded and consider how far the years 1568–72 can be considered years of crisis.

Key questions

- What was the impact of Mary's marriage on foreign affairs?
- What were Elizabeth's diplomatic aims?
- To what extent was Elizabeth's relationship with Spain governed by religious and economic interests?
- How far did she achieve her aims in the period 1558–72?
- What was the impact of religion on foreign affairs?
- How great a threat was England's changing relationship with Spain?
- What were the significant changes in Anglo-Spanish relations in the period 1553–72?

Timeline

1553	July	Accession of Mary I
1554	July	Marriage to Philip of Spain
1557		War against France
1558	January	Loss of Calais
	April	Negotiations with France
	November	Mary's death
		Accession of Elizabeth
1559	April	Treaty of Cateau-Cambresis
	May	Rebellion of the Protestant lords in Scotland
1560	February	Treaty of Berwick
	July	Treaty of Edinburgh
1561	August	Mary, Queen of Scots returns to Scotland
1562	March	Outbreak of religious wars in France
	September	Treaty of Hampton Court
1564	April	Peace of Troyes
1566	Summer	Revolt in the Netherlands
1567	July	Deposition of Mary, Queen of Scots
1568	May	Mary flees to England
	June	Defeat of William of Orange
	November	Seizure of Spanish gold florins
1569	November	Northern Rebellion
1570	February	Papal bull of excommunication
1571		Ridolfi Plot
1572	April	Treaty of Blois
	August	St Bartholomew's Day Massacre

The conduct of foreign affairs in the reign of Mary I

The Spanish marriage and its impact

Reasons for Mary's marriage to Philip of Spain

Mary was determined from the outset of her reign that she needed a husband to offer advice and to father the Catholic heir that was necessary to complete her restoration of Catholicism. It is perhaps natural that the daughter of Catherine of Aragon should have sought a husband among her Spanish relatives, who had been her strongest supporters during the previous two reigns. England had a long history of friendly relations with Spain. A Spanish alliance had first been forged by Henry VII with the marriage between Arthur and Catherine of Aragon, and this had continued during the reign of Henry VIII. Although there had been periods of enmity

4.1 'The Family of Henry VIII: An Allegory of the Tudor Succession' shows Henry and his successors, including Mary and Philip (left)

between England and Spain during her father's reign, by the time of his death in 1547 the wars against France and Scotland ensured that the relationship with Spain was at least cordial, and this situation had continued during the reign of Edward. Thus, in 1553, Mary discussed the possibility of marriage to Charles V's son, Philip, with Renard, the Spanish ambassador. Although the Spanish were not the enemy that they would become by 1588, Mary was ignoring the advice of her Privy Council, including her most trusted Councillor, Stephen Gardiner: that the marriage could prove unpopular with those who objected to Spanish Catholicism and those who suspected that England could become a mere pawn in Spanish ambitions to dominate the continent. The House of Commons also raised strong objections. Nevertheless, Mary stubbornly pursued the marriage and the agreement was reached in January 1554. The marriage treaty did offer some advantage to England as well as safeguards. The heir of Mary and Philip would inherit the Netherlands as well as England and this offered the possibility of England establishing a secure and substantial empire on the continent. Furthermore, Philip was prohibited from exercising any power in England and from appointing any Spaniards to English offices. Nevertheless, it was the proposed Spanish marriage that was the catalyst for the only rebellion of Mary's reign, which is explained in detail on pages 129–131.

The Spanish marriage and foreign affairs

Ultimately, Mary's marriage to Philip in July 1554 was a disaster. In England the match was very unpopular and was blamed, wrongly, by merchants for the decline in the wool trade with the Netherlands at that time. Furthermore, by 1555 it was evident to Philip that there was no possibility of Mary bearing a child and he returned to Spain, which he had inherited on his father's abdication that year. When he returned for a brief visit to England in 1556, it was solely for the purpose of persuading Mary to join him in war against France. The Privy Council was opposed to this but Mary's infatuation with her husband and her sincere belief that she needed his advice led England into a war that resulted in the loss of Calais in 1558, England's last foothold on the continent.

The development of the military and naval system

England's involvement in the renewal of the Hapsburg–Valois conflict would prove disastrous for Mary, but it did lay the foundations of the military and naval system that later enabled Elizabeth to defeat the Armada. The first step towards this was the establishment of a ship-rebuilding programme in 1555, enhanced in 1557 by a repair programme for which the Privy Council allocated funds. Elizabeth would be able to use the vessels supplied by these programmes in her assault on the Scots in 1560. In addition, the war with France revealed the shortcomings of the English military forces and so a new militia system was introduced. The *Arms Act* (1558) provided weapons for troops and so overcame the appalling deficiencies in armaments, while the *Militia Act* of the same year improved efficiency in mustering troops by introducing penalties for failure to respond to the muster.

The French war, 1557–8

War between Spain and France began in January 1557. Initially, England remained neutral but the revelation of French plots to depose Mary tipped the balance and in June 1557 the Privy Council sanctioned the despatch of 7,000 troops, led by Pembroke, to fight in France. Although the major victory of Spain over France had already been achieved, the English were successful in the battle of St Quentin, in which they captured the town and handed it over to the Spanish. If the war had ended at this point, Mary's conduct of foreign affairs would have been regarded favourably. However, unexpectedly, in mid-winter the Duke of Guise led a revenge attack on the fortified town of Calais. The Commander of Calais, Lord Wentworth, was caught by surprise and it seems that it was his failure to take the French threat seriously rather than the condition of the Calais defences that accounts for the defeat and loss in January 1558. While Mary was alive, Philip insisted that the return of Calais to England was included in the peace negotiations, but after her death in November 1558 he ceased to push for it and in the Treaty of Cateau-Cambresis in April 1559 Calais remained in the hands of the French.

An assessment of Mary's marriage and conduct of foreign affairs

The attitude to Mary's marriage may well have been very different if she had produced the longed-for heir. Her religious reforms would have been safeguarded and England's position on the continent would have been significantly strengthened by the takeover of the Netherlands. However, in this she failed and this has led her reign to be regarded as a failure overall.

SKILLS BUILDER

How far did religion shape Mary's foreign affairs?

To address this question you need to list the range of factors that affected Mary's choice of foreign affairs. Religion will be one. You need to identify up to three more factors. Consider what role each factor played in shaping foreign affairs. Which had the greatest influence?

The fear, albeit voiced by a minority at the time, that Philip would use England to pursue his ambitions against France became reality. Although the loss of Calais was not the disaster that it was regarded as at the time, the argument that England would benefit financially because it would no longer need to maintain its three fortresses there could not overcome the sense of national humiliation. By the time Mary died, few people mourned her passing. Her stubborn pursuit of policies without the full support of her Privy Council and her political inexperience that led to ineptitude meant that her reign was not regarded as a success. Consequently, her sister's accession was greeted with celebration and some relief.

What were Mary's achievements?

Mary did not succeed in the twin aims of her reign. Her physical and medical conditions prevented her from bearing a child and the shortness of her reign meant that, although England was largely Catholic in 1558, this situation was only temporary and her half-sister resumed the march towards Protestantism in 1559. Furthermore, her system of government with a greatly expanded Privy Council of 43 members has been described as unwieldy and ineffective. However, in some ways Mary left the country in a better condition than she had found it in 1553. Her Privy Council may have been large, but in effect it operated with an inner core of trusted advisers and special committees to deal with specialised issues. Furthermore, her financial reforms, including the improvement of revenue collection – a more effective collection of customs duties after the introduction of a new Book of Rates – and the plans to revalue the currency, put Crown finances on a more sound footing than they had been in the reign of Edward. Finally, her revival of the army and navy played a vital role in enabling Elizabeth to resist the Spanish in 1588. Therefore, Mary's reign cannot be entirely dismissed as a disaster.

Foreign affairs, 1558–72

Elizabeth's aims

Foreign policy as we know it today did not exist in the sixteenth century and it would not be referred to using this term. The establishment and maintenance of **diplomatic** relations with European neighbours was, however, an essential part of a monarch's role and Elizabeth, like her father and sister before her, reserved the formulation of policy as a royal prerogative. Successful diplomatic relations were judged according to the extent that they met the aims of the monarch; there was little sense of conducting a policy in the broader interests of the country if they did not satisfy the objectives of the Crown. Elizabeth's aims were less ambitious than those of her father. She was not concerned to pursue dynastic claims via marriage into another royal household and, although she desired the return of Calais, lost by Mary in the war against France, she was not interested in asserting the centuries-old claim to the French throne. For Elizabeth, a successful diplomatic policy would be achieved by protecting her realm from invasion from either north or south, thus allowing England

4.2 A portrait of Mary I

to maintain her independence, and by establishing such connections as would allow English trade with the continent to flourish, enriching producers, merchants and particularly the Crown through the collection of taxes and customs duties. Religious issues and the contrasting aims of the other European countries complicated her chances of success in meeting these objectives.

Reformation and Counter-Reformation

The Reformation had destroyed the unity of Christendom and led to the outbreak of religious conflict between and within countries. England was the most important Protestant country in Europe, and Elizabeth's Church settlement confirmed that she intended to return England to Protestantism after Mary Tudor's restoration of Catholicism. This was inevitably a cause for conflict in her relations with the Catholic kingdom of Spain.

4.3 Europe in 1558

Furthermore, when Elizabeth came to the throne, the Counter-Reformation, the Catholic Church's response to the calls for reform, was in full swing. Decisions taken at the **Council of Trent** to establish the training of priests in seminaries, as well as the foundation of the Jesuit order, threatened England. Enthusiastic clerics despatched to England to reignite the spark of Catholicism could trigger the type of religious conflict seen on the continent that had so far been avoided in England.

While Elizabeth was not motivated by religious concerns in her relations with other countries, it is clear from the evidence that members of her Privy Council were. The essential role that religion played in both the internal and external affairs of the state means that a study of Elizabeth's diplomacy is inextricably linked with its domestic impact.

The Hapsburg connection

England had been allied with Spain as a result of Mary Tudor's marriage to Philip II. It appears that Philip briefly considered offering marriage to Elizabeth in 1558. Although the offer itself was rather perfunctory, the desire to maintain peace with England was not. At this time Philip did persuade the Pope not to excommunicate Elizabeth, believing that it was possible that she might be persuaded back into Catholicism. However, the break in relations caused by Mary's death did mean that he ceased to pursue the return of Calais in the Treaty of Cateau-Cambresis in 1559. He was certainly not prepared to fight on England's part to see it returned.

England's relationship with Spain was complicated by four factors.

1. Philip took his role as the leading Catholic monarch in Europe very seriously and, therefore, Elizabeth could not expect that he would tolerate her Protestantism indefinitely.

2. Philip was the ruler of the Netherlands. The Netherlands was important to England as a trading partner; three-quarters of English cloth passed through the port of Antwerp, making the territory essential to the English economy. Moreover, Philip's control of the Netherlands provided him with a base from which to launch an invasion of England and so it was a threat to England's security. The situation was further complicated by the fact that the Netherlands had embraced Protestantism and sought independence from its Catholic master; members of Elizabeth's Privy Council supported intervention to assist them in this quest. Philip would not tolerate this.

3. In 1559 Spain reached an accord with France in the Treaty of Cateau-Cambresis and peace between Europe's foremost Catholic powers was a potential threat if they should decide to make common cause against England.

4. The lure of possessions and wealth in the New World not only significantly increased Philip's wealth but was a cause for competition and hence conflict between Spain and England as seafaring nations.

Definition

Council of Trent
One of the most important councils of the Catholic Church, which met for three sessions in the period 1545–63, during which it condemned Protestant heresies and defined Catholic doctrine.

4.4 Philip II of Spain

4.5 Mary of Guise

However, as emphasised above, in 1558 Philip was not openly hostile to England. He preferred an independent England, albeit ruled by a Protestant and therefore heretic Queen, to the possibility of an England allied to – or even worse dominated by – France. Therefore in 1558 Philip was prepared to tolerate the change of regime rather than intervene in such a way that might drive England into the arms of his enemy.

France

France was England's traditional enemy and English claims to the French throne had sustained conflict for centuries. Furthermore, since the Middle Ages, France had forged an alliance with Scotland that threatened England's northern borders. The Anglo-Spanish alliance forged by Mary had resulted in the loss of the last territory that England possessed in France – Calais. Elizabeth was not prepared to go to war to retrieve it, but she was keen to engineer a situation in which it was returned. The terms of Cateau-Cambresis provided for the return of Calais in eight years or the payment of a French indemnity of 500,000 crowns, provided that England kept the peace. The situation was further complicated because in 1559 the French King, Henry II, died in a jousting accident. Henry's son Francis and his wife, Mary, succeeded him. This was a significant threat to Elizabeth. Francis was married to Mary, Queen of Scots, who had her own claim to the English throne as a great-granddaughter of Henry VII. Furthermore, the accession of Francis I also brought about the ascendancy of the Guise family in France because the young and inexperienced king relied on his uncle, the ultra-Catholic Duke of Guise. **Mary of Guise** was ruling Scotland as regent in her daughter, Mary's, absence. Therefore the new situation threatened England with encirclement, as well as the possibility that Mary, Queen of Scots would assert her claim to the English throne, supported by the Catholic rulers in Scotland. Indeed, at her coronation Mary incorporated the English coat of arms into her own. In time Mary, Queen of Scots would look to Philip of Spain to act as her defender and this played a significant role in the launching of the Armada in 1588.

Scotland

Mary of Guise ruled Scotland as regent for her daughter. After Mary's coronation as Queen of France, the Guise family was keen to advance Mary's claim to the English throne and to use it as a tool in French foreign affairs. However, before progress could be made, Mary of Guise's regency was swept away by revolt in Scotland, as a result of which the Protestant lords took control. This offered a great advantage to Elizabeth in that they could be relied upon to forge friendly relations with England. However, the French were unlikely to allow the **'Auld Alliance'** to be destroyed without attempting to restore it. Therefore, shortly after her accession, Elizabeth was to be confronted with conflict on her doorstep, and one in which it would be difficult to stand aloof.

SKILLS BUILDER

How far was the European situation threatening for Elizabeth in 1558–59?

In order to assess the extent of the threat, you need to review both the dangers to Elizabeth and the opportunities available to her. Study the preceding accounts of the European situation and draw up a table like the one below. Note down the threats and opportunities in the appropriate columns. Once you have examined the content you will be in a position to reach a judgement.

The European situation facing Elizabeth in 1558–59

Country	Threats	Opportunities
Spain France Scotland		

Judgement:

Definition

Auld Alliance

A series of treaties between France and Scotland, first made in 1295–96, directed against England. If England went to war with France, she risked the possibility of a Scottish invasion from the north.

Elizabeth and the Scottish rebellion, 1559–60

Causes of the rebellion

The rebellion began after John Knox returned to Scotland from Geneva. He preached a sermon that encouraged the destruction of church decoration and images. The Protestant Lords of the Congregation took this as a signal to begin military action against the rule of the Guise family. On 21 October 1559 they suspended the regent and took full control. However, it was unlikely that the Guise family would submit to the new situation, and retaliation, with French support, was expected.

The attitude of Elizabeth and her Privy Council

There was great enthusiasm for intervention among the members of Elizabeth's Privy Council. William Cecil, Elizabeth's Secretary of State, in particular, favoured support for the Scottish rebels in order to drive the French out of the British Isles once and for all, and because a Protestant Scotland would be a potential ally for England. Consequently, he sought to persuade Elizabeth to provide aid for the Scottish lords.

The situation was not so simple for Elizabeth. Although she could see the advantage in removing French control in Scotland, she was reticent about involvement in a war with an uncertain outcome, and most importantly she opposed intervention on behalf of rebels who had overthrown their anointed ruler. Diplomatic relations were the Queen's prerogative and ultimately she made the decisions. However, she did take advice from her Council and in the end Cecil persuaded her to support intervention. He drafted a letter that hinted at his resignation and, faced with the loss of her Chief Minister, Elizabeth compromised and acted on the advice she was offered.

Work with a partner to consider the following issues.

- What factors motivated Elizabeth's attitudes and decisions in her relations with Scotland in 1559–60?
- What did she achieve?
- What threats or problems remained?

Definition

Huguenots

Members of the Protestant Church in France who believed in Calvinist doctrine.

Biography

Sir Nicholas Throckmorton (1515–1571)

He was a cousin of Catherine Parr (see p.38) and rose to become a diplomat in Elizabeth's reign. Elizabeth appointed him as ambassador to France. It was in this capacity that he advised support for the Huguenot cause.

English intervention

In February 1560, Elizabeth agreed the Treaty of Berwick with the Scottish lords. It provided for financial and military help from England in order that Scotland should finally be rid of French control. In March, English troops arrived to assist the Scots in their blockade of Leith. This strategy failed but, with the French fleet lost in a storm and the death of Mary of Guise, Cecil was able to bring both sides to negotiations. Under the Treaty of Edinburgh all foreign troops were to withdraw from Scotland and the Scottish Lords of the Congregation were to form a provisional government. Thus Elizabeth's intervention was instrumental in fulfilling one of her key desires, the security of her northern border. Elizabeth could expect to maintain friendly relations with the Protestant government in Scotland and, even though the return of Mary, Queen of Scots in 1561 brought fresh dangers, in the immediate period Elizabeth would benefit from the reality of the Scottish Reformation and Protestant domination in Scotland.

Elizabeth and the French wars of religion, 1562–64

Reasons for intervention

In March 1562, religious civil war broke out in France. Although, on the one hand, this reduced the immediate threat to England since France was focused on its own internal problems, it also raised new issues that Elizabeth's Council were keen to address. Conflicts in the French royal house between the ultra-Catholic Duke of Guise and the House of Bourbon, who supported the French **Huguenots**, drove the religious war. Elizabeth found herself under pressure to intervene on behalf of the Huguenots from Council members, such as Cecil and **Sir Nicholas Throckmorton** as well as Dudley, who was seeking to assert his political power. On this occasion, Elizabeth needed less persuading. The success of the Scottish venture no doubt spurred her on, but she was primarily motivated by the opportunity to retrieve Calais or another similarly useful port. Furthermore, she did not relish the prospect of a Guise victory.

The Treaty of Hampton Court (1562) and English intervention

Under the terms of the Treaty of Hampton Court, Elizabeth promised military aid to the Huguenots. This would take the form of 6,000 troops and a loan of £3,000. In return, England would hold Le Havre and Dieppe until Calais was restored. However, unlike in Scotland, the campaign went badly for the English; the Huguenot army was routed in the field and Elizabeth overstretched herself by trying to exchange Le Havre for Calais. The consequence was that, with the death of the Duke of Guise, the two French parties united to drive out the English. This factor, combined with the onset of plague in Le Havre, led to the surrender of the English in July 1563. The hostilities were brought to an end in the Peace of Troyes in 1564.

The consequences of English intervention

In intervening on behalf of the Huguenots, Elizabeth had broken the terms of Cateau-Cambresis and forfeited her right to the return of Calais. This unsuccessful venture into European diplomacy confirmed her conservative beliefs that intervention should be avoided since the outcome could not be guaranteed. In the future it would be increasingly difficult for the Council to achieve the Queen's agreement for direct involvement.

Elizabeth and the relationship with the Netherlands, 1562–72

Elizabeth's intervention into French internal affairs also offended Philip II, who saw it as clear proof that she was a heretic sponsoring Protestant rebels. Although before 1570 Philip opposed the excommunication of Elizabeth, there was a significant deterioration in their relationship during this period and this had a negative effect on England's trading relations with the Netherlands. In particular, Philip believed that Elizabeth used English traders to foment Protestant rebellion in the Netherlands.

Incidents of piracy in the Channel were common, and Cardinal Granvelle, Philip's ruler in the Netherlands, believed they were carried out with Elizabeth's sanction. In 1563 he used the excuse of an outbreak of plague in London to ban the import of English cloth. Elizabeth retaliated by prohibiting all imports from the Netherlands. The economic consequences were severe as trade in both countries suffered and within the year both sides backed down. However, the resumption of trade did not reconcile the underlying differences and the hostilities escalated in the following years.

Revolt in the Netherlands, 1566

In 1566 there was an outbreak of Calvinist revolts in Dutch towns. Initially Philip responded by allowing a policy of religious toleration, but during this time he gathered his strength and in 1567 he despatched the **Duke of Alba** to the Netherlands with the instruction to crush Protestantism there.

Elizabeth was naturally concerned. The presence of such a large Spanish force across the Channel presented a significant threat to England. Both Elizabeth and her Council feared that once the Netherlands was subdued it could be turned against England. The situation was not helped by the fact that many Protestant refugees from the conflict flooded into England and, although she publicly condemned the revolt of subjects against their anointed lord, the settlement of these Protestants in England looked suspiciously like she was harbouring rebels. Elizabeth's relationship with Philip of Spain went into sharp decline.

Discussion points

In a group, discuss the following points:

- In what ways was Elizabeth's policy towards France a mistake?
- What lessons did she learn for the future?

Biography

The Duke of Alba (1507–1582)
He was a Spanish general and governor of the Spanish Netherlands between 1567 and 1573. The people of the Netherlands called him the 'Iron Duke' because of his harsh methods of ruling and his cruelty, which ultimately inspired the population to rebel against Spanish control.

4.6 The Duke of Alba

William of Orange (1533–1584)

He was brought up as a page in the court of Emperor Charles V. He acted as an adviser to Philip II but his Protestant beliefs led him to become the leader of the party devoted to securing liberties for the Netherlands. He was named as a rebel in 1568 and, although his armies were defeated by 1572, he was able to recover and played a key role in helping establish the brief period of religious toleration in the Netherlands in 1576. He was assassinated in 1584.

4.7 William of Orange

The years of crisis, 1568–72

The Duke of Alba's victory

By 1568, the Duke of Alba had seized the initiative in the Netherlands and his complete victory looked imminent. He had executed leading rebels and defeated **William of Orange** in battle. Elizabeth was under pressure from her Privy Council to intervene, but she was determined to resist. She had learned a valuable lesson from her intervention in the French Wars of Religion and was in no mind to repeat the mistake. She also had a clear perspective on the situation. Although she heartily disapproved of Spanish actions in the Netherlands, she knew that the aid of an expeditionary force from England would not be sufficient to establish the independence of the Netherlands and there was always a chance that it would create a void that the French would step in and fill. On balance, she preferred Spanish control of the Netherlands to the prospect of French dominance of the southern shores of the Channel. It was this consideration that informed her choice of policy.

The policy of harassment

Since Elizabeth could not risk open intervention, she opted instead for a policy of harassment which would make life very difficult for the Spanish. The policy included seamen like Francis Drake attacking Spanish shipping in the New World, but the most explosive episode came closer to home. In November 1568 a storm drove Spanish ships to take refuge in English ports in Devon and Cornwall. The ships were carrying 400,000 gold florins, which were bound for the Netherlands to pay the Spanish army. Elizabeth seized the gold and in doing so struck a great blow against the Duke of Alba. There is some controversy as to what motivated Elizabeth's actions; the gold was a loan from Genoese bankers and, since it was technically still the property of the Genoese, she could justifiably take over the loan herself, which is what she did. However, she had originally agreed to despatch the ships to Alba as quickly as possible and it is difficult to tell whether she decided on seizing the gold herself or whether she was persuaded to do so by Cecil. Whatever the case, it seems she did not expect it to lead to damaging repercussions.

The Spanish reaction

Philip was outraged by the seizure of the gold. On the advice of the Spanish Ambassador to England, De Spes, he responded swiftly and mercilessly. In both the Spanish Netherlands and in Spain itself he ordered the seizure of English ships and property. Within weeks a full trade embargo existed between the two countries. The relationship was plunged into crisis as each side looked for new ways to antagonise the other.

The development of the crisis

Although Philip did not support Elizabeth's excommunication in 1570, he was increasingly ready to support Catholic plots against Elizabeth in England and he not only authorised the Duke of Alba to send financial aid to English Catholics but also promised 10,000 troops to support the Ridolfi Plot of 1571 (see page 95). For her part, Elizabeth continued to encourage the activities of **Sea Beggars** in raiding Spanish shipping, as well as exploring the possibility of an alliance with France, including a marriage to the Duke of Anjou. In 1572 she concluded the Treaty of Blois with France in which the two countries established a league to defend themselves against Spanish aggression (see page 92). In 1572, Elizabeth further inflamed the situation by expelling the Sea Beggars from English ports. They returned to the Netherlands and were instrumental in encouraging renewed revolt with their capture of the port of Brill. Historians are not clear as to Elizabeth's intentions in this expulsion. She may have been tired of the unruly behaviour of the Sea Beggars and mistakenly believed that their expulsion would be regarded favourably by Spain. However, some historians argue that it was a deliberate move to incite further rebellion in the Netherlands. The evidence is too insubstantial for a clear judgement to be made. What is certain, regardless of Elizabeth's intentions, is that the return of the Sea Beggars led to a worsening of Elizabeth's relationship with Philip of Spain.

Results

Although Anglo-Spanish relations had deteriorated to a new depth, it should not be assumed that the two countries were on a course for war, or that either side desired this. Elizabeth's priorities were to preserve the cloth trade, maintain a secure frontier and protect the Channel coastline. None of these objectives would be achieved by open war. The economic consequences of the conflict prompted England to pursue other trading links, and one positive outcome was the opening of trade routes with the Baltic and Russia, as well as directing a greater volume of cloth to the ports of Emden, Hamburg and Middleburg. In this way English trade was secured and dependency on Antwerp was reduced. In the long run this would mean that the maintenance of friendly relations with Spain was no longer essential for trade. However, given the vast wealth and power of the Spanish Empire, the adjustments to English trade routes did not mean that Elizabeth was prepared to incite war. Her priority remained English security and independence.

The renewal of relations with France, 1570–72

The deterioration in Elizabeth's relationship with Philip of Spain led to fresh efforts to woo the French. English security was dependent both on peace in the Netherlands and the prevention of an alliance between Spain and France. The collapse of Anglo-Spanish relations necessitated a fresh accord with France.

Definition

Sea Beggars
Pirates who made a living capturing shipping in the North Sea; they are associated with the struggle for Dutch independence.

SKILLS BUILDER

To what extent was Spain a threat to England in the years 1558–72?

In order to address this question you need to consider:

- What were the threats?
- Which threats could be solved?
- Did the solutions improve the situation or make it worse?
- What could not be solved?

Draw up a table and record your findings. You can add to your table as appropriate as you work through the rest of the chapter.

Biographies

Henry, Duke of Anjou (1551–1589)

The third son of the French King Henry II and Catherine de Medici, he was the leader of the royal army against the Huguenots in the French Wars of Religion. He was Catholic and so a marriage between him and Elizabeth seemed unlikely.

Catherine de Medici (1519–1589)

Catherine was born into the powerful Florentine Medici family in Italy. In 1533, she married Henry, second son of the French King Francis I, who reigned as Henry II of France from 1547 to 1559. Her sons reigned during a period of almost constant civil and religious war in France. She is associated with ordering the St Bartholomew's Day Massacre in 1572.

Definition

Papal bull

A particular type of letter or charter issued by the Pope. A bull is the seal used at the end of the letter to give it authenticity.

Marriage negotiations as a diplomatic tool

In 1570 Elizabeth was still young enough to bear children, and the offer of her hand in marriage was a valuable asset in diplomatic discussions. It also satisfied the desires of her Privy Council, who remained anxious that Elizabeth should settle the question of the succession. Therefore, Elizabeth entered into a round of marriage negotiations with **Henry, Duke of Anjou**, the son of **Catherine de Medici**. It seems unlikely that Elizabeth possessed any genuine desire to marry Anjou, but the negotiations not only led to the signing of the Treaty of Blois, but also reduced the influence of the Guise faction in France, and this was highly favourable to England. As Elton states, marriage negotiations helped to keep France quiet while Cecil was grappling with the greatest crises that had confronted the regime so far – the Northern Rebellion and the Ridolfi Plot (see pages 95–6).

The Treaty of Blois, 1572

Under the terms of the Treaty of Blois:

- France abandoned the claims of Mary, Queen of Scots to the throne of England
- France and England formed a defensive league against potential Spanish aggression directed at either party.

The treaty itself did not last long; it was soon swept away by a fresh insurgence of Catholic violence against Protestantism. But at the critical time when Elizabeth was beset by troubles arising out of the **papal bull** of excommunication of 1570, it provided her with some protection against a potential Franco-Spanish Catholic alliance.

St Bartholomew's Day Massacre, 1572

Events in Paris

The alliance with France was almost immediately put to the test. Catherine de Medici is believed to have instigated the St Bartholomew's Day Massacre. In August 1572, the French Wars of Religion were to be settled by a marriage between the French king's sister and the Protestant Henry of Navarre. Paris was filled with Huguenots who had arrived to celebrate the wedding. However, Catherine believed that the Huguenot leader, Admiral Gaspard de Coligny, was getting too close to her son, Charles IX and she gave orders for his assassination. Although the first attempt failed, the second was successful. This proved to be a general signal for the slaughter of French Protestants, and it is calculated that between 3,000 and 15,000 died, if the massacres elsewhere in France are taken into account.

4.8 St Bartholomew's Day Massacre

The English reaction

Elizabeth's Council was horrified by the turn of events in Paris. To Protestants, the massacre was a clear sign of the fate in store for all English Protestants if Mary, Queen of Scots succeeded to the throne. There were renewed calls for assistance for both the French Huguenots and the Dutch Calvinists by the more militant Protestants on the Council. However, Elizabeth viewed the events more dispassionately; the memory of the disastrous campaign in 1562–63 was still firmly fixed in her mind. Furthermore, she did not want to dispose of the tentative accord forged with France that was such a useful counterweight to the assertion of Spanish hegemony (predominant power and influence) in the Netherlands. Guy has identified six principles of English diplomacy that arose from the events of the massacre:

1. England would not intervene directly in the Netherlands.

2. Volunteers could be used to assist the Dutch.

3. A defensive Anglo-French entente would be deployed against Spain.

4. France should be encouraged to help the Dutch but should under no circumstances embark on a conquest of the Netherlands.

5. Spain should be persuaded to return the Netherlands to its previous semi-autonomous position.

6. French influence in Scotland should be permanently excluded.

Therefore, Elizabeth's policy was directed by the reality of the situation she faced rather than religious passion. Her open stance was one of defensive neutrality and condemnation of rebellions against the appointed ruler, but in private she approved of initiatives to aid the beleaguered Protestants.

Discussion point

Explain why Elizabeth did not resort to direct force as a consequence of the events in France in 1572. Give reasons why members of her Council wanted more direct intervention.

SKILLS BUILDER

Study the six principles identified by John Guy.

- List reasons why these principles arose.

- Support your answer with specific reference to diplomatic events in the period to 1572.

The impact of foreign affairs on domestic events: Catholic opposition in England, 1568–72

The most dangerous effect of the diplomatic situation during this period was its impact at home. The Elizabethan Church settlement had been established successfully as far as her Catholic subjects were concerned. The preservation of the Catholic appearance of Church ceremonies coupled with her subjects' natural loyalty to the sovereign had prevented a backlash that threatened Elizabeth's rule. However, this was all to change as diplomatic events clashed with domestic issues.

The deposition of Mary, Queen of Scots

In 1561, Mary had returned to Scotland to take up her position as Queen of Scotland. The death of her husband, the French king, had left her without support in France. Although her presence in Scotland presented new potential dangers to Elizabeth, she had accepted the reality of the Scottish Reformation and concerned herself with the business of finding a husband. Elizabeth tried to organise a marriage with Robert Dudley, but Mary was in no mind to accept one of Elizabeth's former suitors and instead married her cousin, **Henry Darnley**. In doing this she increased the pressure on Elizabeth, because Darnley also had a distant claim to the English throne. In 1566 Mary gave birth to a son, James, and so further secured her claim to the succession. However, she was beset by her own troubles. Darnley turned out to be an unstable drunk, and the marriage was already breaking down before her son was born. In 1567 Darnley was murdered while recovering from smallpox. The man suspected of his murder was the Protestant Earl of Bothwell. Many believed that Mary was an accomplice and suspicions increased when Mary married Bothwell that summer. The Scottish lords rose against Mary and forced her to abdicate in favour of her son. Mary escaped from her imprisonment across the border to England, where she sought sanctuary in her cousin's realm. Her presence in England was to upset the delicate balance that had been achieved between Elizabeth and her Catholic subjects, and led to the Northern Rebellion. You can read about the rebellion on pages 131–33.

Diplomatic consequences of the Northern Rebellion

The Northern Rebellion demonstrated to Elizabeth and her Councillors the very real danger that arose from Mary's presence in England. Although Elizabeth was able to quash the rebellion (she ordered the execution of 700 rebels), she could not use force to dispose of the Queen of Scots. The greatest problem was the support that Mary would receive from fellow Catholic monarchs in Europe as well as from the Pope. This would in turn impact on the loyalty of Elizabeth's subjects and continue to threaten her from within.

The papal bull of excommunication, 1570

When the northern earls rebelled, they appealed to Pope Pius V for help. In the event this proved of no value in the rebellion because their appeal did not reach Rome until February 1570, by which time the rebellion had

Biography

Henry Darnley (1545–1567)

He was the son of the fourth Earl of Lennox. His grandmother was Margaret Tudor, the sister of Henry VIII. As a consequence he was the cousin both of Elizabeth I and Mary, Queen of Scots and had a claim to the English throne in his own right. He married Mary in 1565 but fell out of her favour because of his drunken behaviour. He was one of those responsible for the murder of Mary's secretary, David Rizzio. Darnley was murdered in Kirk o'Field in 1567.

been defeated. However, Pius V responded with a papal bull of excommunication, *Regnans in Excelsis*, which had far-reaching implications. The bull asserted papal authority and named Elizabeth 'the pretended Queen of England'. The bull deprived Elizabeth of her title to the throne and proclaimed that her subjects were not bound to obey her laws. It went further by stating that those who did continue in allegiance to her were placed under a sentence of **anathema**.

Definition

Anathema

The most serious form of excommunication – anyone under its sentence was damned to hell with the devil.

The Popes bull against the Queene.

4.9 Pope Pius issuing the bull of excommunication

This bull placed Elizabeth's Catholic subjects in an impossible position. They could no longer be loyal to both Queen and Pope. It opened up the door to the influx of missionary priests and later Jesuits, who sought to rekindle Catholicism in England. Although Elizabeth was keen to play down its significance, her Council was not, and Parliament followed their lead. When Parliament met in 1571, all members took the Oath of Supremacy for the first time and they passed a *Treasons Act* making any written or spoken assertion that Elizabeth was not Queen a treasonable offence.

The full consequences of the bull for Elizabeth's diplomatic relations were not fully realised in 1570. Philip of Spain was not convinced of the wisdom of issuing the excommunication at that time. However, the threat became very clear with Spanish involvement in the Ridolfi Plot.

The Ridolfi Plot, 1571

The Ridolfi Plot centred on the plan to free Mary, marry her to the Duke of Norfolk and secure her accession to the English throne. It appears that it was first forged by Florentine banker, **Roberto Ridolfi**, and gained the support of Philip of Spain. Its potential was thus even more threatening than the Northern Rebellion; it was Elizabeth's greatest fear that the Catholic monarchs of Europe should act to replace her. The Duke of Alba was to lead 6,000 Spanish troops to England from the Netherlands.

Biography

Roberto Ridolfi (1531–1612)

Ridolfi was a nobleman from Florence. He was a banker by profession and had business connections in England. He was in Paris when the plot that he masterminded was discovered.

However, either he or Philip backed down at the last moment, for the troops did not materialise and the Council uncovered the plot when Mary's ambassador, John Leslie, was interrogated. This plot marked the end for the Duke of Norfolk. He had been released from the Tower after the Northern Rebellion, but he was rearrested and executed. The Council was anxious to deal the same fate to Mary, but Elizabeth refused. The most she would agree to was a bill that the 'Scottish Queen would be unable to enjoy the Crown of this realm' but she then vetoed it. Mary was to remain in captivity in England.

The discovery of the Ridolfi Plot was followed quickly by the St Bartholomew's Day Massacre. This confirmed Cecil's view that Protestantism was under attack from a murderous Catholic conspiracy and that Mary's presence in England meant that England itself was under threat. Elizabeth, however, would not react with haste. Her natural inclination to prevaricate, coupled with her determination not to provide a reason for France and Spain to ally or Philip to intervene in England, meant that she was determined to maintain a middle path. Thus she prevented a violent diplomatic response to both events. In the long run, however, it was increasingly clear that this would be a difficult position to maintain. According to Guy, in the next stage of diplomacy, Elizabeth's Council would be divided not between pro- and anti-Spanish opinion but between religion and **realpolitik**, that is between intervention or a defensive strategy.

Unit summary

What have you learned in this unit?

- The question of the marriage of a female monarch was a vital one in the sixteenth century. Mary was determined to be married, but her choice of a Spanish prince was not popular.

- Mary's marriage to Philip of Spain led to an alliance between England and Spain that involved England in a war with France and resulted in the loss of Calais, her last continental possession.

- Elizabeth's diplomatic policy was guided by her desire to maintain English independence and security. This necessitated a strategy that would prevent the great Catholic powers – Spain and France – from forging an alliance.

- Religion had a significant impact on the conduct of England's relations with her neighbours as she felt herself to be surrounded by hostile Catholic powers. Key members of the Privy Council were keen to intervene to defend Protestants in Scotland, France and the Spanish Netherlands, while Elizabeth was more concerned not to be seen supporting rebellion against an anointed sovereign.

- Elizabeth preferred to avoid the cost and uncertain outcome of war. Failure in France in 1562–64 enforced this belief and so she preferred to pursue more indirect means to assist Protestants on the continent. These methods often resulted in the escalation of a crisis.

Definition

Realpolitik

Politics and diplomacy that is based on practical considerations and not on ideology or religion.

- Diplomatic events had a significant and dangerous impact at home. The arrival of Mary, Queen of Scots in England in 1568, and the extent to which she attracted support from English Catholics and Philip of Spain, threatened Elizabeth's position as Queen. This problem would get significantly worse in the future.

What skills have you used in this unit?

You have focused your analysis on success and failure in Mary's foreign affairs. You have made decisions about the seriousness of the threats that Elizabeth faced and made a judgement as to how far diplomatic relations had reached crisis point by 1572.

Exam style question

This is the sort of question you will find appearing on the examination paper as a Section A question:

'By 1572, Spain had become an enemy to England rather than an ally.'

How far do you agree with this judgement of English foreign affairs in the period 1553–72?

SKILLS BUILDER

How far do you agree that the years 1568–72 were years of crisis?

- Make a list of all of the diplomatic problems that beset Elizabeth in this period.
- Make a list of all that were solved.
- Make a list of the dangers that remained.
- How significant were the problems remaining?

Exam tips

The key to success is in planning and structuring your paragraphs.

In order to answer this question you should:

- Examine the relationship between England and Spain during the reign of Mary Tudor. Was the alliance accepted entirely? What were the consequences?
- Examine the threat from Spain during the reign of Elizabeth (including the extent of support for Mary, Queen of Scots) and consider the nature of the threat by 1572.
- Weigh up the relative threats and make your judgement based upon the evidence.

You are now ready to write your answer.

RESEARCH TOPIC

Work with a partner to investigate the threat posed by Mary, Queen of Scots in more detail. Use the Internet to research:

- the murder of Lord Darnley and its consequences
- Mary's escape from Loch Leven in 1568 and the outcome
- the York Conference 1568–69
- Mary's role in the Northern Rebellion and the Ridolfi Plot.

Consider: Was Mary a greater threat in Scotland or in England?

5 Controversy: How seriously did the rebellions of 1536–69 threaten the Tudor state?

What is this unit about?

From 1536–69 there were five major rebellions in England, as well as a number of smaller protests and plots. This unit is concerned with how seriously these outbreaks threatened the authority of the state and the ability of the monarch to govern effectively. It examines the events and causes of each one, considers the extent of unrest and the impact and significance of each rebellion in the context of its time. This involves relating the rebellions to the stability of the government that came under attack, as well as the rebels' aims and objectives. The unit also addresses the nature of rebellion in the Tudor era. To do this, it invites you to analyse the rebellions and compare them with each other, to trace the changing patterns of unrest and relate them to wider developments in state and society.

In this unit you will:

- investigate the rebellions of 1536–37, 1549, 1554 and 1568–69
- assess the impact and significance of each rebellion in its own context
- compare the rebellions to identify similarities and differences, and to define the criteria that could make rebellions a threat to the state
- use the criteria to evaluate the extent to which the Tudor State was threatened by rebellion in the years 1536–69.

Key questions

- What were the key features of the rebellions of 1536–69?
- In what ways did the rebellions of 1536–1569 threaten the monarch or the state?
- How far did the nature and causes of rebellion change in the years 1536–69?
- How far did rebellion influence the development of the Tudor state?

Timeline

1536–37	The Lincolnshire Rising and the Pilgrimage of Grace
1547	Death of Henry VIII and accession of Edward VI
1549	The Year of Commotions: The Western Rebellion and Kett's Rebellion
	The fall of Somerset
1553	Death of Edward VI; the 'Nine Days Queen'; accession of Mary I
1554	Wyatt's Rebellion
1558	Accession of Elizabeth I
1569–70	Northern Rebellion

What features made protest and rebellion likely to occur?

England in 1536 was a country of villages and small towns, some of which held the status of a borough, enabling the wealthier citizens to take over local government as a corporation or council, and to choose one or two MPs. The only large city was London, although towns like Norwich and Hull had a population of several thousand and some merchants who had acquired considerable wealth. The vast majority of the population, however, were farmers who might vary from labourers and smallholders to quite substantial **yeomen**. Alongside them there were tradesmen and craftsmen who might also be relatively prosperous compared to their neighbours. Despite differences in wealth, they all formed a part of the commons or common people, distinguished from the social and political elite by the need to work with their hands. The gentry and nobility, who made up the governing class, derived their income from the ownership of land and the collection of rents, or from a profession such as the law or the Church.

Despite their lack of representation in government, the commons were not without a voice in affairs. They could, and often did, make their presence felt by **popular** protest, for example by dismantling fences or filling in ditches where land had been enclosed, or by occupying a disputed area. Such protests were generally small in scale, but could spread to different areas and sometimes led to riots and attacks on property or individuals. These activities did not threaten the government, and were often intended as an appeal to higher authority against local abuses. This was recognised in the government's response, which was often surprisingly tolerant, with punishment restricted to a few ringleaders if imposed at all. Popular protests were, in effect, a safety valve by which the poor and powerless could make their views known to those who exercised authority over them.

Nevertheless, it could not be ignored, because protest provided the raw material for something far more dangerous. If protests were widespread then law and order could break down. Without a standing army or police force, Tudor rulers had to rely on respect for authority to regain control. This was made easier because most protests had limited aims, and respect was quickly restored if some of them were met. If, however, popular discontent was exploited or channelled by members of the elite into more significant political issues, then protest could become rebellion, and rebellion could pose a serious threat to the government, the monarch or even the state itself. This is summarised in Source A.

Definitions

Yeomen

A class of prosperous peasants who worked their land themselves, so were not gentlemen. They often took on parish offices and had some education.

Popular

In the sixteenth century this meant 'of the people', that is, outside of the elite who normally made political decisions.

Source A

Tudor politics operated on two levels, which we can crudely label the high and the low . . . High politics [operated in] the world of the nobility and gentry . . . [and] the issue here was who would run the country. Low politics [existed] at a local level, where a good deal of power and responsibility was held by people . . . that we can style yeomen, but they might run businesses as well as farms. Particularly if they were involved in the cloth or the meat trade, they might travel round the country a good deal; they were well informed, independent-minded, used to dealing with a wide variety of people, and used to running their own and other people's affairs. These were the people who led popular Tudor rebellions . . . If high politics was about *who* should run the country, low politics was about *how* the country should be run. High taxes, perversion of justice, aristocratic high-handedness, hoarding of food supplies; these were the issues that brought periodic eruptions of fury . . . Religion mattered in low politics as well as high . . . Government reactions to rebellion repeatedly revealed the gulf between the two worlds of politics, and the fear that the high had of the low. It is this gulf which helps us to explain both success in staging rebellions and success in preventing them. It came from bridging the gulf between the two politics.

From A. Fletcher and D. MacCulloch, *Tudor Rebellions*, fifth edition, published 2008

SKILLS BUILDER

One of the few successful 'rebellions' in Tudor England came in 1525, with the protests against the Amicable Grant (a planned tax). In that instance, popular protests were widespread in south-east England, and the Dukes of Norfolk and Suffolk relayed the protesters' grievances to the King. After some consideration the King withdrew the grant and blamed Wolsey for the problem. What made this protest successful? There are some clues here, but you could also find out more about what happened and analyse the information to see how far it supports the arguments put forward in Source A.

Although the rebellions of 1536–69 each had particular causes, there were also some underlying features in Tudor society that help to explain them all and demonstrate why they might pose a threat to the government. The main priority in this unit is to assess the extent of that threat, but the causes of a rebellion do have some relevance to the threat it posed. A rebellion caused by significant and deep-seated problems was likely to gain widespread support. The causes of the unrest could also influence the demands that the rebels made, and the actions that they were prepared to take in pursuit of them. The causes of a rebellion influence its nature, or character, and that in turn affects the seriousness of the threat that it could pose. It is, therefore, useful to begin by considering the features of Tudor society that were likely to cause unrest or motivate rebellion.

Economic and social problems

Population and food

In the years 1536–88 Tudor society underwent rapid change, brought about by a combination of economic and political factors. Probably the single most important fact about Tudor England was that between 1500 and 1600 the population virtually doubled. The inevitable result was pressure on resources (especially land), rising prices and periods of scarcity. In addition, a rising population meant a plentiful supply of labour, downward pressure on wages and periodic unemployment. In the words of an anonymous pamphlet addressed to the government in 1549, 'There is nothing that will sooner move the people unto sedition than the scarcity of food.' More importantly, they expected the government to help them. As the pamphlet explained, 'What faith and allegiance will men observe towards their prince and governor who have their children famished at home for lack of meat? The people, for the most part, do impute the cause of dearth [scarcity] unto their rulers.' Shortages, of food and other essentials, were only a part of the problem, as explained in Source B.

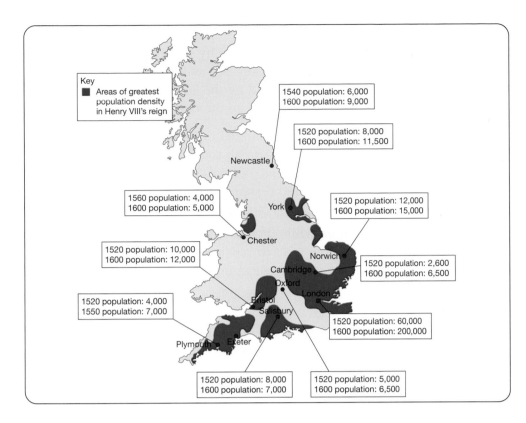

Table 5.1 Population growth in the sixteenth century

Year	Population estimate (in millions)
1524	2.3
1541	2.7
1551	3.0
1561	3.0
1571	3.2
1581	3.6
1591	3.9
1601	4.1

5.1 Population density in the sixteenth century

Source B

The doubling of the population in the 120 years before the civil war [1642] is the critical variable of the period, [with effects that] spread out into every aspect of society and [were] causally related to major changes in agriculture, trade, industry, urbanisation, education, social mobility and overseas settlement. It gave a tremendous stimulus to agricultural output, which increased sufficiently fast to feed twice the number of mouths, although undoubtedly at a reduced standard of living . . . This remarkable achievement was partly a result of an expansion of the area under cultivation, eating into the wastes, the forests, the hillsides and even the fens. But it was also the result of improvements in agricultural techniques . . . This expansion of agricultural output could only be achieved, however, at the cost of upsetting the former social balance. There was a massive shift to economic rents, accompanied by a reorganisation of property rights, by which more and more land fell into private control through enclosures of both wastes and common fields. As a result of this process and of the **engrossing** of farms into larger units of production, there began to emerge the tripartite pattern of later English rural society – landlord, prosperous tenant farmer, and landless labourer. Tens of thousands of small-holders were driven off the land or reduced to wage labourers, while others found their economic position undermined by encroachment on, or over-stocking of, the common lands by the big farmers and landlords. Enclosure became a popular scapegoat for the dislocations inevitable in so major a reallocation and redistribution of the land, but there can be no doubt that the extra millions were only fed at the cost of much individual hardship suffered among the small peasantry.

From Lawrence Stone, *The Causes of the English Revolution, 1529–1642,* published 1972

Definition

Engrossing
Gathering more land to expand an individual's holding, often implemented using enclosure.

SKILLS BUILDER

Summarise in no more than 100 words the main changes identified by Stone in Source B.

5.2 The Great Chain of Being, from a document written in 1579

Definition

Customary rights

Rights based on custom, or long usage, rather than written law.

The Great Chain of Being

None of these changes were easily controlled by government, but, as the pamphleteer of 1549 suggested, they could not avoid some blame. In part, this was because of attitudes encouraged by the government itself around the concept of a natural hierarchy based on the Great Chain of Being.

- Society was envisaged as a series of linked units, stretching from God himself down through the various human social orders to the natural world of animals and plants. Within this structure each unit had a fixed place, carrying its own rights and responsibilities.

- The higher orders, who wielded power, had responsibility for the well-being of those below them, while the lower orders, who laboured and obeyed their betters, had the right to receive protection and care in the 'commonweal' or commonwealth, meaning the community as a whole.

Tudor governments accepted this responsibility, as shown in attempts to regulate enclosure and manage treatment of the poor, as well as the toleration of limited protest. Nevertheless, enclosure legislation was difficult to enforce, and treatment of the poor focused as much on brutal measures to control vagrants as on care for the distressed. In some areas the Church did much to fill the gap, and private charity was encouraged as a Christian duty, but when the interests of the common people clashed with those of the gentry and nobility on whom the government relied, they were often abandoned. By 1536 there were already numerous complaints that the 'commonweal' was endangered by landlords enclosing land, the spread of sheep, the decline of **customary rights** and changing social relationships, when a new threat appeared in the shape of religious reform and an attack on the traditional Church.

Religious conflicts

Until the outbreak of rebellion in 1536 there was a surprising lack of opposition to the religious changes introduced by the Reformation. Opposition came largely from individuals, such as Sir Thomas More, Bishop John Fisher and a few Carthusian monks. Historians have offered different explanations for this. For Elton, Dickens, and those who believe that the Church was already weakened and lacking support, the lack of opposition is not difficult to explain. For Haigh, and others who perceive the Church to be popular, there is more of a problem. They have pointed out, however, that new treason laws made it dangerous to be openly critical, and that Cromwell's informers were known to be widely active.

More important, perhaps, was the fact that the changes were made in a piecemeal process, with the direction of developments only becoming gradually apparent. For the higher clergy and the political nation, the establishment of royal supremacy over both Church and state was a momentous change, bordering on revolution, but for many of the laity and even the lower clergy its impact was muted. Church services, rituals, holy days, the collection of tithes, baptisms, marriage and funerals continued uninterrupted in many places.

Only in 1535–36 did the implications of the political Reformation begin to take on distinct religious forms, with the issue of new articles of faith, injunctions to the clergy, and the dissolution of the smaller monasteries and transfer of property to the Crown. At this point threats posed by religious changes became apparent and began to provoke complaint. In most rural areas and in small towns the parish church formed a valued centre for community life. The numerous gifts, endowments and offerings made to local churches show the respect in which they were held, and that the role of the Church within local communities was central.

A growing conflict became apparent between those who welcomed the new religious forms, responded to the opportunities for Bible reading and a private relationship with God, and those who remained loyal to the traditional forms and priorities. More importantly, the monarch's new role as head of the Church meant that he carried responsibility for ensuring that the correct forms were followed and the rules enforced. The distinction between religion and politics became blurred so that private faith could become a political crime. The reaction of those who suffered was to protest and to seek redress from those responsible. When this failed at local levels, they could appeal to higher authority. Lacking alternatives, their methods were often riotous, potentially or actually violent, and the outcomes unpredictable. Whether they constituted a threat to the state depended on the scale and complexity of the problems, the attitudes of the ruling elites in the country, and the response of central government to both. Whatever the impact, the significance of both religious conflict and economic pressures in stimulating popular protest is undeniable.

The Pilgrimage of Grace, 1536–37

Outline of events

The Pilgrimage of Grace was not so much a single rebellion as a series of outbreaks that spread across northern England between October 1536 and February 1537. It had its origins in Lincolnshire, where there were three separate sets of royal commissioners at work in 1536. One commission was engaged in dissolving the smaller monasteries, another in collecting taxes granted by Parliament in 1534 and the third was inspecting the quality of the clergy. Both individually and collectively, they signalled the presence of an increasingly active and intrusive central authority.

Protest began in Louth, when the bishop's registrar arrived to inspect the local clergy. On the night of 1 October a group of local men arrived to guard the church and, when the registrar arrived the following day, he was seized by the commons, led by a shoemaker named Nicholas Melton. Having burned the registrar's papers and forced the waiting clergy to swear loyalty to them, the protesters marched to Legbourne nunnery nearby and captured the royal commissioners at work there in the process of dissolution. This was a signal for a general rising.

Although Melton, now calling himself 'Captain Cobbler', received a message on 2 October saying that Yorkshire was not yet ready to rise, he marched on to Caistor, where the tax commissioners had arranged a meeting with local residents in the hope of dispelling the wilder rumours about their work. When the commons of Louth arrived, the commissioners tried to flee, but several were captured and forced to write a letter to the King outlining the discontent and recommending that popular grievances should be considered and the protesters granted a general pardon.

By 4 October the local gentry had assumed leadership of the rising. Violence escalated and Dr Raynes, the Bishop of Lincoln's unpopular Chancellor, was brutally beaten to death by the muster of local militia at Horncastle. His clothes and money were distributed among the crowd, while the gentry drew up a formal list of demands in which the commons' grievances were combined with their own concerns. Around 10,000 rebels marched unimpeded towards Lincoln. There they were joined by the principal nobleman of the county, Lord Hussey, who had links to the **Aragonese faction** at court, and new articles listing their grievances were drawn up and sent to London. A general muster was planned to take place at Ancaster, near Grantham, on 8 October, but the gentry persuaded the commons to wait at Lincoln for the King's reply. On 10 October they received a letter from the King threatening harsh punishment if they did not disperse. For the gentry, with a great deal to lose, the choice was stark and a royal army led by the Duke of Suffolk was only 40 miles away at Stamford. By the time the King's official herald reached Lincoln on 11 October, many of the 18 gentry leaders had already left, and the rising had dissolved amid bitter recrimination between the gentry and the commons. Those who remained were persuaded to return home. Later the King ordered the arrest and execution of the ringleaders and about 100 death sentences were imposed, although only 57 were actually carried out. Many of these were clergy.

The collapse of the Lincolnshire rebellion did not mark the end of Henry's problems in the north. On 4 October a Yorkshire lawyer, **Robert Aske**, had been returning to London for the law term and (according to his account) heard of the unrest when he crossed the Humber. He visited the rebels, read their list of grievances and took their oath, before returning to Yorkshire. Arriving at his native Howden, on the road towards York, he found local men about to call a muster and after some hesitation he seems to have taken charge, calling on support from Beverley and Howdenshire before marching on York.

It was at this point, while in York from 16 October, that the character of Aske's rising became more clearly defined as a 'pilgrimage', with the adoption of the Pilgrims' Oath and banner of the five wounds of Christ. Aske emphasised the pilgrims' peaceful intentions and kept his men under good discipline, ensuring that goods were paid for and property left untouched.

Definition

Aragonese faction

Officers and courtiers who sympathised with Catherine of Aragon and opposed Henry's plans for divorce, marriage to Anne Boleyn and the religious changes enacted by Henry and Thomas Cromwell.

Biography

Robert Aske (c.1500–1537)

Aske was the younger son of a gentry family from Howden in the East Riding, with a successful legal practice in York. He had wide contacts among northern gentry and lawyers, and was also employed as a legal agent by Henry Percy, the Earl of Northumberland.

He began the restoration of religious houses that had been dissolved and encouraged the Prior of Holy Trinity Priory in York to resist dissolution. Meanwhile, risings had broken out across much of the north. In the North Riding, Durham and Northumberland there was local violence and companies were formed under gentry leadership, which began to move towards York. The town of Barnard Castle was forced to surrender and the Bishop of Durham's palace at Bishop Auckland wrecked, but Skipton Castle, under the control of the Earl of Cumberland, held out against them. Similarly, the Earl of Derby remained loyal to the King and used his influence in Lancashire, Cheshire and North Wales to maintain royal authority. There were musters of rebels in Cumberland and Westmorland, but efforts to take control of Carlisle failed and on 27–28 October the main body of north-western rebels moved on towards Pontefract.

5.3 The Pilgrimage of Grace

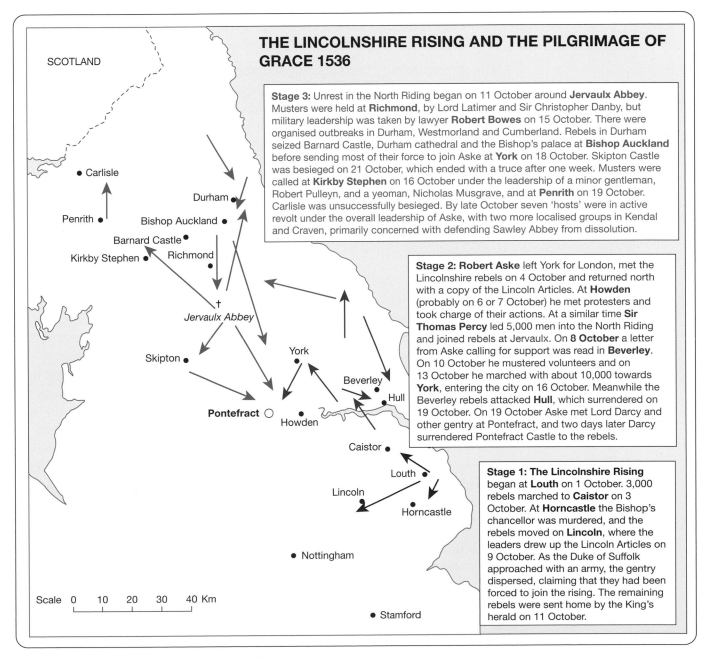

THE LINCOLNSHIRE RISING AND THE PILGRIMAGE OF GRACE 1536

Stage 3: Unrest in the North Riding began on 11 October around **Jervaulx Abbey**. Musters were held at **Richmond**, by Lord Latimer and Sir Christopher Danby, but military leadership was taken by lawyer **Robert Bowes** on 15 October. There were organised outbreaks in Durham, Westmorland and Cumberland. Rebels in Durham seized Barnard Castle, Durham cathedral and the Bishop's palace at **Bishop Auckland** before sending most of their force to join Aske at **York** on 18 October. Skipton Castle was besieged on 21 October, which ended with a truce after one week. Musters were called at **Kirkby Stephen** on 16 October under the leadership of a minor gentleman, Robert Pulleyn, and a yeoman, Nicholas Musgrave, and at **Penrith** on 19 October. Carlisle was unsuccessfully besieged. By late October seven 'hosts' were in active revolt under the overall leadership of Aske, with two more localised groups in Kendal and Craven, primarily concerned with defending Sawley Abbey from dissolution.

Stage 2: Robert Aske left York for London, met the Lincolnshire rebels on 4 October and returned north with a copy of the Lincoln Articles. At **Howden** (probably on 6 or 7 October) he met protesters and took charge of their actions. At a similar time **Sir Thomas Percy** led 5,000 men into the North Riding and joined rebels at Jervaulx. On **8 October** a letter from Aske calling for support was read in **Beverley**. On 10 October he mustered volunteers and on 13 October he marched with about 10,000 towards **York**, entering the city on 16 October. Meanwhile the Beverley rebels attacked **Hull**, which surrendered on 19 October. On 19 October Aske met Lord Darcy and other gentry at Pontefract, and two days later Darcy surrendered Pontefract Castle to the rebels.

Stage 1: The Lincolnshire Rising began at **Louth** on 1 October. 3,000 rebels marched to **Caistor** on 3 October. At **Horncastle** the Bishop's chancellor was murdered, and the rebels moved on **Lincoln**, where the leaders drew up the Lincoln Articles on 9 October. As the Duke of Suffolk approached with an army, the gentry dispersed, claiming that they had been forced to join the rising. The remaining rebels were sent home by the King's herald on 11 October.

SCOTLAND

Carlisle

Durham

Penrith
Bishop Auckland

Barnard Castle
Kirkby Stephen • Richmond

† Jervaulx Abbey

Skipton
York

Beverley
Hull

Pontefract ○
Howden

Caistor

Louth
Lincoln
Horncastle

• Nottingham

Scale 0   10   20   30   40 Km

• Stamford

Government reaction to the Yorkshire rising was slow, partly because officials were distracted by events in Lincolnshire. The Earl of Shrewsbury had forces at Nottingham, but was waiting for the King's orders, while Lord Darcy, at Pontefract Castle, complained that he lacked forces and weapons and was besieged by the townsmen, who supported the rising. On 19 October Aske met with Darcy, Edward Lee, the Archbishop of York and other leaders in Pontefract Castle. He emphasised his loyalty to the King, his belief that the King had been misled, and argued that the abbeys were essential for the northern economy. Lee rejected the rebellion, but Darcy, Sir Robert Constable and the others present joined the rebels and Aske formed a Council to share the leadership. Many of these men held important positions within regional government, but the great magnates of the region remained aloof, like the Earl of Northumberland, or loyal to the King like Cumberland and Derby. Pontefract Castle, which controlled the Don river crossings and the road south, was surrendered and became the focal point for a pilgrim army of approximately 30,000 men.

The government at last began to act. Shrewsbury advanced towards the River Don with an army of 8,000 and the King's northern commander, the Duke of Norfolk, invited the pilgrim leaders to meet with him at Doncaster to discuss their grievances. Before the meeting, on 27 October, Norfolk assured the King that he would not need to keep any promises he made to the rebels. He then tried to persuade the leaders (Aske did not attend) to abandon the campaign and, when he failed, he agreed to send their petition to the King and to maintain a truce in the meantime. Henry rejected the petition but, on Norfolk's advice, delayed his response and suggested further negotiations. However, news of the King's rejection reached Skipton, and it took all of Aske's authority and persuasion to hold the commons in check.

On 21 November Aske agreed to a further meeting with Norfolk, to be held at Pontefract in early December. From 2–4 December the pilgrims' council met and finalised their demands – the Pontefract Articles (see Source C). On 6 December their leaders met with Norfolk, who agreed to a free pardon and a free Parliament. Henry had been demanding that at least ten of the leaders should not be pardoned, but Norfolk's apparent generosity put him in a strong position. He persuaded the leaders that most of their complaints should be dealt with by a Parliament and offered that, if the abbeys would formally surrender to the King's commissioners, they would be granted special permission to continue until Parliament met. The next morning Aske persuaded the reluctant commons at Pontefract to accept the terms and go home, while he and the gentry rode to Doncaster and submitted to Norfolk.

Aske thought they had won, and the north confidently waited to hear from Norfolk that the King had agreed to their terms. Instead, nothing happened. The King celebrated Christmas, and neither rejected nor ratified the agreement that Norfolk had created. By early January frustration was growing, and on 16 January a rising was attempted under the leadership of Sir Ralph Bigod in the East Riding.

The intention was to capture Hull and Scarborough, and hold them to force the King to act. The rising was a pathetic failure and Bigod fled to Cumberland, where unrest was increasing, as the commons despaired of their gentry leaders. He was arrested on 10 February. An attack on Carlisle by the commons failed miserably: they were routed and scattered. These actions, however, gave the King a pretext for reneging on his supposed promises and launching retribution. Norfolk imposed martial law in Cumberland and hanged the captured rebels. The rebel leaders were gradually rounded up, brought to London and put on trial. A total of 178 executions are recorded, including those of Bigod, Lord Hussey and Lord Darcy, while Aske himself was hanged, drawn and quartered in York.

SKILLS BUILDER

What do the articles suggest about the causes of the rebellion? How reliable are they as evidence of who participated and why?

Source C

1 . . . to have the heresies of Luther, Wycliffe, Huss [and others] . . . within this realm to be annulled and destroyed.

2 . . . to have the supreme head of the Church touching the care of souls [i.e. spiritual care] . . . restored unto the see of Rome . . .

3 . . . that the Lady Mary be made legitimate . . .

4 To have the abbeys suppressed to be restored . . .

5 To have the tenth and first fruits and tenths clearly discharged, unless the clergy choose to pay a rent to the crown.

6 To have the Observant Friars restored to their houses again.

7 To have the heretics . . . [have] punishment by fire . . .

8 To have the lord Cromwell, the Lord Chancellor, and Sir Richard Riche . . . [receive] punishment for undermining the good laws of this realm and maintaining heretics.

9 That the lands in Westmorland, Cumberland and other districts . . . may be held by tenant right, and the lord to have at every change two years gressom [entry fine] and no more . . .

10 The statutes preventing the carrying of handguns and crossbows to be repealed and apply only in the royal forests and parks . . .

11 That doctor Leigh and doctor Layton . . . [receive] punishment for their extortions in their time of visitations to the abbeys.

12 Reformation for the election of knights of shire and burgesses . . . as in the ancient way.

13 Statute for enclosures and intakes to be put into execution and the enclosures pulled down.

14 To be discharged and relieved of the quindine [a form of tax] and taxes now granted . . .

15 To have the parliament in a convenient place at Nottingham or York . . .

16 The Statute of the Succession of the Crown by will [Act of Succession, 1534] . . . be repealed.

17 . . . that all the recognisances, statutes, penalties new forfeited during this time of commotion may be pardoned . . .

18 The privileges and rights of the Church to be confirmed by Act of Parliament [including Benefit of Clergy] . . .

19 The liberties of the Church [areas run by the Church, e.g. Palatinate of Durham] to have their old customs . . .

20 To have the statute that no man shall will his lands [Statute of Uses] to be repealed.

21 That the statutes of treasons for words and such like [Treason Act, 1534] . . . [be] repealed.

22 That the common laws may have place as was used in the beginning of your grace's reign . . .

23 That no man from the Trent north, who is summoned by a writ of court, appear anywhere but at York unless it is a matter directly touching the King . . .

24 A remedy against escheators [officers who collected land that reverted to the Crown] who find false cases or charge extortionate fees.

From The Pontefract Articles, written by Robert Aske with the help of Lord Darcy, December 1536

SKILLS BUILDER

To understand what happened between October 1536 and February 1537, you should draw up a timeline or flow chart to summarise the main stages of the rebellion.

Source D

[The Pontefract Articles] formed as sweeping a statement of sheer conservatism as could be imagined. Henry could not reasonably have been expected to accept such an indictment of his entire regime, especially as many of the changes had been introduced for good and sufficient reasons – and, of course, with the consent of Parliament . . . In spite of the pilgrims' professions [of loyalty] Henry had little choice but to treat them as his enemies, because what they were demanding amounted to a complete retraction of twenty years of policy and an unthinkable surrender to democratic dictatorship.

From David Loades, *Henry VIII: Court, Church and Conflict,* published 2007

The Pilgrimage of Grace: Causes, nature and significance

Historians disagree about the causes of the Pilgrimage of Grace, the relative importance of economic, religious and political motives, and the aims of its leaders. The issue has some importance in assessing how seriously it threatened the monarch and the state. The causes of the rebellion influenced the aims of the rebels, the extent of their support and the actions that they were prepared to take. Some historians believe that the rebellion was essentially spontaneous, an outbreak of popular resentment against change, led by the yeomen and tradesmen who were the natural leaders in a society of villages and small towns. Others point to the rapid intervention of the gentry and suggest that the rebellion reflected the anger of an entire community. As such it would 'bridge the gap between high and low politics' and pose a serious threat to the King's government. Even if the rebels did not seek to challenge him directly, the demand that he reverse his policies and dismiss his closest advisers would, if conceded, leave him effectively unable to rule even though he might reign, as Source D explains.

Was the Pilgrimage of Grace a spontaneous popular rising?

There is widespread agreement among historians that, by 1536, government policies were causing considerable popular resentment. It is probably no coincidence that when the first outbreaks occurred in Lincolnshire, there were three different sets of government commissioners at work there, dealing with the monasteries, the parish clergy and the collection of taxes. Sources E, F and G explain their impact in the county.

Source E

In early 1536, Parliament passed an act dissolving all minor monastic houses in England and Wales. Prior to its passage rumours had circulated amongst the population of the 'putting down' of the monasteries and of the imposition of new taxes upon christenings, marriages and burials, sheep, cattle and basic foodstuffs. Some even said that the King's Councillors intended to carry religious change as far as the destruction of all parish churches . . . The planned removal of minor monastic houses seemed, therefore, to confirm a wider set of popular anxieties . . . In early October 1536 the 'commons' of Lincolnshire rose in armed demonstration against such policies. Although public leadership came from the greater gentry of the county, the main movers of rebellion were men such as Nicholas Melton, known as 'Captain Cobbler': relatively prominent, prosperous villagers. Far from providing the real leadership to the rebellion, 'the first many of [the Lincolnshire gentry] knew of the rising was when their own bailiffs, tenants and serving-men confronted them with the demand that they swear the rebel oath' . . .

From Andy Wood, *Riot, Rebellion and Popular Politics in Early Modern England,* published 2001

Source F

The commons in Lincolnshire and across the north were subject to the poor harvest of 1535 and the indifferent one of 1536. In some areas, they were aggrieved by enclosures and oppressive landlords. Above all, they were struck by the arrival of unprecedented displays of government interference, which impinged directly upon them in the form of tax, in the dissolution of the smaller local monastic houses and, most urgently, in the form of disturbing rumours. The commons feared the loss of their local church property, further tax demands, and were ripe for agitation by their natural leaders among the priests and gentry.

From Paul Thomas, *Authority and Disorder in Tudor Times*, published 1999

Source G

Monks and parish clergy were heavily involved in spreading rumours, encouraging the revolt, and drawing up programmes. The clergy clearly resented the increased taxation which the Reformation had involved for them, the threat that their morals would be investigated, and the blow to their status involved in the recognition of a layman as Head of the Church. This, rather than a positive feeling in favour of the Pope seems to be behind the demands about the supremacy.

Nevertheless, both gentry and clergy had to work through the common people, had to manipulate popular prejudice to their own ends; and the way they did so can tell us something about popular attitudes. A conservative revolt could be mobilised in terms of defence of local rights and opposition to religious change; and these motives could hold together, briefly, social groups with differing, even contradictory, aspirations . . . The heart of the matter, the issue on which these two aims fused, may have been the defence of the parish church; the embodiment of the village community, the centre of its pride, the symbol, too, of the belief that there may be more to life than an unending and precarious fight for subsistence.

From C.S.L. Davies, *Peace, Print and Protestantism 1450–1558*, published 1977

Source C, however, reveals a much greater range of grievances, some of which seemed to relate more closely to gentry concerns and court politics than to the problems of the lower orders. In addition, the course of the rebellion revealed a considerable degree of organisation and communication across a wide geographical area, suggestive of leadership at a high social and political level, and possibly of a significant degree of pre-planning and readiness for the outbreak. In the aftermath of the risings, many of the gentry claimed to have been coerced into participation, but the reliability of such claims is obviously debatable. In the face of conflicting evidence, the role of the gentry needs to be carefully assessed. If the argument in Source A is valid, the nature and extent of gentry participation in the rebellion is directly linked to its significance as a threat to the monarch and the Tudor state.

What was the role of the gentry in the Pilgrimage of Grace?

Although the early protests in Lincolnshire were led by yeomen and tradesmen, within days the gentry had taken charge and, as the unrest spread, there was clear evidence of involvement from the landowners and lawyers who made up the provincial elite. In both Lincolnshire and

SKILLS BUILDER

How far do Sources E, F and G suggest that the northern risings of October 1536 were both spontaneous and popular?

Definitions

The 'assembled commons'

Mainly farmers, labourers and tradesmen, but joined by members of the local clergy as well as monks from the threatened abbeys.

Statute of Uses

A Use was a legal arrangement used by the gentry and nobility to give property to their heirs without paying feudal dues. In 1536 Cromwell enacted a law against them which landowners resented; it was repealed in 1540.

Yorkshire, musters of the local militia (traditionally used for defence against the Scots) were used to gather support for the rebellion and this required the participation of local gentry. There is evidence of pre-planning in Lincolnshire and the East Riding. On 2 October Captain Cobbler had been informed that Yorkshire was not ready to rise, suggesting contacts north of the Humber, and Aske's account of meeting rebels by chance on both sides of the Humber does not bear scrutiny. His movements around the Humber estuary and his meetings with the rebels make far more sense if he was an organiser and point of contact between potential rebel groups. The claims of the Lincolnshire gentry to have been coerced into participating in the revolt might be supported by the rapidity with which they abandoned it at the approach of royal forces. Nevertheless, it was the gentry who drew up the Lincolnshire articles of grievance, and apparently took the opportunity to insert some grievances of their own. The Horncastle priest, Nicholas Leche, described how the Lincolnshire gentry drew apart to compile the list, and when the Sheriff read the articles to the **assembled commons** he had to explain what the **Statute of Uses** was. The names of Cromwell and Rich, and the list of reforming bishops singled out for criticisms, are unlikely to have come from the Lincolnshire peasantry, although their dislike of religious changes had been amply demonstrated. While Leche's claim that the gentry controlled the rising may have been intended to shift responsibility, there is no reason to doubt this part of his account.

In Yorkshire, contact between rebel hosts in different areas testifies to gentry leadership within a short time of the first eruption. It was Aske, having raised a force in his native Howdenshire, who called for support from Beverley, where another gentleman lawyer, William Stapleton, gathered a rebel force. In the North Riding the various rebel forces were co-ordinated by a third lawyer, Robert Bowes, with the help of the Percy connection. Sir Thomas Percy, brother of the Earl of Northumberland, led a force of about 600 rebels from the East and North Ridings to join the rebel centre at Jervaulx, while it was predominantly Percy tenants who formed the force in Durham and later moved south. This may not be the result of active participation by the Percys – their tenants in North Yorkshire, Durham and Northumberland formed a significant proportion of the population – but they were the centre of a network that certainly did help to manage the revolt. Aske and Bowes both served the Earl as legal agents and would have been familiar with both his family and tenant relationships. Although there had been some spontaneous protests around Kendal and in north Lancashire, the main risings in Cumbria and the musters at Kirby Stephen in Westmoreland were instigated by letters from Bowes. There can be little doubt that the Yorkshire risings were orchestrated and that they were orchestrated by members of the elite.

It has been suggested, however, that most of the gentry who became involved in the risings were coerced by popular pressure, and joined only to try and control the actions of the commons. There is significant evidence to support this. Claims of coercion were widespread in the aftermath of the rebellion, but given that the alternative could be a charge of treason, such claims have to be treated with a measure of caution. The 18 gentlemen who joined the rebels in Lincolnshire seem to have had no forewarning and certainly experienced some pressure from the commons. They later claimed that they had joined the rising to control it, and the fact that they restrained the commons from joining the Ancaster muster and kept them at Lincoln supports this interpretation. There is also evidence that the commons' leaders were decidedly suspicious of their intentions, not least Captain Cobbler, who later regretted that they had not killed all the gentlemen while they could, since he 'thought always that they would betray us'. Despite this, concepts of natural hierarchy encouraged the commons to seek leadership from the elite and this may have been encouraged by the clergy, who played an active role in events. On balance it seems likely that the majority of the gentry in Lincolnshire were pressurised into the rising, but that having become involved they sought not only to restrain the commons' anger but also to channel it towards grievances that they shared as well as some of their own.

Across Yorkshire and the border counties the picture is more mixed. Most of the major nobility held aloof and, in the north-west, large numbers of gentry took refuge with the Earl of Cumberland in Skipton Castle, fighting off a rebel siege when other strong points were surrendered. This does suggest that those who refused to participate faced danger and more isolated members of the elite may have had little choice. Sir Thomas Percy claimed that he had been forced to lead his tenants, but he played an active role thereafter. Given that his brother, the childless Earl of Northumberland, had been forced to name the King as his heir (see Unit 1 page 24), Sir Thomas had a great deal to fight for and, perhaps, little to lose. There is also evidence of wider discontent among the elite. When Darcy surrendered Pontefract to the rebels he was joined on the pilgrims' council by Sir Robert Constable (a member of the Council of the North), Robert Lascelles and William Stapleton, with more tacit support from Lord Latimer, Lord Lumley, Baron Scrope of Bolton and Lord Conyers. All shared a link with the Percy interest, but they were also religious and political conservatives.

Source H

The gentry were an important group because they were a more visible form of government than the nobility. As landowners in their own right, they came into contact with those beneath them through tenancy agreements and any specific obligations written into these contracts (such as offering military help when requested). More broadly the gentry were also the agents of central government . . . as Justices of the Peace, with wide responsibilities for administering the law, hearing cases and regulating aspects of village life. In this position the gentry were one of the groups trapped between the commons and the crown. On the one hand they owed allegiance to the government and their conduct could be the reason for [popular] rebellion . . . On the other, they were as likely to be affected by the direction of royal policy as the people they governed, so could share the anger at rapid changes to the traditions that gave them status in their community.

From Tony Imperato, *Protest and Rebellion in Tudor England, 1485–1601*, published 2008

Source I

The arrival [in Yorkshire] of copies of the Lincolnshire rebel demands inspired a much larger, co-ordinated rising of the counties of Yorkshire, Westmorland, Cumberland, and Lancashire. Over three weeks in mid-October 1536, a large-scale rebellion was mounted, organised via Hundreds (the administrative entities into which counties were divided) from which men were mustered into nine rebel hosts . . . In some areas the local gentry proved willing to lead the rebels; in others, gentlemen had to be forced into this role; while in the Lake counties, loyalist gentry were singled out as the rebels' main target. The rebels swore oaths to maintain the commons, the King and the Church against the 'enemies of the commonwealth' (that is, the King's advisors) and circulated handbills and ballads [which] reflected both the micro- and macro-politics of the rebellion. Upon the establishment of a Council at York, rebel demands were homogenised around a set of complaints addressed to the Privy Council. By this point, the northern gentry had assumed leadership of the rebellion.

From Andy Wood, *Riot, Rebellion and Popular Politics in Early Modern England*, published 2001

SKILLS BUILDER

To what extent do Sources H and I support the idea that the local gentry played a leading role in the Pilgrimage of Grace?

Definition

Escheator

A royal official with the power to execute wills and deal with property issues where estates were reverting to the Crown. There were significant opportunities for corruption and for making large profits from the role.

Many of the higher classes shared the commons' grievances, although not necessarily in the same form. The Pontefract Articles refer to the Statute of Uses, the activities of **escheators**, traditional 'liberties' such as the Palatinate of Durham, the working of the common law, the need for both Parliaments and central law courts to meet at York, and a demand for parliamentary elections to be free of government interference. These were secular concerns, like the commons' economic grievances, but they applied primarily to the lawyers and gentry who led the revolt. What seems to have united the pilgrims across all social classes were two issues: the future of the Church and the future of Thomas Cromwell. Of the twenty-four articles drawn up at Pontefract, no less than 11 were concerned with religion. By his own admission Aske had included the demand for the restoration of papal authority without consultation, and he may have been responsible also for the listing of heresies to be punished, specifically naming Luther, Wycliffe and Hus. Four articles were concerned with the restoration of the abbeys and the punishment of Leigh and Leighton, whose evidence of corruption had enabled Cromwell to draw up the act against them. Other articles demanded the restoration of clerical privileges, including benefit of clergy, clerical jurisdiction and the burning of heretics, while Cromwell and Rich were specifically named as deserving punishment for 'maintaining heretics' and 'undermining the good laws of this realm'. As with the Lincolnshire articles, it is likely that many of the specifics came from the ranks of the gentry and possibly the clergy, but the behaviour of the commons throughout the revolt testifies that they shared these religious loyalties. The defence of local churches, the demand for (and actual examples of) restoration of the abbeys and the attacks on clerical commissioners trying to enforce Cromwell's injunctions leave no doubt that religious issues were of immediate concern to the community as a whole, and that the different classes were united in religious conservatism. Combined with social deference and belief in a natural hierarchy, this allowed the gentry to take the lead and bring the whole force of the community to challenge the government. It also, of course, allowed those who had a separate agenda to exploit popular grievances for their own purpose.

Was the Pilgrimage of Grace brought about by a political conspiracy?

As Source H points out, the status of the gentry did not prevent them from being a part of the local community and their leadership was broadly welcomed. Although there could be some clash of interests between the gentry and the commons, there was also unity, and gentry leadership undoubtedly enhanced the organisation and effectiveness of the risings and the extent to which they could threaten the government and the monarch. Some historians, however, have challenged the idea that the rebellion was genuinely popular and argued that it was created and manipulated by a conservative faction among the nobility, fearful of losing influence and determined to reverse the direction of political development in the 1530s. The influence of the Percys, their links with both Aske and Bowes, and the prominent role of Northumberland's disinherited brothers, led to suggestions that the rebellion was a conspiracy hatched by a disgruntled feudal aristocracy, fighting to maintain their regional independence in the face of an encroaching central government. This argument was reinforced by Mervyn James, who studied the role of Lord Hussey, one of the principal nobles in Lincolnshire and a member of the Aragonese faction at court. Hussey was able to stir up resentment among the Lincolnshire gentry of Charles Brandon, Duke of Suffolk, who had estates in the county and had used his friendship with the King to monopolise patronage. An alliance of regional nobility with locally minded gentry and lawyers would account for several of the pilgrims' demands, notably for legal sessions and a Parliament in the north.

A more direct challenge to the authenticity of the pilgrimage as a popular movement came from the work of Geoffrey Elton, who argued that it originated in the 'high politics' of the court, and was devised by the defeated supporters of Catherine of Aragon and Princess Mary. According to Elton, 'the pilgrimage originated in a decision by one of the court factions to take the battle out of the court into the nation, to raise the standard of loyal rebellion as the only way left to them if they were to succeed in reversing the defeats suffered at court and in Parliament, and in forcing the King to change his policy.' Elton argued that the pilgrimage had two key objectives: the restoration of Princess Mary to her place in the succession and the destruction of Thomas Cromwell. He was able to show that the main leaders of the rebellion had long-standing personal links, both with each other and with Aragonese interests. This included Robert Aske, whose work as a lawyer took him to London on a regular basis, and Sir Robert Constable. Hussey was closely linked to Lord Darcy, who surrendered Pontefract Castle to the rebels, had served Catherine of Aragon and Mary, and opposed the King's divorce from as early as 1527. Hussey had also been Chamberlain of Mary's household from 1535 until he was dismissed and his wife imprisoned. They had encouraged Mary's refusal to accept the royal supremacy, and blamed Cromwell for pressurising her to do so.

Eustace Chapuys (1489–1556)

Chapuys was the Imperial ambassador and representative of the Hapsburg Emperor and King of Spain, Charles V. Charles was the nephew of Catherine of Aragon and the leading Catholic ruler in Europe. For both reasons he was deeply opposed to Henry VIII's actions between 1529 and 1536 and, as the Emperor's ambassador, Chapuys sought to encourage any form of resistance to royal policies, including rebellion and treason.

Both Hussey and Darcy had been engaged in talks with **Eustace Chapuys**, in 1535, about the possibility of a co-ordinated rebellion and imperial invasion to reverse the changes that had been made since 1533. This would have been treason by any standards, reflecting the anger and despair felt by Catherine's friends at the course of events. Since then Cromwell and his allies had only grown stronger and their policies more radical. By 1536, according to Elton, Darcy, Hussey and their associates despaired of arresting the process through normal court politics and were ready for a more desperate strategy. There was evidence of discontent in the north throughout 1536 and it was hoped that, by showing the King the strength of feeling against Cromwell and his allies, they could persuade or force him to reverse the direction of his policy. While not denying that popular discontent existed, Elton argued that the rebellion was organised and manipulated by a court faction for their own ends.

Elton's work has been challenged as failing to explain the scale and spread of the rebellion, and as insufficient to account for its impact. While not denying the possibility of a conspiracy among those who took charge of the rebellion, critics argue that the numbers involved, the range of localised activity and the obvious difficulty experienced by the leadership in holding back the angry commons on several occasions all testify to more deep-seated causes of unrest. Source J illustrates the debate.

Source J

Elton did raise questions that should warn us against taking any one simple explanation of the risings. He drew attention to those he saw as key figures: Aske himself, Lord Darcy and Lord Hussey. Aske's story of how he was forced to join the rebels makes no sense at all . . . Darcy pretended at first that he was opposed to the rising . . . Yet he surrendered Pontefract quite extraordinarily quickly. Moreover, when he did so he was ready to distribute to the rebels numerous badges of the Five Wounds of Christ [selected by Aske as the rebels' badge when in York a week earlier] . . . None of these men, Professor Elton argues, can seriously be thought to have been taken entirely by surprise in October 1536. But can we see this as a decisive argument that their political disaffection lay at the heart of the rising?

From A. Fletcher and D. MacCulloch, *Tudor Rebellions*, fifth edition, published 2008

Elton's argument, therefore, serves to moderate claims that the rebellion was simply the spontaneous eruption of discontent against the actions of an isolated and deeply unpopular regime. However, the existence of a conspiracy is clearly insufficient to explain the revolt as a whole, or the nature of the threat that it posed to the King and his government. It can be argued that far from manipulating the situation, the conspirators were inspired by it – that the existence of discontent encouraged their hopes and the outbreak of popular unrest spurred them into action.

What is most important is that all of these elements were necessary to create a significant threat to the authority of Henry VIII.

How seriously did the rebellion threaten Henry's government?

The range and scale of grievances and the ability of the pilgrims to paralyse government in the north created a significant challenge to the King's authority. They revealed widespread hostility to the changes introduced in the 1530s by Henry and Cromwell. An army of 30,000 men was a threat by any standards, and Norfolk and Shrewsbury would have struggled to contain the threat had the pilgrims begun to march south. While the claims of historians like Haigh that they would have gathered further support from 'widespread sympathy in southern counties for the pilgrim cause' may be overstated, the government was in serious trouble. Although Henry seems to have underestimated it at first, and belittled it in public, his letters betray anger and anxiety. According to Nicholas Fellowes, 'the whole of northern society was out of joint, and a remedy was needed' if the regime was to survive.

It did so because of a combination of ruthless duplicity on the part of Norfolk and the King, and the reluctance of the pilgrim leaders to pursue their cause to its logical end, which was treason. When Aske declared his loyalty to the King and demanded the removal of evil Councillors, he was probably sincere. The purpose of the pilgrim army was not to depose Henry, but to force him to restore traditional rights and relationships. This strategy had worked well in 1525 in resisting the Amicable Grant, but that was a limited demand, the greater nobility were sympathetic and the King's face was saved by a convenient scapegoat. In 1536 some of the nobility were sympathetic, and many, including Norfolk, disliked Cromwell enough to relish him as a scapegoat, but the range and scale of the rising made that impossible. The King's authority could not survive the concessions demanded and he had no choice but to pursue victory by whatever means were necessary. The very scale of unrest undermined its chances of success, and the naivety of the rebel leaders and the indiscipline of some elements within the rebel coalition gave Henry the opportunity.

5.4 The Pilgrims' banner, depicting the five wounds of Christ

The bloody suppression of the 1537 rising led the pilgrimage to be considered, in general terms, a failure. Michael Bush has argued that, by raising so large an army and forcing the government to negotiate, the pilgrims demonstrated such potential for resistance that Henry was forced to bring the process of reform to a halt. Although the Bigod rising allowed Henry to renege on his promises, he slowed the pace of change. However, as you have seen in Unit 1, the reasons for Henry's desire to slow the pace of reform are unclear, and the extent to which he did so before 1539 was limited. Moreover, government control of the north was strengthened as a result of the rebellion and many of those who participated were harshly punished. Source K develops the point, although Source L offers a different assessment of the situation.

Source K

No Parliament met in the north, and within a few months all the leaders of the original pilgrimage, including Aske, Darcy and Hussey, had been rounded up and executed. The north was not to rise again for another 30 years. In due course some of their demands were quietly accepted: Cromwell fell; Mary was restored to the succession; and the *Act of Wills* followed the *Statute of Uses*. But none of these things were the direct result of the rebellion. Had the pilgrims attempted to declare Henry deposed, or summoned the aid of the Emperor [Charles V], or even dealt directly with Reginald Pole, they would have been much more clearly the King's enemies in the traditional sense. They did none of those things, and yet paid as high a price as if they had . . .

Not many of those who disliked the King's proceedings were prepared to stand up and be counted – except inadvertently when their grumblings were detected . . . The pilgrimage is a test case. However strongly most of the participants disagreed with the King, they were not prepared to push their discontentment into an open confrontation. They did not want another King, they wanted the King to behave in a different way and they were, in their own eyes, demonstrators and not rebels.

From David Loades, *Henry VIII: Church, Court and Conflict*, published 2009

Source L

Given this combination of protest from a wide geographical and social spectrum of northern society . . . the pilgrimage could have been fatal for Henry's government: it came perilously close to succeeding and was [according to C.S.L. Davies] 'the largest popular revolt in English history'. If more leading noblemen of the north had backed it, all would have been lost for the evangelical clique around Cromwell in London. This was the most dangerous of all the unsuccessful rebellions of the Tudor period. Yet in the end, not enough of the north's natural leaders were prepared openly to support the movement: they were probably frightened by the fact that too many leaders had emerged from outside their charmed circle, and by the very provisional nature of the deference which they discovered in the lower orders. With many of those gentry and noblemen who did assume leadership roles using their position to slow the momentum of the rebel crowds, the Westminster government was given its chance to play for time and take the initiative. As C.S.L. Davies suggests, 'the end result of the pilgrimage may have been to sow such distrust between clergy and commons, and between gentry and commons, as to prevent any repetition for a generation'.

From A. Fletcher and D. MacCulloch, *Tudor Rebellions*, fifth edition, published 2008

Conclusion: The impact of the rebellion and the development of the Tudor state

The rebellion posed some danger to the King, if not to his person then at least to his authority. The pilgrimage had clearly demonstrated that, if government decisions alienated too great a proportion of the King's subjects, then the King could face a serious challenge. They reflected a deep-seated conservatism that remained strong in many parts of the kingdom and, whatever the particular objectives of the rebels, they shared a desire to defend a way of life whose traditions they respected and valued. Some of the rebels' aims were partially fulfilled, although there is some debate about the role of the rebellion itself in achieving this. However, the rebellion failed to reverse the direction in which the Tudor state had developed under the control of Henry VIII and his advisers. It can be argued that there was some slowing in the pace of change, but 1537–40 were years of consolidation rather than reversal. The greater nobility and many of the gentry had demonstrated their loyalty to the Tudors, or at least their fear of the alternatives.

SKILLS BUILDER

Analyse Sources K and L. How far do they agree about the nature of the threat to Henry VIII created by the Pilgrimage of Grace?

The royal supremacy in state and Church remained intact, the wealth and status of the Church was significantly diminished (as explained in Unit 1) and the ability of central government to enforce its authority across the kingdom was significantly enhanced. In withstanding a serious challenge, the Tudor state created by Henry and Thomas Cromwell emerged with greater strength and stability. The opportunity had been taken to demonstrate the government's power, to remove some of its enemies and intimidate others, and to strengthen the machinery on which government relied. The danger posed by rebellion to both the political and social order had been clearly demonstrated. Its legacy would become apparent when further unrest broke out in 1549.

The Rebellions of 1549

In 1549 the Tudor monarchy was vulnerable, with a child King represented by his Lord Protector, Edward Seymour, Duke of Somerset. Somerset was the King's uncle, but a Protector could never exercise the same personal authority as a mature, adult King, particularly when faced by rebellion. Serious economic pressures had been building up with both enclosures and price inflation bearing heavily on the lower orders and this was compounded by the government's religious policies. Most historians have treated the rebellions of 1549 as separate and distinct events, with the Western Rebellion reflecting the religious tensions of the period and Kett's Rebellion being attributed almost entirely to economic problems. However, recent research into the 'low politics' of local communities has uncovered a much greater range of unrest. It is suggested that the threat posed by the accumulation of protest, and the ability of leaders from the 'middling sort' to establish links and organise action across a wide geographical area, made the situation much more dangerous than is often allowed.

The Western Rebellion

Background to the unrest

There were signs of upheaval as early as 1547, with a riot in Penryn. This was sparked by the activities of William Body, described by MacCulloch as 'an unscrupulous and avaricious careerist', who had secured the post of Archdeacon of Cornwall by dubious means and apparently exploited religious reform as a means of enriching himself. In April 1548 he was attacked and killed by a mob in Helston, led by Martin Geffrey, the priest of St. Keverne, which lay in the Lizard peninsula, where Cornish was still widely spoken. The cause of unrest there was the government's religious policies, but this was exacerbated by the actions of local gentry. The principal families of the Helston area, the Godolphins and Reskymers, had purchased Church lands and had close links with Protestants in Devon led by Sir Peter Carew, who had done much to anglicise the eastern part of Cornwall. Religious divisions in Cornwall were closely linked with cultural and economic changes, which were undermining ancient traditions to the detriment of many inhabitants.

> **Discussion point**
>
> Did the Pilgrimage of Grace 'come perilously close to succeeding'? If it really posed a serious threat to the King or the state, why was it not more successful?

On this occasion in 1548 the mob were persuaded to return to their homes, and the ringleaders hanged for the murder, but it is clear that resentment continued to grow and a year later it erupted in a much more serious form.

Outline of events

The rebellion began in the spring of 1549, when it was ordered that the new Prayer Book must be used across Cornwall on Whit Sunday. Its leader was Humphrey Arundell, who gathered forces around Bodmin and drew up articles of grievance with the help of a small group of conservative clergy. Early in June he led his forces into Devon, where a separate rising had broken out at Sampford Courtenay. There the local priest had been forced by the villagers to ignore the new Prayer Book and return to the traditional mass. The local gentry seem to have been intimidated by the murder of a Justice of the Peace who had sought to quell the unrest, and did nothing to interfere. Hence the two groups of protesters met up at Crediton, where they were visited by **Sir Peter Carew**, whose presence merely inflamed the situation. The rebels then moved to Clyst St Mary. There they met with Sir Thomas Denys and Sir Hugh Pollard, who sympathised with their desire to prevent further religious reform until King Edward came of age, and persuaded them to petition the government in an orderly way. However, further interference by Carew and the sheriff of Devon, Peter Courtenay, prevented a truce, and the rebels moved to besiege Exeter on 2 July.

The government reacted very slowly. When Lord Russell was sent to restore order Somerset seems to have believed that the rebellion was still confined to Sampford Courtenay and provided Russell with a small and

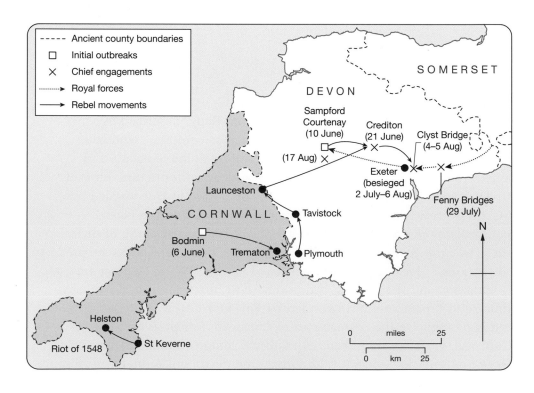

5.5 The Western Rebellion

inadequate force. Government resources were already stretched in dealing with riots in the south, east and the Midlands, and an additional force under Lord Grey, which was sent to the west on 12 July, had to be diverted to deal with unrest in Oxfordshire. Russell tried to recruit men in Dorset and Somerset, but without success. A determined march towards London by the rebels might well have been successful and possibly gained support along the way. No such attempt was made, however, and on 28 July Russell was able to attack and defeat parties of rebels around Fenny Bridges and along the river Otter. When Grey and his force of Italian mercenaries finally arrived on 3 August the government forces were able to lift the siege. The rebels, who numbered about 6,000 at this time, appeared to disperse into the West Country and with Russell reluctant to follow, Somerset was concerned that rebel possession of Plymouth would allow them to make contact with the French, who declared war on 8 August. However, there is no evidence that any contact was made, and on 16 August Russell caught the main rebel force at Sampford Courtenay once more and defeated them there. In the chase that followed, it has been estimated that about 4,000 West Country inhabitants died.

What did the rebels want?

During the course of the rebellion the rebels produced three sets of articles, which demonstrate the mixture of concerns that brought about the unrest. The first was drawn up by the Cornish leaders and a second, drawn up by the Devon rioters, was incorporated when the rebels were at Sampford Courtenay. The final, and only surviving, version was compiled during the siege of Exeter, mainly by Robert Welsh, a Cornishman who was Vicar of St Thomas's in Exeter. There can be no real doubt that religion played a significant part in causing the rebellion, but any precise estimate of its significance is complicated by the existence of different versions of the articles and by the existence of different factions among the rebels. A call for the Church to revert to the ceremonies and procedures used at the end of Henry VIII's reign runs through all three versions of the articles, and both the Cornish rebels and the villagers of Sampford Courtenay had insisted that there should be no significant changes until King Edward came of age. This suggests a preference for traditional forms, but also an acceptance of royal supremacy and respect for the Crown. However, the final version goes much further, demanding the recall of the English Bible, limitations on lay communion and the restoration of abbey lands. Calls for the removal of proposed taxes on sheep and woollen cloth that appeared in the first two sets of articles now disappeared, as did complaints about food prices. Where the Cornish had requested a liturgy in the Cornish language, the third set of articles demanded only a return to Latin. They also included a demand that 'Lord Cardinal Pole' should be pardoned for his opposition to King Henry and brought back from Rome to take charge of the King's Council. Contemporary letters written from Lord Russell's camp indicate that there were serious divisions among the rebels over the final articles.

How far is it possible to treat the rebel articles as reliable evidence of rebel aims?

Discussion point

What similarities can you find between the Pilgrimage of Grace and the Western Rebellion? What were the main differences? How far do they explain why the Western Rebellion appears to have been much less of a threat to the government?

It seems likely that the original grievances of the commons were being set aside by their leaders – the conservative clergy and the Courtenay-Arundell faction.

In the south-west, as in the Pilgrimage of Grace, it appears that religious conservatism had the power to unite communities in opposition to unpopular changes. Arundell, the only gentleman of note to join the rebels, had strong religious convictions. It is also likely, however, that his religious views coincided with his personal interests and the impact of factional rivalries among the elite. The Arundells of Trerice and Lanherne were cousins of the Courtenay Earls of Devon. They had been the pre-eminent family in Cornwall, holding office both locally and at court, but their Catholic sympathies had led to loss of influence, and Arundell's brother and cousins had been removed from the list of JPs in Cornwall shortly before the rebellion. With the disgrace of their Courtenay cousins in 1538, power in the south-west had passed from this conservative faction to Protestant newcomers like Sir Peter Carew. The government's problems in Cornwall and Devon were compounded by the failure of the resident gentry to contain the rising, partly because the more tactful and sympathetic of them gave way to men like Carew. MacCulloch describes the western gentry as 'polarised' by a feud between 'a clique of convinced evangelical gentry on the one hand and the remains of the Courtenay clan on the other'. On both sides, religious preferences, family status and personal interest helped to shape rival political objectives, and infiltrated the rebellion. Like the Pilgrimage of Grace, the Western Rebellion was an initially spontaneous outbreak of popular resentment, caused by a combination of economic pressure, a desire for social justice and hostility to religious changes. This popular resentment was encouraged by the conservative clergy and channelled by gentry leadership into a political attack on those held responsible – the King's advisers and chief administrators. The removal of 'evil advisors' was a central plank of the rebels' demands in both cases, which avoided an overt attack on the monarch himself while forcing him to concede control of policy and decision-making. According to Source M, however, the Western Rebellion was much less of a threat.

Source M

The breakdown of local government in Devon and Cornwall had now lasted almost two months . . . [and] Russell delayed in Exeter during the second week of August, beset by problems of money and supplies . . . Somerset was unnecessarily worried since the rebels lacked the organisation to hold Plymouth, which they had taken earlier in the summer, and were not even in contact with the French. But they showed courage and determination in facing the overwhelming royal army of about 8,000 men that marched west from Exeter on 16 August. The final struggle at Sampford Courtenay was prolonged . . . and it required a threefold attack by Russell, Grey and Herbert in the evening to force the rebels to retire. [Yet] the rebellion never had a real chance of forcing the government to make concessions in its religious policy, and its suppression was only so prolonged because the Western Rebellion coincided with the various 'rebellions of Commonwealth' to the east and north.

From A. Fletcher and D. MacCulloch, *Tudor Rebellions*, fifth edition, published 2008

Kett's Rebellion

Background to the unrest

The suppression of the rebellion in the west was made more difficult by the outbreak of similar upheavals elsewhere. As in the west, the events of 1549 that became known as Kett's Rebellion had already been foreshadowed at Northall in Hertfordshire, where – in May 1548 – an unpopular landlord, Sir William Cavendish, triggered a riot in which his property was attacked and his fences pulled down. Cavendish had been about to enclose an extensive area of common land near the Middlesex/Essex borders, affecting villagers in three counties, who celebrated their success by blowing up his **rabbit warren**, killing over two thousand rabbits. They then set up camp on the disputed land and forced the royal officials who had been overseeing the enclosure to leave, but not before promising to bring the protesters' concerns to the attention of the government. Some 95 of the protesters were later indicted, but were never punished, and a week after the incident the Lord Protector, the Duke of Somerset, set up a commission under John Hales, an idealistic Protestant reformer, to investigate illegal enclosures in the Midlands. The economic causes of the incident, the use of 'camping' as a form of protest, and the government's response all foreshadowed the events associated with Kett's Rebellion.

In May 1549 there were attacks on enclosures in Somerset and Wiltshire. On 1 July the government summoned gentry from the south-east and Midlands to Windsor, probably with the intention of raising forces to go west. The absence of the gentry seems to have sparked action in a number of localities, especially Essex and Oxfordshire. These demonstrators also pulled down fences, demanded an end to enclosures and began to gather in camps to assemble petitions to the Lord Protector. By 7 July the movement had spread throughout the area from which the gentry had been summoned – the Thames valley, the home counties, north to the Midlands and east to Suffolk and East Anglia. Given the upheavals taking place in the south-west, it could be claimed that the whole of southern England and a significant part of the Midlands were in a state of unrest. On 8 July Somerset appointed a new enclosure commission under Hales, with greater powers than had been given in 1548. By coincidence, this was the same day that trouble broke out in Wymondham, Norfolk, leading to Kett's march to Norwich and the events that became known as Kett's Rebellion.

Outline of events

Wymondham lay within the wooded pasturelands of Norfolk, where enclosures had caused much resentment. The problems of 1549 were sparked by a quarrel between the residents of Wymondham and John Flowerdew, a local lawyer and escheator. Flowerdew had enclosed several areas of woodland pasture and also claimed ownership of the land and church belonging to the dissolved abbey at Wymondham. The residents believed the church had been purchased by the parish and wanted to use it, while Flowerdew intended to pull it down.

Definition

Rabbit warrens
Enclosed and artificial creations like deer parks, which ensured that the hunting and eating of rabbits was confined mainly to the upper levels of society.

During a local feast on 6–8 July, Flowerdew's fences were attacked. He seems to have attempted to turn the protest against the property of Robert Kett, a local tanner who had bought and enclosed parts of the manor of Wymondham. Kett had led complaints about the destruction of the church and quarrelled bitterly with Flowerdew. He now responded by sympathising with the demonstrators and assuming leadership of their movement. Supported by yeomen and farmers from the area, he organised a march on Norwich, gathering considerable support along the way. The rebels arrived at Norwich on 10 July and were denied entry to the city. By 12 July they had set up camp on nearby Mousehold Heath with around 16,000 men, where Kett drew up a list of grievances (the Norfolk Articles) and sent them as a petition to Somerset.

At this point there was little sign of violence and no direct threat to the government, as Kett seems to have expected a favourable response. There had, however, been some significant incidents in which unpopular gentry were humiliated and property attacked or looted as the rebels moved through the county.

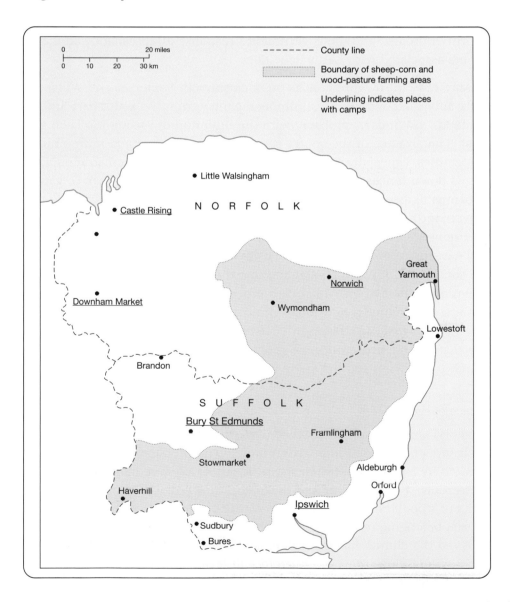

5.6 Kett's Rebellion – the area affected

While they waited, further camps were set up at Downham Market in Norfolk and elsewhere in Suffolk, Kent and Cambridgeshire. With many of the gentry away at Windsor, they were powerless to resist, as was the corporation of Norwich. There is no sign that any attempt was made to recruit leaders from the ranks of the gentry, and the camps appear to have been well disciplined and organised. Kett made agreements with the Mayor and Aldermen to provide food for the insurgents, and two of them, Mayor Thomas Codd and Alderman Thomas Aldrich, signed the rebels' petition. They later claimed to have been forced to do this.

The atmosphere changed on 21 July, when a government herald arrived to offer a pardon to the rebels if they would disperse. Unlike many of the other camps around the country, the Norfolk rebels refused. There is evidence that memories of Henry VIII's betrayal in 1537 were still strong, but this does not explain why the Norfolk rebels should be exceptional. Something can be attributed to Kett's influence and it may also reflect the level of bitterness that existed among villagers and townsmen in a highly commercialised county where traditional communities were under threat. When the pardon was rejected, the city authorities began to prepare defences and the rebels attacked. By the evening of 22 July, Norwich was in the hands of the insurgents, although the city authorities were treated with some respect. The leading Aldermen were imprisoned in Surrey Place, previously the residence of the Earl of Surrey, but they were kept in some comfort and allowed to maintain outside contact. The ease with which the insurgents took control suggests that they had the sympathy of many in the town.

Somerset abandoned his conciliatory approach and ordered a force under the command of William Parr, Marquis of Northampton, to cut off the rebels' supply lines and negotiate a surrender. Northampton entered Norwich on 30 July and on the following day he offered a full pardon to those who would disperse, but then failed either to act decisively or to negotiate. Deprived of supplies, the rebels were forced to attack and, in a far bloodier encounter, re-took the city, forcing Northampton and many of the gentry to flee in disarray. His second-in-command, Lord Sheffield, was killed. With this action the rising had become a full-scale rebellion. While the government commissioned a more substantial force under the command of John Dudley, Earl of Warwick, Kett made some attempt to gain further support, for example from Yarmouth, but made no move to take the initiative and advance towards London. Hence, when Warwick's force arrived on 23 August, the rebels were trapped. Warwick offered to pardon all except Kett, but when Kett agreed to negotiate on that basis, he was held back by his own men, leading to a skirmish. The chance of a peaceful outcome had now passed. On 26 August, the arrival of more mercenaries to join Warwick and military miscalculation by Kett led to bloody defeat at Dussindale, with as many as 3,000 rebels killed. Kett was condemned for treason on 26 November and hanged at Norwich Castle on 7 December. His brother William was hanged from the spire of Wymondham Abbey.

What did the rebels want?

Kett's Rebellion was largely confined to East Anglia, which was a region of dense population and developed industry as well as agriculture. The coast and fens meant that fishing had some importance, and there was mixed arable and pastoral farming. Norwich, the second largest city in the kingdom, was home to around 16,000, but the 1540s had seen serious disruption of trade and a collapse of the local textile industry that brought large-scale unemployment. The city was troubled by serious social divisions, with six per cent of the inhabitants who were prosperous merchants owning about 60 per cent of the land and goods assessed for taxes. About 35 per cent of residents were too poor to pay any tax in 1525, and by the 1540s the Common Council of the town were complaining of the loss of craftsmen and the growth in the number of 'foreigners and beggars'. The events at Wymondham suggest that economic changes were a significant cause of the unrest, and that there was a perceived threat to traditional communities and social relationships. Conditions around the region reinforce this argument, and are reflected in the articles drawn up by the rebels at Mousehold Heath in July 1549.

The Norfolk Articles

Definition

Hundreds

Areas of administration.

The 29 articles each begin with the words 'We pray that . . .', giving the document the clear character of a petition. They are signed by representatives from 22 **hundreds** in Norfolk, some from Suffolk, and the city of Norwich. Three of the articles (numbers 8, 15 and 20) focus on the quality of clergy, asking that priests should reside in their parish, serve the whole community and not act as chaplains to the wealthy, be able to preach and teach poor children their catechism. Article 22 sought a reduction in the proportion of tithes taken. Articles 12, 18 and 27 were concerned with the conduct of royal officials, who were mostly local gentry and lawyers, and abuse of their powers, while Article 24 was against the sale of wardships, and the need for those who had been wards, other than of the King, to have freedom in deciding to marry. Again, this suggests a level of corruption and exploitation among the educated elite.

The remaining 21 articles were all focused on economic rights and social justice. Some were quite specific, for example Article 23, which asked that none below the rank of gentleman should be allowed to keep a dovecote, or to keep 'conyes' (rabbits) on his land unless they are fenced in so that they cannot be a nuisance to others. Articles 3 and 16 refer to particularly local problems. Article 3 asked that 'no lord of the manor shall common upon the commons', referring to the practice of landlords grazing their stock on the lands of their tenants by claiming their traditional grazing right of 'foldcourse'. Article 16 asked that 'all bondmen should be free', referring to restrictions still placed on some tenants as a legacy of ancient feudal practice. This was particularly common on lands previously held by the Duke of Norfolk until his attainder in 1547. Articles 5, 6, 7 and 14 asked that land prices and rents should revert to the levels used in the reign of Henry VII, while

Articles 2, 9 and 21 were concerned with the terms on which land was rented, seeking to prevent abuse of landlord powers and restore customary rights. There was some respect shown for traditional symbols of gentry status, such as the possession of a dovecote or rabbit warren, but there was also some concern that different social and functional roles were becoming blurred. Article 4 objected to priests buying land, Article 25 to manorial lords acting as bailiffs for one another, and Article 26 asked that 'no lord, knight nor gentleman shall have . . . spiritual promotion'.

The remaining articles were concerned with enclosures and restrictions on access to land. Article 1 sought to protect the existing enclosures for the production of saffron, which was both expensive and essential for the cloth trade. The other items sought to prevent enclosure of commons, to ensure that profits from common land were fairly distributed, to stop the wealthy from amassing large flocks and herds to graze on them (overstocking), and to ensure open access to rivers and the coasts for the purpose of fishing and 'passage'.

The actions of the rebels and the evidence of the Norfolk Articles allow some definite conclusions to be drawn about the nature and significance of the rebellion. Its causes were mainly economic. Andy Wood's comment that 'a strong current of class conflict' ran through parts of the Pilgrimage of Grace certainly applies to the Norfolk rebellion, where gentry leadership was never sought and where local landlords were often the cause of the complaints. Many of the articles were concerned with local abuses and even the more general complaints, for example over prices and rents, would be seen in a local context. The articles on religious issues were also tinged with a sense of class, for example in the demand that priests serve the whole community and offer support and education to the poor. This is backed up by research carried out by Diarmaid MacCulloch, who found some evidence of radical Protestant influence among the camps in East Anglia.

A second feature is the underlying conservatism of the rebels: the emphasis on traditional rights, the perception of a more prosperous past and the conviction that recent changes were the cause of distress. The rebellion began, and remained for much of the time, as a traditional protest in which the commons sought to draw attention to their difficulties and to appeal to the higher authority of the central government over the heads of their local rulers, whom they believed to be responsible. It can therefore be suggested that the Norfolk rebellion did not constitute a direct threat to central government, let alone the Tudor state. The more obvious aspect of the rebels' rhetoric was their concern with the 'commonwealth' or 'commonweal'. By this they meant the traditional community of village and town, which they believed to have been destroyed by government neglect and gentry greed. Their views were shared by Protestant reformers like John Hales and Bishop Latimer and, more importantly, by the target of their appeals, the Duke of Somerset. His sympathy for the problems of the lower orders has been seen as a major cause of the rebellion, just as his removal from power in its aftermath provided a quick and relatively easy solution. Sources N and O reflect recent research.

SKILLS BUILDER

What do the demands of the Norfolk rebels suggest about their aims and attitudes, and the causes of the revolt?

Source N

By the late spring of 1549, disorder was widespread south of the Trent. Crowds of rebels, said to number hundreds or thousands, knocked down recent enclosures. The houses of unpopular gentry were plundered; wine cellars were emptied; estate archives selectively cleared of documents that prejudiced tenants' rights; deer parks were denuded by mass poaching . . . The first [phase] in the spring, represented a continuation of the earlier troubles of 1548. The second phase began with Somerset's fatal decision to issue a second enclosure commission on 8 July, 1549. This was responsible for the spread of the insurrection into East Anglia. The first rebel camps within East Anglia were formed in western Suffolk, possibly by late May. By July, rebel camps had been established in Norfolk at King's Lynn, Downham Market, Norwich and Hingham, and in Suffolk at Ipswich, Melton and Bury St Edmunds. In Essex there may well have been a camp at Colchester. Urban insurrections failed in Cambridge and Yarmouth . . . It was from these camps that the rebels took their name: the 'camp men'. And for a generation the East Anglian rebellions were remembered as 'the camping time' or the 'commotion time', rather than as Kett's Rebellion.

From Andy Wood, *Riot, Rebellion and Popular Politics in Early Modern England*, published 2001

Source O

[By offering the rebels significant and genuine concessions] Protector Somerset had isolated himself from all those who mattered in English high politics . . . [but] it nearly worked. After all, every commotion in the south, east and the Midlands dispersed without much bloodshed except the Mousehold camp. The Protector might, indeed, have got away with the gamble if the Marquis of Northampton had not blundered when he led his force from London into Norfolk, combining lack of local knowledge with political ineptitude. His mishandling transformed the Norwich encounter from negotiation to bloody battle. Once Norfolk exploded into really murderous violence, Somerset's strategy came crashing down, and the privy Councillors could vent their feelings on him, and on the commons of England.

From A. Fletcher and D. MacCulloch, *Tudor Rebellions*, fifth edition, published 2008

SKILLS BUILDER

To what extent do Sources N and O agree with one another about Somerset's handling of the rebellions?

How serious was the threat caused by the 1549 rebellions?

By July 1549 most of southern England was in a state of unrest, but very little is known about the individual risings and demonstrations. Most were suppressed locally, with very few executions after the event. Outbreaks in Oxfordshire and Buckinghamshire were more prolonged, apparently led by conservative clergy, but when a force of mercenaries on route for the West Country with Lord Grey was diverted to the area, the rebels quickly dispersed and were mopped up by local gentry using their own retainers. The government appears to have played down the problems and very few of the rebels left any documentary evidence. Therefore, until new research was carried out by Diarmaid MacCulloch, Ethan Shagan and Amanda Jones, many historians were unaware of the wider context in which the Western Rebellion and Kett's Rebellion took place. Source P is a good example of the way in which both rebellions tended to be interpreted, as isolated outbreaks that did not significantly threaten the government. Source Q illustrates the new perceptions produced by recent research.

Source P

The Western Rebellion erupted as a result of the attempts of Protector Somerset to compel all parishes to use the 1549 Prayer Book, which represented a discernible shift towards Protestantism . . . Does the Prayer Book rebellion, then, deserve its title? Certainly, of the 16 demands almost all are religious . . . written by clerics who believed that no religious changes could legally take place while Edward VI was still a minor – in other words, the 1549 Prayer Book was the work of 'evil counsellors'. Only one article is clearly secular, demanding a limit to the size of gentry households. One is struck by the lack of gentry support for the movement – in contrast, of course, to the Pilgrimage of Grace. Most of the rising's leaders were yeomen or tradesmen, from just outside the gentry class . . .

While the Western Rebellion was at its height, a series of anti-enclosure riots in Norfolk rapidly grew into a major protest . . . Somerset himself has often been blamed for inciting the movement through his social policy, and it is quite true that he had set up a commission on enclosures, which was still at work. Some of the rebels do seem to have believed that they were simply anticipating government policy; in other words, that they were doing what the government wanted them to . . . Time and again the rebels demands harked back to some golden age during Henry VII's reign. This was the protest of a local community mainly directed against the exactions of landlords, and thus it was difficult for it to evoke a national response . . .

From J. Lotherington (ed.), *The Tudor Years*, published 1994

Source Q

With astonishing speed from 7 July and during the following week, mass uprisings swept through precisely the areas from which the gentry had been summoned to Windsor on 1 July . . . Much will probably remain concealed from us for ever. We only know of the northernmost rising, at Seamer near Scarborough, because the martyrologist, John Foxe, was given papers about it and chose to write it up in his *Book of Martyrs* as an example of the disorder which popish rebels could cause . . . Similarly, it was only the recognition of the notebook of a Buckinghamshire JP from 1549 [by Diarmaid MacCulloch] that revealed the scale of events in Buckinghamshire. It has now been thoroughly analysed by Dr Jones, revealing that 134 men from twenty different parishes in the county and a few from elsewhere were bound over to keep the peace late that July. Their rising was paired with that in Oxfordshire, and a large number of those involved seem to have marched on Oxford just as the westerners marched on Exeter and the East Anglians did on Norwich. The rising in this area was (as we have seen) serious enough to cause the government to divert the army intended for the West Country under Lord Grey to quell the disturbance. The only comparative success for the government was in keeping London quiet . . . There was a good deal of support in London for the programme of religious reformation that the government was promoting, and none of the agrarian grievances like enclosures, which could rally popular anger.

From A. Fletcher and D. MacCulloch, *Tudor Rebellions*, fifth edition, published 2008

The nature and significance of the 1549 rebellions

The events of 1549 highlight the importance of economic factors in causing both protest and rebellion in Tudor England. The scale and extent of upheaval and the involvement of the commons can be directly related to problems such as enclosure, rents and prices, tenants' rights and taxation, while taxation, land tenures and feudal payments also affected the gentry. However, the relationship is more complex than a simple correlation between hardship and unrest. As in the northern risings of 1536–37, the protestors in the East Anglian rebellion of 1549 were not motivated only by hardship, but also by a sense of injustice, of rights ignored and customary

SKILLS BUILDER

How far does the evidence given in Source Q challenge the claims made in Source P about the limited threat posed by the 1549 rebellions?

protection lost. The concept of the commonweal in danger appears in both areas and did much to justify men who accepted the idea of a natural hierarchy in challenging the authority of their rulers. The same is true of the western rebels. While it is more difficult to assess the impact of economic pressures in the Western Rising because of the unreliability of the evidence, it is clear that the initial outbreaks in Cornwall were caused by a popular reaction to the destruction of valued and cherished institutions. The arrogance and rapacity of William Body, the intrusion of an apparently mercenary and to some extent alien gentry, and the widespread hardship caused by rising prices combined to create a belief that a familiar way of life was under threat.

What had changed since 1536–7 was the role and outlook of the gentry, and the attitude of the commons towards them. The signs had been there in 1537, but by 1549 the gap between social classes had widened further. Government propaganda and the developing role of the gentry in the administration and Parliament had cemented the relationship between the political elite and the Tudor state, while economic change highlighted class conflict and elite fear of popular violence. To a much greater extent than in 1536, the commons acted alone and did not seek gentry leadership. Their failure and the role of the gentry in suppressing their protests had significance for both the rebels and the state. Although Wood and MacCulloch have shown that the commons could mount significant and well-organised protests across quite wide geographical areas, the 1549 rebellions lacked political focus and made no real attempt to challenge the government. Somerset did not fall from power because the rebels threatened him, but because he failed to satisfy the ruling elite, who demanded rapid suppression and the restoration of control. The removal of an adviser, however key, did not threaten the authority of the monarch or the state unless it was forced upon them by rivals with a political agenda, such as religion, faction or the role of the nobility in relation to royal authority. Noble and gentry leadership had provided elements of this in 1536, but in 1549 there was little evidence of any such intentions. In 1553 they re-emerged from the religious conflicts that surrounded Henry VIII's two daughters.

Rebellion in the reigns of Mary and Elizabeth, 1553–1569

The succession problem: Conspiracy and rebellion

Whatever the preferences of the gentry and nobility in terms of religion and the succession, there could be no challenge to the right of Edward VI to succeed his father. At the time of his parents' marriage both Catherine of Aragon and Anne Boleyn were dead, and as a widower Henry had every right to remarry. As a male, Edward took precedence over both of his sisters. In 1547, therefore, rival factions sought to control the King rather than challenge him, and his Seymour relatives won the battle. However, the accession of Mary in 1553 and the place of Elizabeth as her successor by their father's will reopened the issues of legitimacy and religious belief that had shaped factional struggles since the 1530s. In 1553 the leader of the Protestant faction, the Duke of Northumberland, had tried to retain power by replacing Mary with Lady Jane Grey, and his failure left his allies without hope of influencing events through the normal political channels. As a result, Sir Thomas Wyatt and his associates turned to rebellion in 1554, as did the northern earls in 1568. There are distinct similarities between the two rebellions.

Wyatt's Rebellion

Outline of events

Although Sir Thomas Wyatt sought to appeal to religious fears in the wake of Mary's accession, and many of his Kentish rebels do appear to have had Protestant sympathies, the revolt originated among courtiers and Councillors who feared losing influence if the Queen proceeded with her planned marriage to Philip of Spain. The leading conspirators alongside Wyatt were Sir James Croft, who had been Lord Deputy of Ireland during Northumberland's administration, and Sir Peter Carew. He was a close associate of Edward Courtenay, Earl of Devon, who had been imprisoned in the Tower of London since his father's execution in 1538. The original plan was to marry Courtenay to Mary, which was in accordance with his Aragonese links and his family's history. However, Mary's insistence on the Spanish match seems to have persuaded the conspirators to substitute Elizabeth, and when protests in Parliament failed to change her mind, to turn to rebellion. The plot was also encouraged by the French ambassador, who feared the growth of Spanish influence in England.

5.7 Thomas Wyatt

Plans were made to co-ordinate risings in Herefordshire under Croft, Devon under Carew, Leicestershire under the Duke of Suffolk (father of Lady Jane Grey) and Kent under Wyatt, but news and rumours of the plot leaked in January 1554, before the preparations were complete. The Imperial ambassador, Simon Renard, seems to have alerted Bishop Stephen Gardiner, the Queen's adviser, who extracted details from Courtenay himself. Although all the plotters left court in early January, it was only Wyatt in Kent who was able to raise a significant force, taking advantage of unrest caused by a depression in the cloth industry and strong anti-Spanish attitudes there to raise a force of about 3,000. Compared to the numbers involved in 1536 and 1549 this was a tiny force, but proximity to London and the unpopularity of Spanish influence allowed him to march unimpeded towards the city after a force of 500 London Whitecoats (the trained bands of London militia) sent to stop him at Rochester deserted and joined the rebels. His plan was to seize the Queen and force her to change her intentions. If she refused, he would proclaim Princess Elizabeth in her place, and may well have secretly intended this anyway. The threat was real enough for Mary to consider leaving London, but an offer to negotiate delayed Wyatt's force at Blackheath and gave Mary time to appeal to the citizens of London for support.

When Wyatt reached Southwark on 3 February he was unable to cross London Bridge, but no attempt was made to stop him moving on. The rebels crossed the Thames at Kingston and marched towards the City, with royal forces under the Earl of Pembroke allowing them to pass. Only when they reached Ludgate and found the gates closed did they meet real opposition. Wyatt was forced to retreat, and the citizens began to harry his forces until he became trapped with about 300 of his men. Of these, about 40 were killed before Wyatt surrendered. The government behaved with cautious leniency towards the rebels. For once executions were largely confined to the political leaders who were undoubtedly guilty of conspiracy, though the unfortunate Lady Jane Grey and her husband, who were in prison because of the earlier plot, were also executed to stop Lady Jane becoming the focus of any further rebellion.

Discussion point

Why did the Wyatt rebellion fail?

What did the rebels want?

The immediate cause of the rebellion was Mary's decision to marry King Philip of Spain. Wyatt appealed to patriotism, claiming that the Spanish marriage would subject England to Spanish methods and interests. Although many of the Kentish rebels were Protestant, little was made of the religious issue – in fact he disclaimed any religious motives after his surrender and arrest. Nevertheless, it is difficult to dismiss its significance as a cause of the revolt. All of the rebel leaders had Protestant credentials, with the possible exception of Courtenay. However, Courtenay had been imprisoned for a number of years, and his confession to Gardiner suggests that he was not difficult to manipulate. Far more significant is the role of Carew, a convinced Protestant who had gained both economically and politically from the Edwardian regime. Although the failure of the other risings tends to emphasise the importance of Wyatt, the likelihood is that the real author of the rising was Carew, who had the necessary political contacts to draw in Croft and Suffolk as well as Courtenay. However, as an absentee landlord in Devon, detested by the commons of both Devon and Cornwall for his role in inflaming the discontents of 1549, he had little chance of raising support there. Meeting hostility in the west, and possibly aware that the conspiracy had been discovered, he fled to Normandy before the Kentish rising began. But if religion was significant, why then did Wyatt deny it? The main reason seems to be that patriotism and anti-Spanish sentiment offered a better way of raising support.

Source R

Mary's marriage plans had given some of her Protestant opponents the chance to pose as patriots and mobilise support under the guise of outraged nationalism. Sir Thomas Wyatt's Rebellion lasted only two weeks and recruited less than a tenth as many supporters as had the Pilgrimage of Grace, but it still caused some sticky moments for the government, especially when a force of 500 Londoners sent against the rebels defected to Wyatt at Rochester, crying (allegedly) 'We are all Englishmen'.

From R. Lockyer and D. O'Sullivan et al, *Tudor Britain*, published 1997

Source S

The most plausible motivation of those who led Wyatt's Rebellion and its associated conspiracies was an attempt to restore the Protestant ascendancy of the reigns of Edward VI and Jane. Why did the conspirators not publicise this religious and political motivation? For the same reason that the Lady Mary remained silent about the religious theme during the July 1553 coup d'etat, which successfully overturned the reign of Queen Jane. England was a deeply divided country in terms of religion in 1553: it made no sense to limit the appeal of any rebellion by appealing to only one side of the religious divide.

From A. Fletcher and D. MacCulloch, *Tudor Rebellions*, fifth edition, published 2008

Wyatt warned a Protestant supporter not to 'so much as name religion, for that will withdraw from us the hearts of many'. The significance of his comment is two-fold. First it reveals the divisive nature of religion as an issue, in that to identify with one theology was to incur the enmity of the other, automatically limiting the support available. The second point is that, in this context, religion cannot be separated from political power. Since the 1530s both religion and the ambition for power had defined political faction, and the evolution of politics in the later years of Henry and the reign of his son had merely strengthened the links between them. In 1553 the link between monarch, government and religious development was completed by the death of Edward. In the place of a minor who could be considered, however inaccurately, not to be responsible for religious developments, there were now two daughters of Henry VIII whose claim to legitimacy, and therefore loyalty, depended at least to some extent on the religious views of their subjects. Whatever else this did, it made rebellion both more justifiable and more dangerous to the monarch. The unrest of 1536 and 1549 could be focused on 'evil counsellors' and avoid a direct challenge to the monarch. Despite Wyatt's disclaimers, if the rebels had captured Mary in 1554, the rebellion would almost certainly have ended in her deposition and replacement with the Protestant Elizabeth. In 1568–69 the northern earls appealed for Spanish aid and sought the approval of the Pope. Although they claimed only to be seeking the acknowledgement of Mary, Queen of Scots as Elizabeth's successor, the papal bull that arrived too late to help them called on Elizabeth's subjects to depose her. It was fortunate for both queens and for the Tudor state that the widespread popular unrest that had characterised the rebellions of 1536 and 1549 failed to materialise.

The Northern Rebellion, 1569–70

Outline of events

The trigger for the rebellion was the arrival in England in 1568 of Mary, Queen of Scots, Elizabeth's cousin and potentially a Catholic heir to the throne. The origins of the rebellion lay in a plan for Mary to be married to the Duke of Norfolk, but they were not necessarily based on disloyalty to the Queen. Elizabeth had already suggested a safe Protestant marriage for Mary to her own favourite, the Earl of Leicester, and Leicester was among those privy to Norfolk's plan. It is more likely that both Leicester and

Discussion point

How far can religious loyalties and nationalist sentiments be treated as separate issues in this period?

SKILLS BUILDER

Working with a partner, compare the threats to the monarch from the following rebellions:

- The Pilgrimage of Grace, 1536
- The Western Rebellion, 1549
- Kett's Rebellion, 1549
- Wyatt's Rebellion, 1554.

Which rebellion was the most significant and why?

5.8 The Northern Rebellion

Norfolk saw it as a way of increasing their influence on the Privy Council at the expense of William Cecil. The Queen, however, was furious that such plans had been discussed and, after Leicester confessed to his part on 6 September, Norfolk fled to his estate at Kenninghall in Norfolk, and considered his options. These included joint action with his brother-in-law, Charles Neville, Earl of Westmorland, and other northern magnates including Thomas Percy, seventh Earl of Northumberland and brother of Lady Westmorland. The northern nobility were characterised by traditionalist attitudes in both religion and politics, as they had demonstrated in 1536–7, and were already disenchanted with Elizabeth. Having been restored to their old positions on the Council and as Wardens of the Marches by Mary Tudor in 1557, they were disappointed to be overlooked by Elizabeth and thoroughly opposed to the Elizabethan settlement in the Church. When Mary, Queen of Scots arrived in England, Northumberland had visited her at Carlisle, and the two had corresponded thereafter. By August/September 1568 the north was rife with rumours of a marriage between Mary and Norfolk, and a plan to force Elizabeth to declare Mary as her heir.

When Norfolk found that his own gentry and tenants were reluctant to take action on his behalf, he sent a message to Westmorland, warning him against a rising, and returned to court to throw himself on Elizabeth's mercy. He was dispatched to the Tower of London. Meanwhile the northern earls hesitated, torn between local Catholic allies who urged them to act and reluctance to challenge the Queen's authority. On 9 October they met with the Council of the North in York, where they admitted having heard rumours of a rising but denied any knowledge of what lay behind them. However, when a suspicious Elizabeth demanded that they appear at court, they failed to respond. Finally, after strong persuasion from Lady Westmorland, who accused her husband and brother of shameful cowardice, the earls began to raise forces. On 14 November they forced the hearing of Mass in Durham Cathedral and began to march south. By 22 November they had reached Tadcaster, south of York, with about 5,500 men, but then turned aside and retreated north-west to Knaresborough. There they waited for Spanish help and reinforcements from Lancashire, neither of which arrived.

The reasons for their hesitation are unclear, but they may well have become aware that Mary, Queen of Scots was to be moved south, out of their reach, and they may also have heard rumours of a massive force being put together by the Earl of Warwick to move against them. Even more importantly, the response to their call to arms had been decidedly lukewarm in many quarters. Whatever the reasons, they began to retreat into the heart of Percy country, and demonstrated some effectiveness in besieging and capturing Barnard Castle. It was clear, however, that they could not move beyond the far north-east, and any hope of help from Mary's supporters in Scotland had already disappeared. By 16 December, with the royal army nearing the Tees, the earls were ready to give up hope, and both fled north to Scotland. Westmorland escaped to Holland, where he lived as a pensioner of Spain, but Northumberland was handed over to the English in 1572 and executed for treason.

How serious were the threats posed by the rebellions of 1554 and 1568?

Despite the direct threat to the monarch's safety, it can be argued that neither revolt posed a serious challenge, because both lacked widespread popular support. This was perhaps more surprising in the north, where the earls attempted to appeal to traditional loyalties. To the horror of the magnates, their appeal was received with indifference and even hostility outside their own associates and dependants. They still had some basis for action. The Percy family alone still owned 40 townships, two key castles at Alnwick and Warkworth, and had over 2,000 tenants scattered across the north-east, Cumbria and Yorkshire. They were supported by the Nevilles, some of the Dacres and a proportion of north-eastern gentry. They were eventually able to raise a reasonable troop of horses from the north-eastern gentry and their servants, but contemporaries commented on the poor quality of their infantry who were described as having to be paid or 'brought forwards by coercion'. Even the appeal to traditional religious loyalties had mixed results. At Darlington, according to Sir George Bowes, 'John Swinburn, with a staff, drove before him the poor folks to hasten them to hear Mass.' The earls had expected the attack on Durham to bring out support in north Yorkshire, but had to offer money, and when that was insufficient, the threat of 'spoil and burning' to force the commons to join them. Since 1536 a whole generation of tenants had experienced the rule of law from Westminster in the form of the prerogative courts of equity as well as the common law, and found it both more neutral and more consistent than the application of customary rights by feudal landlords. In the same period the gentry had been promoted and trusted to organise defence and maintain order under the supervision of central government. In 1536 the pilgrims raised an army of 30,000, without the direct intervention of the earls. In 1568, at most they put together around 6,000 men, many of them reluctant to engage. The earls and their gentry retainers, according to Wood, 'were fighting to preserve a world that was already lost'. Sources T and U examine the threat from Wyatt's Rebellion and Source V draws comparisons with the Northern Rebellion.

Source T

Unlike the rebellions of 1549 this was a political conspiracy among the elites, and there was little popular support. The rebellion was led by Sir James Croft, Sir Peter Carew and Sir Thomas Wyatt, who feared that growing Spanish influence at court could endanger their own careers . . . Simultaneous rebellions in the West Country, the Welsh borderland and Kent were to be supported by a French fleet. The plan failed because the inept Courtenay disclosed the scheme to his patron, Gardiner, before the conspirators were ready. In any case Carew, Croft and the Duke of Suffolk bungled the uprisings. Wyatt succeeded in raising 3,000 men in Kent and this caused real fear in the government because the rebels were so close to London. Royal troops sent to crush the revolt deserted to the rebels . . . [but] an over-cautious Wyatt failed to press home his advantage and although he led his motley troops with some dash, his delay in marching on London gave Mary time to see to its defence . . . Paget suggested leniency for the rebels for fear of provoking further revolts. Fewer than a hundred executions took place among the commons, and most were pardoned. As for the rebel elite, apart from Wyatt and Suffolk, only Jane Grey and her husband, Guildford Dudley, were executed.

From R. Turvey and K. Randell, *Henry VIII to Mary I: Government and Religion, 1509–58*, published 2008

Source U

Sir Thomas Wyatt gained from the proximity of Kent to the capital. The trained bands led by the semi-retired Duke of Norfolk failed to put up significant resistance . . . and Londoners displayed curious ambivalence towards the rebels as they approached the city. Only at Ludgate was it clear that the city would back the monarch. Significantly, because Wyatt was very much a member of the ruling elite, and had used anti-Spanish propaganda with particular effectiveness, the elite failed to close ranks with the unanimity displayed against the northern pilgrims, the distant Cornish and the commoners of East Anglia . . . Mary's new regime was pushing its luck, not so much with a policy of Catholic restoration as with the Spanish marriage and the provocation of those members of the court elite who either felt excluded or feared imminent exclusion.

From Paul Thomas, *Authority and Disorder in Tudor Times*, published 1999

Source V

The foundation of Tudor authority was the dynasty's hold on the confidence of London and the south-east. The Londoners' attitude at Rochester showed that Mary had temporarily lost it. Wyatt came nearer than any other Tudor rebel to toppling a monarch from the throne. Yet in the political development of the century, the rebellion's significance is that it failed [and] demonstrated the bankruptcy of rebellion as a way of solving this kind of political crisis. The [northern] rebellion failed primarily because of its incoherence and aimlessness, but also because its support remained geographically limited. It had not even mobilised the full resources of the two earls . . . The strength of the rebel army lay in their horsemen, who were 'gentlemen and their household servants and tenants'. Such men joined the earls through bastard feudal allegiance [but] the appeal to bastard feudal loyalty was insufficient in itself to raise a large army . . . Unlike the Pilgrimage of Grace, the rebellion failed to find a wide basis in society . . . In the aftermath of the rebellion there were bitter recriminations against the earls for leading humble people into disaster . . . The failure of the rebellion, its feebleness and its disorganisation all proved that northern feudalism and particularism could no longer rival Tudor centralisation.

From A. Fletcher and D. MacCulloch, *Tudor Rebellions*, fifth edition, published 2008

Conclusion: The impact of rebellion on the Tudor state

There were a number of reasons for rebellion in mid-Tudor England: underlying economic and social changes, religious conflicts and political rivalries. Protest was endemic, usually caused by economic problems, but also at times because of social changes and religious loyalties. Only when these elements combined with political rivalries and ambitions, to provide political leadership, did protest become rebellion. Generally, rebellion required an element of 'high politics', such as problems in the relationship between the nobility and the Crown, between local or regional loyalties and central government, or between religious loyalties and the power of the state. With the possible exception of Kett's Rebellion, the major upheavals of the period involved some element of all three, and even the events at Norwich were influenced by Somerset's actions and the rivalries around him. However, rebellion also required an element of 'low politics', such as economic hardship or a perceived threat to the 'commonweal' in order to rouse the commons and create significant popular support.

In 1536 all of these elements were present in the north of England, creating a significant threat to the monarch. Although the rebel leaders did not intend to directly threaten the King, the range and scale of their grievances made it unavoidable. Northern society was structured around precisely the institutions and individuals who were likely to suffer from the changes introduced by Henry VIII and Cromwell: great territorial magnates, powerful abbeys, a strong regional identity and a deeply conservative population. Their attempts to defend their way of life posed a direct and fundamental challenge to the state that Henry had created, and the range of support that the rebel leaders were able to harness made it a serious one. The rebellion failed because of distance from the centre of power, the naivety of the rebel leaders and the ruthlessness of both Henry and his northern commanders, especially Norfolk. Above all, it

SKILLS BUILDER

Interpreted in the context of your wider knowledge, how far do Sources T, U and V support the argument that neither revolt posed a serious challenge to the monarchy because they were both political conspiracies among 'the excluded', lacking widespread popular support?

Discussion point

How far can the major rebellions in 1536–68 be linked to the Henrician Reformation and the changes made in the years 1533–36? Should the mid-Tudor rebellions be seen as separate events, or as part of a deeper, underlying conflict based on both religious and political rivalries?

failed because the leaders lacked the necessary intent to commit treason. The rebellion was essentially conservative and defensive, and this was even more the case in 1549.

The Pilgrimage of Grace allowed Henry to remove its leaders, weaken his enemies and strengthen the apparatus of the state in the north and elsewhere. It also left a legacy of bitterness and suspicion between the commons and the political and social elites. A further decade of economic and social change, religious reform and government propaganda widened the gulf between high and low politics, and bound the elite more firmly to the state rather than the community.

As a result the rebellions of 1549 were essentially movements of the commons in defence of the commonweal, and lacked the high political leadership to constitute a serious threat. Nevertheless, the response of the state was repressive. Over 3,000 rebels died at Dussindale, and over 4,000 in the west, most of them men of ordinary income and status. In the west this came on top of the 6,000 who had died at **Blackheath** in 1497. These are significant figures among a sparse population and represent a severe loss to the communities for whom they spoke. The failed rebellions of 1549 were the last example of large-scale independent action by the commons under the leadership of the yeomen, tradesmen and lower clergy who had been so significant in 1536.

This was partly because of disillusionment with the results of rebellion in both 1536 and 1549, and partly because the 'middling sort' were also

Definition

Blackheath

The site of a battle just outside London, where Cornish rebels were attacked and defeated by Henry VII in 1497, with heavy casualties. They had marched to the capital to protest against harsh taxes, but were no match for the royal army.

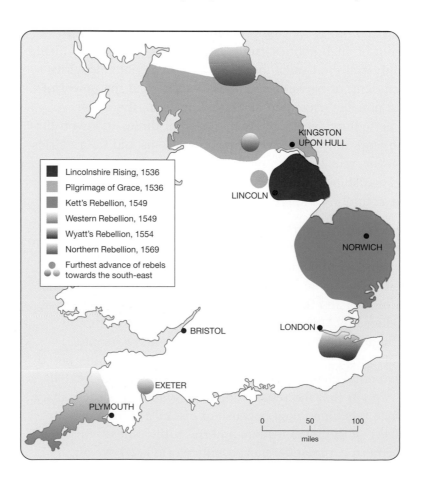

5.9 Mid-sixteenth century rebellions

Lincolnshire Rising, 1536
Pilgrimage of Grace, 1536
Kett's Rebellion, 1549
Western Rebellion, 1549
Wyatt's Rebellion, 1554
Northern Rebellion, 1569
Furthest advance of rebels towards the south-east

KINGSTON UPON HULL
LINCOLN
NORWICH
BRISTOL
LONDON
EXETER
PLYMOUTH

gaining greater prosperity and a more secure place within the Tudor state. Those who had led the protests of 1536 and 1549 in defence of the 'commonweal' were increasingly the men who began to take on local office, as bailiffs, churchwardens, and, later, overseers for the poor. As the state expanded in the localities it began to bridge the gap between high and low politics, and draw into itself the erstwhile leaders of popular protest. According to Wood: 'The central irony of the history of the 1549 rebellions is that so many of the rebel leaders were beneficiaries of the very economic changes that the rebellions sought to prevent. After 1549 . . . the successors of Robert Kett placed an increasing distance between themselves and the rural poor . . . [particularly] in southern and eastern England. As wealthier villagers and townsfolk . . . gradually removed themselves from the organisation of protest, large-scale, open riot diminished and poorer plebeians lost public, political agency.'

Rebellion did not end in 1549. The death of Edward VI meant that political and religious rivalries among the elite hardened around two contrasting queens, and the rebellions of 1553–54 and 1568–69 were more directly focused attacks on the reigning monarch than had been seen since the reign of Henry VII. What they lacked was the support of the wider community, even in the north where conservative religious and regional loyalties still lingered. The rebellion of the northern earls showed that in the more remote parts of the kingdom the greater nobility could still call on sufficient loyalty to pose a threat to the Queen, but any comparison with the events of 1536 serves to highlight its limitations and the strength that the Tudor state had acquired. By trying, and failing, to mount a significant challenge to its authority, the northern earls emphasised the futility of rebellion as a means of pursuing political objectives and helped to ensure that it did not happen again within the sixteenth century. While low politics could still erupt in localised outbreaks, the high politics of the elite were increasingly played out within the confines of the state, in Parliament.

How seriously did rebellion threaten the Tudor state?

Source W

In 1536 the Pilgrimage of Grace mustered enough support to take control of the north of England away from the King and his county administrators. There was little possibility that Henry could regain control and re-impose his will without prolonged fighting . . . Rebellion had cornered him into what for a monarch was an unfamiliar and humiliating position – having to listen to the demands of people from parts of the country that he had only recently described as 'one of the most rude and beastly of the whole realm', and offer a compromise . . . In 1549, much of southern and central England was convulsed by protests as a combination of radical religious reforms, festering problems about land use, price rises, war, and a young King without the presence to control government formed a 'mid-Tudor crisis' of sorts . . . In 1554, Wyatt's Rebellion, despite its low numbers and insufficient preparation, was able to march into London and confront the Queen over her marriage plans . . . In the right hands and with the right circumstances, popular protest in the sixteenth century could pose a dangerous challenge to the monarch and the state.

From Tony Imperato, *Protest and Rebellion in Tudor England, 1485–1601*, published 2008

Discussion point

How far are the judgements offered in Sources W and X conflicting? Do they apply the same criteria in making their judgements?

Source X

Each Tudor monarch faced at least one serious revolt and encountered significant military problems in suppressing them . . . [Yet] one cannot but be struck by the provincialism of most rebellions. Almost every rising was the response of a local community to purely local grievance, and hence co-ordination with other areas hardly ever happened, if it was even tried. Peasants were reluctant to stray far from their fields, especially at harvest time. Only the gentry could have organised a more widespread uprising, and gentry leadership of popular revolts was by no means universal.

From J.Lotherington (ed), *The Tudor Years*, published 1994

Unit summary

What have you learned in this unit?

Historians differ and will continue to differ in their judgements about the significance of rebellions in Tudor England because of the complex nature of the events, the problems involved in interpreting the evidence, and the criteria that they have to use to make a judgement. Evaluating a threat involves looking at what could have happened, and to do this you have to understand what created the threat and what those involved in it intended to do, as well as what they did. Therefore judgements about the significance of rebellions have to be based on understanding of their causes, aims and intentions as well as the actions taken and the eventual outcomes. You have learned about these aspects of each of the five major rebellions that took place in 1536–69, but you have also learned that the rebellions had complex effects, and that across the sixteenth century the legacy of failed rebellions helped to develop and strengthen the Tudor state.

What skills have you used in this unit?

You have researched the events relating to a number of rebellions and cross-referenced between them in the context of your wider knowledge. You have developed criteria for making a judgement and learned to weigh conflicting elements in order to come to an overall conclusion. You have analysed and evaluated the views of historians against each other and against your wider knowledge of the period, and you have begun to reconcile different and conflicting views to develop a judgement of your own. You can now apply these skills to practise the kind of question that you will face in Part B of the Unit 3 exam.

SKILLS BUILDER

Developing a judgement

The analysis of rebellions offered in this unit has drawn on a number of criteria that can be used to assess the significance of the threat that they posed. To make your own judgements you can re-read the outlines of what happened, and apply the criteria as set out below. You can also do further research using the work of different historians, particularly those mentioned in the sources, which will give you the context in which the selected extracts were written, and more detailed information about the rebellions. To develop your own judgement you can utilise two questions:

1. How seriously did any of the rebellions threaten the monarch or their personal authority?

2. How far do you agree with the view that, in 1536–69, rebellion strengthened rather than threatened the Tudor state?

Criteria

1. Unless the government was particularly weak or vulnerable, a successful rebellion would require considerable physical force. This could come from foreign intervention, but was most likely to be based on *widespread popular support*.

2. To achieve this, there would need to be *significant popular grievances*.

3. Leadership was necessary, and the examples of unrest in 1536–54 suggest *that leadership of the commons by some of their own village elite was crucial*. However, it is also clear that for a rebellion to be sustained and widespread, the rebels *required leaders with some access to the structures of power*. In effect, a serious threat to central government was unlikely *without noble, or at least gentry, participation*. Not least, they also needed some military experience or training.

4. This, however, could give rise to problems. Different groups and interests could combine and compromise, but there was also considerable distrust if one section was deemed to be coercing or exploiting another. A successful rebellion required a *measure of unity, and leaders with the political skill to sustain it*.

5. *Geography and practical logistics* were important. Proximity to London was one factor, but access to and contacts with foreign aid could also be significant.

6. *Of crucial importance were the aims of the rebels, or at least of their leaders*. Did they wish to threaten the government, or merely to pressurise it into changing policy? How easily could they be placated, sidetracked or divided?

7. *How was the government able to handle the situation?* How decisive were those in power, and what support could they rally? At times Tudor governments lacked easy access to military resources, but they had enormous reserves of power, patronage and propaganda. Economic changes, religious zeal and political rivalries could cut both ways, and as the Tudor State grew in strength and efficiency, they increasingly cut in the government's favour.

You may find it useful to discuss which of the criteria seem most significant and what weighting should be attached to them, but in forming your judgement you should remember that the final outcome depended above all on the way that different factors interacted and how the different criteria impacted in practice.

Exam style question

This is the sort of question you will find appearing in the examination paper as a Section B question:

'Popular protest in the sixteenth century could pose a dangerous challenge to the monarch and the state.'

How far is this statement accurate in relation to the years 1536–69? Explain your answer, using the evidence of Sources W and X and your own knowledge of the issues related to this debate.

Exam tips

Success in Part B questions in Unit 3 does not depend on your knowledge of historians and historiography, but on your ability to analyse and cross-reference sources in the context of your knowledge about the period. Sources W and X offer a range of different points about the nature and significance of rebellions, which can be linked into conflicting arguments. In this way the response is 'source driven', i.e. using the arguments provided by the sources to set up different interpretations and then use your own knowledge to evaluate them against each other and develop your own judgement from the process. You are **not** required to describe historical debates or the arguments put forward by other historians, and if you choose to make reference to any historians' views beyond those offered in the sources you should keep your points brief and link them into the main arguments that you are developing from the sources and your own knowledge. To address this question:

1 Analyse the question and define the issue clearly in your own mind. This can also provide a useful introduction when you start your answer.
2 Read all the sources and break them down into points for and against the statement in the question. Then link up the points on each side into a coherent argument.
3 Plan your response to develop and explain each of the arguments by taking points from the sources, building on them (and, when appropriate, challenging them) with examples from your own knowledge. To do this well you need to begin with the sources, but you also need to go beyond them and use your wider knowledge to develop your arguments fully.
4 Finally, offer your own judgement and support this with evidence from the sources and your own knowledge. Your judgement may be based on a preference for one of the arguments, or it may draw from both of them by showing that the apparent conflicts can be reconciled. Explain this fully in a developed conclusion.

Key advice: Don't start to write your response until you have analysed, cross-referenced and planned it, and know where you are going!

Bibliography

Wood, Andy, *Riot, Rebellion and Popular Politics in Early Modern England*, published 2001

Fletcher, Anthony and MacCulloch, Diarmaid, *Tudor Rebellions*, fifth edition, published in 2008

Davies, C.S.L., *Peace, Print and Protestantism 1450–1558*, published in 1977

Loades, David, *Henry VIII: Church, Court and Conflict*, (2009)

Smith, A.G.R., *The Emergence of a Nation State*, second edition, published 1997

Lotherington, J. (ed.), *The Tudor Years*, published 1994

Stone, Lawrence, *The Causes of the English Revolution, 1529–1642*, published 1972

Thomas, Paul, *Authority and Disorder in Tudor Times, 1485–1603*, published 1999

Turvey, Roger and Randell, Keith, *Henry VIII to Mary I: Government and Religion, 1509–1558*, published 2008

Turvey, Roger and Heard, Nigel, *Change and Protest, 1536–88*, fourth edition, published 2009

Imperato, Tony, *Protest and Rebellion in Tudor England, 1485–1601*, published 2008

Lockyer, Roger and O'Sullivan, Dan et al, *Tudor Britain*, published 1997

UNIT 6 Anglo-Spanish relations (2): Conflict, crisis and triumph, 1573–88

What is this unit about?

This unit focuses on the increasing difficulties that Elizabeth faced in her diplomatic relations, particularly with Spain in the middle years of her reign, and highlights the reasons why, in spite of her determination to avoid conflict, she found herself facing the Spanish Armada in 1588. This period saw a significant decline in Anglo-Spanish relations as a result of three key factors: religious differences; the revolt in the Netherlands; and the presence of Mary, Queen of Scots in English captivity, and her role in a series of plots to remove Elizabeth from the throne. Religion underpinned the growing animosity as Philip II, supported by the Pope, became less tolerant of Elizabeth's Protestantism, particularly because of the growing English support for the Calvinists in the Netherlands. Although Elizabeth was disinclined to support rebellion against an anointed lord, her Privy Council was not so principled and this resulted in a significant struggle between 'neutralists' and 'interventionists', which would result in an English expedition to the Netherlands and the consequent launching of the Spanish Armada. The crisis was intensified by the continued plotting by Mary, Queen of Scots and the approval and involvement of the Spanish ambassador in these plots. The years 1573 to 1588 are, therefore, ones of developing crisis in which Elizabeth struggled to avoid open conflict but which ultimately led to war. The great triumph of her reign, the defeat of the Armada, concludes these years.

In this unit you will:

- discover the key reasons for conflict and the way in which they combined to push England and Spain on a collision course for war
- consider and discuss key issues that initially delayed but finally drove the two countries into war.

Key questions

- What factors prevented open conflict between England and Spain in the years 1573–87?
- How great was the threat from Spain?
- What role did religion play in shaping foreign affairs?
- Why did England and Spain end up at war by 1588 and why did England triumph?

Timeline

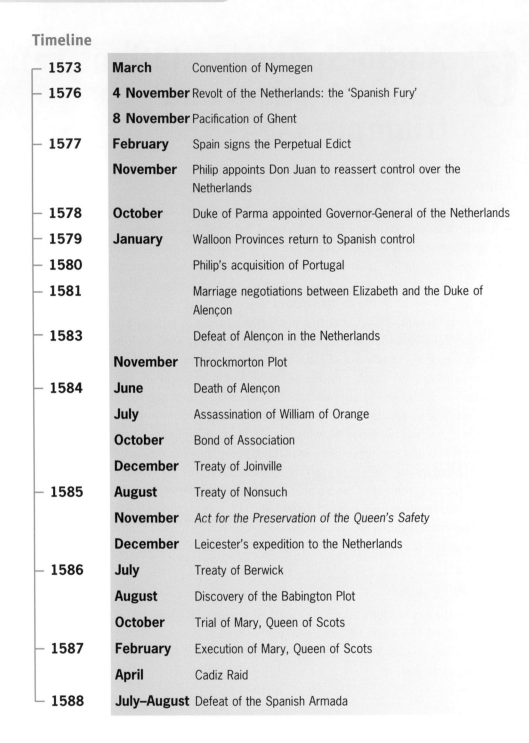

1573	March	Convention of Nymegen
1576	4 November	Revolt of the Netherlands: the 'Spanish Fury'
	8 November	Pacification of Ghent
1577	February	Spain signs the Perpetual Edict
	November	Philip appoints Don Juan to reassert control over the Netherlands
1578	October	Duke of Parma appointed Governor-General of the Netherlands
1579	January	Walloon Provinces return to Spanish control
1580		Philip's acquisition of Portugal
1581		Marriage negotiations between Elizabeth and the Duke of Alençon
1583		Defeat of Alençon in the Netherlands
	November	Throckmorton Plot
1584	June	Death of Alençon
	July	Assassination of William of Orange
	October	Bond of Association
	December	Treaty of Joinville
1585	August	Treaty of Nonsuch
	November	*Act for the Preservation of the Queen's Safety*
	December	Leicester's expedition to the Netherlands
1586	July	Treaty of Berwick
	August	Discovery of the Babington Plot
	October	Trial of Mary, Queen of Scots
1587	February	Execution of Mary, Queen of Scots
	April	Cadiz Raid
1588	July–August	Defeat of the Spanish Armada

Diplomatic situation by 1572

Elizabeth's diplomacy up to 1572 had succeeded in avoiding direct conflict, but her relations with the great Catholic powers of Europe had deteriorated significantly by that point. The upheaval in the Netherlands drew England into the religious wars on the continent, in spite of Elizabeth's desire to avoid this at all costs. Furthermore, the arrival of Mary, Queen of Scots in England had led to Spanish interference on the domestic scene in the most dangerous of ways.

The involvement of the Spanish in the Ridolfi Plot (page 95) was clear evidence to members of Elizabeth's Council that the Spanish threat could not be ignored and needed prompt action. Elizabeth's policy of harassment had only succeeded in antagonising Philip II without providing a solution to the problem. Finally, her efforts to court the French, as a counter-weight to the Spanish threat, via a round of marriage negotiations with the Duke of Anjou had come to an abrupt end in August 1572 with the Massacre of St Bartholomew's Day. The wholesale slaughter of French Protestants raised fears of a Catholic onslaught on England. Therefore, Elizabeth's position must be regarded as very precarious.

Elizabeth's diplomatic intentions, 1572–1585

In spite of her difficulties, Elizabeth was not inclined to respond aggressively. Guy has claimed that her preferred tactic during the decade of the 1570s was what he calls 'defensive neutrality'. She refused to be persuaded by her Council to declare support for the Calvinists in the Netherlands and she sought to persuade Philip II to withdraw his forces from the provinces, and to allow the Netherlands to settle back into the semi-autonomous position it had enjoyed under Charles V. In order to achieve this desired result she had to keep more than a watchful eye on the ambitions of the French. It was even less desirable that the French should gain control of the Netherlands and extend their mastery of the southern Channel coast even further. The policy was not, however, successful in achieving its aims. By the 1580s, Elizabeth's schemes, while still avoiding direct intervention in the Netherlands, would be sufficient to persuade Philip that England was the greatest stumbling block to his attempts to pacify the region. With the growth in influence of the **Catholic League** in France, Philip would embark on the 'Enterprise of England' – the preparations for a great **armada** to invade England. By 1585, Elizabeth's diplomatic position would reach crisis point.

The resumption of diplomatic relations with France: Marriage negotiations 1573–81

Although the St Bartholomew's Day Massacre marked a significant crisis in relations with France, Elizabeth refused to allow it to dictate policy. As Guy says, 'moral outrage was tempered by realpolitik'. France was necessary to England to balance Spanish aggression. Elizabeth, therefore, continued to court the French by means of marriage negotiations. The new suitor was the **Duke of Alençon**, brother of Charles IX and the youngest of Catherine de Medici's sons. It seems that in the early years Elizabeth was genuinely interested in the prospect of marriage but, as time progressed, this waned and by the time of the last visit of the Duke, in 1581, both sides regarded the marriage alliance as a purely diplomatic expedient. The Privy Council certainly had grave misgivings about Elizabeth's marriage into the Catholic House of Valois. They feared French domination of English policy and the destruction of the Protestant Church.

Definitions

Catholic League
An extremist group established by Duke Henry of Guise, whose main purpose was to destroy the French Huguenots. After 1584 it was subsidised by Philip II as the means of stopping the spread of Protantism in the Netherlands.

Armada
The Spanish word for navy.

Biography

Duke of Alençon (1555–1584)
Francis, Duke of Alençon, was the youngest son of Catherine de Medici and Henry II of France. He became Duke of Anjou in 1574. (Alençon is referred to as Anjou in many books; for the purpose of simplicity he will be referred to as Alençon in this text.) He was Elizabeth's suitor from 1579 to 1581. There was a considerable age difference between the two; she was 46 and he was 24. In spite of this, Elizabeth seriously considered marrying her 'frog', as she called him.

Discussion point

Why did Elizabeth want the Netherlands free from interference from France and Spain?

With a partner, make a list of the disadvantages to England if either country had complete domination of the Netherlands.

Discussion point

Why did Elizabeth use marriage as a means of diplomacy but never actually marry?

Definition

Privateer

A person or a ship that was given written permission by the government to attack enemy vessels in a time of war. It was cheaper than retaining a navy to carry out the task.

Although a marriage would offer the opportunity to control Alençon's interference in the Netherlands, as well as reducing the power of the Catholic League, the disadvantages outweighed the gains that could be made. Consequently, Elizabeth gave way to the will of the Council and no marriage took place. However, Alençon was used as a tool to bind France to England and prevent the development of a Franco-Spanish alliance. This is seen most obviously during the revolt of the Netherlands from 1576 to 1583, when Elizabeth subsidised his expedition instead of providing her own troops (see page 147). Alençon died in June 1584 and after this date Elizabeth no longer used marriage as a diplomatic tool.

The deterioration in relations with Spain, 1573–1585: The conflict over the Netherlands

It would be wrong to assume that England and Spain were set on an inevitable collision course in the 1570s and 1580s, and that the launching of the Spanish Armada was a certainty. It was not in the interests of either country to go to war and both sides sought to avoid it through diplomatic activity. Like Elizabeth, Philip II did all he could to avert the crisis. However, like her, he also indulged in secret schemes to undermine his adversary's power and consequently helped to fan the flames of conflict. It was the precarious position of the Netherlands that was the catalyst for that collision.

The uneasy peace, 1572–75

The relationship between England and Spain had declined in the years after 1570 as a result of Elizabeth's excommunication, Spanish involvement in the Ridolfi Plot and the policy of harassment that Elizabeth had pursued which antagonised Philip II and led to him imposing an embargo on English trade. However, since neither side was prepared to do battle, a compromise had to be reached. Elizabeth's policy of allowing English **privateers** to close the Channel to Spanish ships helped to persuade Philip that concessions were necessary and so, in 1574, he lifted the trade embargo. Under the terms of the Treaty of Bristol the gold dispute was settled and English rebels were banished from the Netherlands. Furthermore, English Protestants in the Netherlands were permitted to practise their religion. In return, Elizabeth closed her harbours to Dutch rebels and refused them any assistance. She had also agreed to withdraw support for raids on Spanish shipping in the Indies in the Convention of Nymegen in 1573. Therefore, at this point, it appeared that diplomacy could settle the dispute to the satisfaction of the monarchs, if not to that of the Protestant members of Elizabeth's Council, who sought to give direct support to the Dutch rebels to overthrow Catholicism in their state.

6.1 Scenes of the Spanish fury at Antorff, 1576

The revolt of the Netherlands, 1576–79

Causes

It was the unstable condition of the Netherlands that led to the resurgence of hostility between England and Spain. Philip's subjugation of the Netherlands after the revolt in 1566 had been incomplete. William of Orange may have been defeated in battle but he stubbornly refused to give up the fight. He actively sought assistance in his struggle against Spanish control in the Netherlands. The opportunity arose in 1576 when the Spanish army in the Netherlands mutinied because they had not been paid. This act, known as the 'Spanish Fury', resulted in Spanish troops sacking Antwerp and so united the seventeen provinces of the Netherlands in rebellion against their overlords.

The Pacification of Ghent

The Estates General (the Parliament) of the Netherlands demanded that all foreign troops should be expelled from the Netherlands and that their 'traditional liberties' should be restored. Elizabeth supported these demands and offered a loan of £100,000. She also warned **Henry III of France** not to intervene in the Netherlands, threatening force if he did. Thus, she was moving further towards supporting the Netherlands than she ever had before. She interceded with the Spanish to persuade them to accept the treaty known as the Pacification of Ghent. In fact, the reality of the situation dictated that Spain had little choice; with its army in disarray, Spain was obliged to accept the situation for now. In February 1577 Elizabeth signed an accord, called the Perpetual Edict, agreeing to comply with the terms of the Pacification of Ghent.

Biography

Henry III of France

Henry (Duke of Anjou, see page 92). He ascended to the French throne in 1574. Although he was Elizabeth's suitor in 1570, his strong Catholic faith meant that marriage to her was never realistic.

Don Juan of Austria (1547–1578)

Don Juan or Don John, as he is more commonly known, was the illegitimate son of Charles V, born in 1547. He was the military leader assigned to the Netherlands in 1576. He broke the terms of the Pacification of Ghent and was successful in defeating the armies of the Netherlands, but he died of camp fever in 1578 before the Netherlands had been completely subdued.

John Casimir (1543–1592)

John Casimir was a convinced Calvinist and was commissioned by Elizabeth to fight on behalf of the Dutch Protestants in 1577. However, his destruction of Catholic churches in the Walloon provinces led to division among the rebels and encouraged the southern states to reach an accord with Spain.

Walloon

Refers to the region in the south of what is now Belgium; also the language spoken by many in that region.

Renewal of the conflict, 1578–80

By the autumn of 1577 Spanish finances had recovered to a degree that permitted a renewed campaign in the Netherlands. A new commander arrived; Philip appointed **Don Juan of Austria** as Governor-General of the Netherlands and he brought a new Spanish army with him. Thus, war broke out in the Netherlands. Elizabeth warned Philip to withdraw Don Juan and abide by the Pacification of Ghent to no avail. The Privy Council discussed terms for an Anglo-Dutch entente and Guy suggests that they were unanimous in their support for it, but Elizabeth maintained her stance against a war that would have an uncertain outcome. Instead, she opted for a new version of harassment: she sanctioned the use of a mercenary force in the Netherlands, of up to six thousand English and Scottish volunteers, led by the mercenary **John Casimir**. Furthermore, she financed **Francis Drake's** circumnavigation of the globe, which included a voyage to the Spanish Indies where he was authorised to attack Spanish shipping. Drake did considerable damage to Spanish finances when he captured a galleon carrying silver bullion off the Pacific coast. When she knighted Drake in April 1581, Elizabeth was, in effect, giving her approval to piracy.

The role of the Duke of Alençon

William of Orange was disappointed by the lacklustre response given by Elizabeth to the plight of his people. He therefore turned to France for aid and found it in the form of the Duke of Alençon, who accepted sovereignty over the Netherlands with the title 'Defender of the Liberties of the Low Countries'. This was potentially even more dangerous for Elizabeth than the complete restoration of Spanish control. As a result, she resumed marriage negotiations with Alençon in order to achieve a measure of control over his actions in that region.

The resumption of Spanish control, 1578–79

Alençon had little impact in the Netherlands on this occasion. In October 1578 Don Juan died and the more capable Duke of Parma replaced him. Furthermore, the Catholic **Walloon** provinces in the south did not fully support the objectives of the revolt and they separated themselves from the Estates General and the northern provinces, and made their peace with Spain in January 1579. Elizabeth's policy of sponsoring John Casimir instead of sending her own forces had backfired disastrously in this region. Casimir and his troops were fervent Calvinists. Their violent attacks on Catholic churches in the Walloon provinces had alienated the population there and driven them back into Spanish arms. Alençon withdrew from the Netherlands and the United Provinces – the remaining seven provinces in the north of the Netherlands – were left to fend for themselves, assisted only by the fact that Philip II was too occupied by events in Portugal and **the Azores** to give the Netherlands his full attention at that time.

Spanish ascendancy, 1580–85

Elton claimed that by 1585 a clear situation had emerged in the relationship between England and Spain: 'England grew stronger as Spain grew weaker'. It is difficult to justify this view by a study of the events of this period and their consequences without any recourse to hindsight. William Simpson, by contrast, has described England's condition in this period as one that grew 'steadily more acute'. While Spain grew in wealth and developed an accord with France through the Catholic League, Elizabeth was beset with problems for which she failed to find adequate solutions, each decision tending to escalate rather than reduce the threat.

The acquisition of Portugal, 1580

Philip's power was significantly enhanced in 1580 when he added Portugal to his empire. This latest addition gave Philip control over the Portuguese navy, which meant he now had command of sea forces comparable to those of England. Moreover, Portugal had a prosperous trade with the east and Philip would now enjoy its profits. Elizabeth was alarmed by this new development and initially authorised Drake to seize the Azores as a base from which England could assist Don Antonio – Philip's rival for the crown of Portugal. However, when Philip announced that this would amount to a declaration of war she backed down.

Parma's re-conquest of the Netherlands

Elizabeth was unable to combat Philip over the question of Portugal and so she fell back on supporting Alençon in a renewed attempt to establish independence in the Netherlands. Elizabeth agreed to new subsidies to fund his expedition there, when he visited England between August and October 1581. The visit was supposedly to conduct marriage negotiations, although, in reality, it seems that neither party was serious on this issue. According to Guy, Elizabeth privately rejoiced at his departure. More importantly, he left with £70,000 towards the cost of his campaign. However, Elizabeth was still not prepared to give wholehearted support to the United Provinces in their struggle. She retained her view that they were rebels against their anointed sovereign. As a consequence, she refused to be drawn into a full alliance against Spain, even though there was much support for this in the Privy Council.

In the event, Alençon failed in the Netherlands. His leadership proved incompetent. He soon quarrelled with the Estates General and abdicated his position of sovereign of the United Provinces. He returned to France in 1583 and died in June of the following year.

Biography

Sir Francis Drake (1540–1596)

He was a celebrated sea captain, privateer and pirate in the Elizabethan era, and second in command of the English fleet against the Armada in 1588. He became renowned for attacking Spanish shipping. His raid on Cadiz in 1587 delayed the Armada by a year. He was responsible for using the fire ships that caused the Spanish to break anchor and later led to the Armada being scattered by the wind.

6.2 Sir Francis Drake

Definition

The Azores

A group of nine volcanic islands in the north Atlantic Ocean that were colonised by the Portuguese in the fifteenth century.

Discussion point

Look back at the different opinions on the situation in the Netherlands held by Elizabeth and her Privy Council. What can you learn about the nature of royal power at this point in Elizabeth's reign? Make a bullet point list.

Biography

Alexander Farnese, Duke of Parma (1545–1592)

He was Duke of Parma and Piancenza from 1586 to 1592, and Governor-General of the Spanish Netherlands from 1578 to 1592. He replaced Don Juan after his death. He defeated the Dutch rebels in the Siege of Antwerp in 1584.

Definition

Tercios

A mixed infantry formation of 3,000 professional soldiers (pikemen and musketeers).

One of the key reasons for Alençon's defeat in the Netherlands was the presence of the **Duke of Parma**, Philip's nephew, in the region. Parma was an excellent commander and he used the much-feared and seemingly invincible Spanish **tercios** to subdue the Dutch rebels. Parma took Brabant and Flanders by force and then moved onwards to Antwerp. Alençon, aware that the 'game was up', returned to France and Parma was able to establish Spanish hegemony over the Netherlands once more. According to Guy, Philip devoted all his resources to the recovery of his position in the Netherlands; bribes were apparently as effective as his armies, with many rebels prepared to switch sides for the right price.

Elizabeth has been greatly criticised for failing to follow advice and enter into a full alliance with France in favour of the Dutch rebels. She has been regarded as too hesitant. However, as Guy says, the alliance would not have outlived the death of Alençon in 1584 and her subsequent approval of an expedition to the Netherlands only served to further antagonise Philip. It is therefore hard to see what options Elizabeth did have in her diplomacy that would have maintained English interests, while not serving to offend Philip.

SKILLS BUILDER

How far did events in France affect England's relations with Spain after 1572?

Draw up two spider charts entitled: 'Events threatening relations with Spain' and 'Events that could lead to improved relations'.

Summarise the key points from this chapter relating to Anglo-French relations with regard to Spain on the charts.

Write a developed conclusion with a judgement focused on the question above.

The assassination of William of Orange, July 1584

The situation in the Netherlands took another turn for the worse in July 1584 when a French Catholic assassinated William of Orange. Philip had declared William an outlaw and offered a reward of 25,000 crowns for his assassination. French Catholic Balthasar Gerard ingratiated himself into William's circle and, on 10 July, shot him at close range. This plunged the Netherlands into crisis. The Protestant rebels had lost their leader and the manner in which he had died confirmed the significance of the threat posed to all Protestants from Catholicism. In England, the Privy Council was convinced that Elizabeth herself was directly threatened and that the advance of Philip in the Netherlands had to be checked.

6.3 The assassination of William of Orange

The Treaty of Joinville, December 1584

The death of Alençon had significant consequences in the internal affairs of France, as well as leaving a void in the leadership of the Dutch rebels. The heir to the French throne was now the Protestant Henry of Navarre. This alarmed the Guise faction, who sought to strengthen their position by reviving the French Catholic League. In a secret agreement, the Treaty of Joinville, Philip II pledged to assist the Guise party in its plan to disinherit Navarre. The religious wars were thus revived in France, to Philip's satisfaction since it limited the chances of French interference in the Netherlands, and to Elizabeth's great dismay since it not only meant that she could no longer rely on French help in the Netherlands but perhaps, more significantly, because it carried the threat of a full Franco-Spanish alliance that posed the greatest danger of a Catholic attack on England from the continent. This fear was enhanced by Philip's seizure of English shipping docked in Spanish ports. The move coincided with Walsingham's discovery of the secret Treaty of Joinville and roused great suspicion that it marked the imminent launch of an armada against England. The Privy Council was convinced that decisive steps needed to be taken and that Elizabeth must prevaricate no longer.

Discussion points

In groups discuss the following points:

- Why did Alençon fail in the Netherlands?
- Why was Philip able to reassert control over the Netherlands by 1585?

Why did the assassination of William of Orange cause such panic among Elizabeth's Councillors?

Working with a partner, try to come up with at least three reasons.

SKILLS BUILDER

Define the following terms:

- neutralist
- interventionist.

Discussion point

What were the pros and cons of intervention in the Netherlands?

In your groups identify as many as you can. Compare your list with that of another group. Alter your list as appropriate.

The reaction of the Privy Council

The Privy Council was united in its opposition to Spain but still divided as to the measures that should be implemented. Up to 1585, the so-called 'neutralists', represented by William Cecil, Lord Burghley, had prevailed. They believed that England needed to build up her defences against a possible attack, but that she should not take any action that could actually provoke such a response from Spain. Elizabeth tended to side with this group, whose ideas were closely aligned to her own. However, in 1585, the 'interventionists' – spearheaded by Walsingham and Leicester – gained the upper hand in the debates. They were certain that, if Parma gained complete control of the Netherlands, the next step would be an attack on England and thus it was imperative that England should intervene on behalf of the rebels. Elizabeth was finally persuaded to take action.

The Treaty of Nonsuch, August 1585

The Estates General, seeking to heal the chasm created by the loss of its leaders, William of Orange and the Duke of Alençon, offered Elizabeth sovereignty of the Netherlands. She was not prepared to accept such a position, proffered by rebels, but she was now prepared to engage in direct intervention in the region. Under the terms of the Treaty of Nonsuch, she promised to send 6,400 foot soldiers and 1,000 cavalry under the command of an Englishman of 'quality and rank'. In return she demanded the ports of Flushing and Brill as security for her expenditure. Elton has criticised Elizabeth for this demand. Her dealings with the Netherlands were, he claims, 'constantly bedevilled by her refusal to sink money in that country without such securities'. She was perhaps more sensibly cautious than Elton allows in this statement. Elizabeth did not have unlimited funds and she could not afford to devote the bulk of her finances into a campaign in which victory could not be guaranteed, and which could leave England exposed.

Leicester's expedition to the Netherlands

The Queen's former favourite, Robert Dudley, Earl of Leicester, was appointed as the commander of the English forces and he arrived in the Netherlands in September. Meanwhile, Drake was instructed to put pressure on the Spanish by conducting raids on towns on the north-west coast of Spain. The expedition to the Netherlands was not a success. Elizabeth was not enthusiastic and soon got cold feet. After only six weeks she rejected the arguments of the interventionists and opted once more for realpolitik; she wanted to bring the Spanish back to the negotiating table. She gave orders that Leicester was not to attack the Spanish but only to defend the Dutch. She was outraged when Leicester accepted the position of Governor-General from the Estates General, which she claimed was explicitly against her orders and gave the impression that she had accepted sovereignty over the Netherlands, and that Leicester was acting as her viceroy. Secretly, behind Leicester's back, she sanctioned Burghley's commission to reopen talks with Parma.

Meanwhile, Leicester's campaign floundered; his enthusiasm for the Calvinist cause sponsored by the provinces of Utrecht and Friesland alienated the rich provinces of Holland and Zeeland, and this was exacerbated by his order to suspend trade with the Spanish. This angered the wealthy businessmen of the region. Finally, his lack of judgement was confirmed by his appointment, in 1587, of the Catholic Sir William Stanley to control Deventer. Stanley had fought as a mercenary on the Spanish side and he soon outraged the Estates General by handing the town over to the Spanish. Leicester returned to England having failed to achieve his mission. The whole expedition had succeeded, however, in pushing Anglo-Spanish relations to a crisis point.

Guy suggests that one of the key reasons for Leicester's failure was a fundamental incompatibility between Elizabeth's aims and those of Leicester. Leicester wanted to establish control over the Netherlands by driving out the Spanish and then forging a Protestant coalition with the United Provinces. However, Elizabeth, it appears, still hankered for a semi-autonomous Netherlands, which she believed could be achieved by using threats against the Spanish in order to persuade them back to the negotiating table. In this she also failed. In fact, her diplomacy yielded the worst possible result; it seems that it was during this period that Philip was persuaded to embark upon the 'Enterprise of England', the construction of a great armada to invade England and overthrow Elizabeth.

SKILLS BUILDER

What factors enabled England to avoid war with Spain for so long?

Review the material in this unit. Identify a range of at least four factors and draw up a table in your notes like the one shown below. Develop the reasons with detailed examples and reasoning:

Factor	Developed explanation
1	
2	
3	
4	

The catalyst to war: The diplomatic impact in England, 1580–87

The Catholic threat

The tension had increased from the moment Mary, Queen of Scots had stepped onto English soil. The events of 1569–70 had already demonstrated that there were Catholics who were sympathetic to her cause and regarded her claim to the throne as more legitimate than that of Elizabeth.

William Allen (1532–1594)

William Allen was born in Lancashire. He refused to take the Oath of Supremacy after Elizabeth's succession and left England. He set up a college at Douai to train missionary priests who subsequently travelled to England to re-convert the population to Catholicism. He wrote in support of Philip's plan to invade England and was made a cardinal in 1587.

Society of Jesus (the Jesuits)

St Ignatius Loyola founded the Society of Jesus in 1534, originally to do missionary work in Jerusalem. However, the Jesuits were soon directed to focus on stopping the spread of Protestantism in Europe.

Although the Earl of Sussex had been able to crush the Northern Rebellion on Elizabeth's behalf and the later execution of Norfolk for his part in the Ridolfi Plot sent a strong message to those contemplating treasonous acts, Elizabeth and her Councillors did not underestimate the threat that came from those Catholics who gave their loyalty to the Pope first, and whose opposition to Elizabeth was justified by the papal bull of excommunication issued in 1570. The majority of the Catholic population, even during the Northern Rebellion, remained loyal to Elizabeth, but she could not guarantee that this would not change. As long as Elizabeth remained in conflict with Philip II, he would seek to manipulate her own subjects against her. For this reason, diplomatic events had very real consequences for Elizabeth in her own realm. This is shown very clearly in the arrival of Catholic priests and Jesuits with their mission to rekindle Catholicism in England.

The seminary priests

Acting upon the orders of the Council of Trent to re-convert the Protestants of Europe, in 1568 **William Allen** had set up a college in Douai, in the Netherlands. The college enjoyed the patronage and protection of Philip II. The first of these seminary or missionary priests arrived in England in 1574, and by 1580 there were approximately one hundred. These priests were particularly dangerous to Elizabeth because they were trained in the scripture so that they could rise to the challenges posed by Protestants well versed in the Bible and thus undermine the Church settlement, which was still in the process of being embedded in England. They offered confession – an attractive prospect to those who had not fully accepted the Settlement and who feared for the condition of their souls.

The Jesuits

Perhaps even more alarming was the arrival in 1580 of members of the **Society of Jesus** or Jesuits, as they are more commonly known. The Jesuits were trained to carry out spiritual exercises designed to cultivate a profound religious experience. They were very effective in reviving latent beliefs in former Catholics and hence were a significant threat to the stability of Elizabeth's realm. The first two Jesuits to arrive in England were **Robert Parsons** and **Edmund Campion**. They immediately began establishing a series of safe houses where Jesuits could hide from the authorities.

Biography

Edmund Campion (1540–1581)
Born in London in 1540, Campion was converted to Catholicism at Douai and entered the Jesuit order. He accompanied Robert Parsons on his mission to England in 1580. He was captured and taken to the Tower of London. Questioned in Elizabeth's presence, he affirmed her as the rightful queen but, although she offered him title and wealth, he refused to renounce his Catholic faith. He was racked twice and executed by hanging, drawing and quartering at Tyburn on 1 December 1581.

How significant was the risk?

In hindsight it is easy to say that the threat from the priests was exaggerated. Both the seminary priests and the Jesuits rejected a political agenda. Their interest was in religion, not in stirring up treason against Elizabeth. However, as the conflict in the Netherlands intensified, it was impossible for Elizabeth's government to ignore its 'enemy within' and indeed the priests themselves became increasingly embroiled in the struggle. In 1588, when the Armada was ready to launch, William Allen called upon English Catholics to rise up against the 'usurper' Elizabeth.

In the event, Elizabeth's government was well equipped to combat the danger. Walsingham's network of spies proved very adept at tracing Jesuit priests; Edmund Campion was arrested in July 1581 and executed in December after refusing to reject his faith and accept a position in the Anglican Church. Acts were passed in Parliament to outlaw the actions of the priests and Jesuits. In 1581 the *Act to retain the Queen's Majesty's Subjects in their due Obedience* declared it was treason to seek to convert a subject to Catholicism, while the 1585 *Act Against Jesuits, Seminary priests and such other like disobedient persons* ordered any Catholic priest who had been ordained since 1558 to leave the country within forty days or be declared a traitor. Overall, it has been calculated that 250 people were executed as a result of these acts, 180 of these being priests. Crucially, however, the acts had the desired effect. The population remained loyal to Elizabeth. The recusancy fines, which were significantly increased from the shilling set in 1559 to £20 a month, ensured that the majority of Catholics attended Anglican services and were encouraged to develop allegiance to their monarch. In 1588 Catholics ignored Allen's calls to revolt against Elizabeth and support Philip's invasion.

Biography

Robert Parsons (1546–1610)
Robert Parsons was the senior Jesuit who travelled to England in 1580. He fled the country after Campion's arrest and execution. He supported William Allen's stance over the Spanish Armada, believing that only armed intervention would restore Catholicism to England.

Discussion point

How great a threat did the seminary priests and the Jesuits pose to the stability of Elizabeth's realm?

Divide your group into two halves. Prepare arguments for and against a significant threat and discuss them in order to reach a judgement.

The Throckmorton Plot and its consequences, 1583–6

The plot

The discovery of the Ridolfi Plot and the subsequent execution of Norfolk had not dampened Mary, Queen of Scots's determination to assert her claim to the English throne. She now had powerful friends on the continent who were prepared to plot on her behalf to remove Elizabeth since this would satisfy their diplomatic objectives. In 1583 Walsingham uncovered just such a plot. The Catholic Duke of Guise and the Spanish Ambassador Mendoza conspired to reassert Catholic control of Scotland and use it as a base for an invasion of England, with the intention of putting Mary on the throne. Walsingham uncovered the plot after he arrested Francis Throckmorton, an English Catholic who acted as an intermediary between Mary and Ambassador Mendoza. The plot confirmed the Privy Council's worst fears that an alliance between France and Spain would be directed against Protestant England. The reaction was therefore severe. Although Mary once again escaped with her life – Elizabeth maintained her attitude that nothing could touch one of 'God's anointed' – Mendoza was expelled from England and the Privy Council drew up the Bond of Association.

The Bond of Association, 1584

The danger to Elizabeth loomed large by 1584: Parma was successfully re-conquering the Netherlands; in October 1583 John Somerville, a young man from Stratford who had married into the old Catholic Arden family, was arrested for waving a pistol at Elizabeth and declaring his intent to kill her; in November 1584 William of Orange was assassinated; and the interrogation of Throckmorton had implicated the Earls of Northumberland and Arundel in the Ridolfi Plot and led to their arrest. Burghley and Walsingham drafted the Bond of Association. The signatories to the Bond swore to defend Elizabeth's life and to prevent a 'pretended successor' from attempting to take the throne by means of plots and assassination. The original wording implied that not only Mary but also her son, James VI of Scotland, would be destroyed if a plot, successful or not, was uncovered.

Discussion point

Did 1583–84 represent a turning point in Elizabeth's foreign affairs?

John Guy has described the association as a 'political vigilante group'. Thousands of men flocked to sign the bond. Elizabeth claimed to be ignorant of its existence until she saw members' seals attached to it. The situation was grave. This was not an act drawn up by Parliament; instead it was 'lynch law'. Nevertheless, the threats to Elizabeth's life and the consequences this would have for a realm without a clear succession were apparent. The problems would have to be solved politically and diplomatically.

The *Act for the Preservation of the Queen's Safety*, 1585

The bill for the *Act for the Preservation of the Queen's Safety* was presented to Parliament when it opened in November 1585, along with the bill to outlaw Jesuits and seminary priests. Its original wording was altered so that when it became law, **James VI of Scotland** was exempted from the penalties of the act, unless he was privy to the crime. Thus, Mary, Queen of Scots would be barred from the succession if Elizabeth were to be killed.

The Treaty of Berwick, 1586

The Guise plan to retake Scotland failed and Scotland remained firmly in Protestant control. This afforded the Privy Council the opportunity to consider both the security of the realm and the question of the succession. England and Scotland signed a mutual defensive alliance pact to guarantee aid should an invasion of either homeland take place. Furthermore, under the terms of the Treaty of Berwick, James was to be paid an annual pension of £4,000 from the English state. He was also won over by a letter from Elizabeth promising that nothing would be done that threatened his title to the English throne. Indeed, as Elton says, 'the English diplomats found James much readier to abandon his mother than they had expected'. The Treaty of Berwick, therefore, secured the border and went a long way to easing fears about the succession.

The Babington Plot and its consequences, 1586–87

The Babington Plot

Walsingham was convinced that there were men plotting to kill Elizabeth and replace her with Mary, but he needed proof. Mary had been moved into the custody of Sir Amyas Paulet, who kept her isolated from the outside world in Chartley Hall in Staffordshire. Paulet was a radical Puritan and proved impervious to Mary's charm. He was not prepared to trust her as previous jailers had done and so inspected all correspondence to and from Mary.

Walsingham's opportunity to trap Mary came after he had arrested a Catholic exile, Gilbert Gifford, in 1585. Gifford confessed to having plotted on Mary's behalf and agreed to act as a double agent for Walsingham as a condition of his release. Gifford was instrumental in setting up a method of communication between Mary and the French ambassador by concealing letters in a watertight box in a beer cask. Mary was under the impression that she could now correspond freely, having circumvented Paulet's inspections.

Mary's complicity in the plots against Elizabeth was finally uncovered when she agreed to the terms of the Babington Plot hatched in 1586. A member of the Catholic gentry, Anthony Babington, was persuaded to lead an insurrection of English Catholics to coincide with an invasion led by the Catholic League. The plot had Spanish and papal support and the services of assassin John Savage, an ex-soldier who had sworn to kill Elizabeth.

> **Biography**
>
> **James VI of Scotland and I of England (1566–1625)**
>
> The son of Mary Queen of Scots and Henry Darnley, James became king of Scotland in 1567 after his mother was forced to abdicate. He was recognised as Elizabeth's heir in the Treaty of Berwick in 1586, as long as he was not involved in plots against her. He acceded to the throne of England in 1603 after Elizabeth's death.

6.4 The execution of Mary, Queen of Scots

Mary agreed wholeheartedly to the plot and wrote emphasising the need for foreign help. Walsingham now had the proof he needed to remove the Queen of Scots.

Trial and execution of Mary, Queen of Scots

In spite of Elizabeth's very vocal reservations, Mary was sent to Fotheringhay Castle for her trial, which opened in October 1586. She questioned the legality of the trial by saying that, as a Queen of Scotland, she was not subject to English law. However, she was persuaded to mount a defence since failure to do so might appear as an admission of guilt. Mary's guilt was evident from her letter to Babington and her judges, appointed under the terms of the *Act for the Preservation of the Queen's Safety*, would have sentenced her to death at once had they not been stalled by Elizabeth because the letter had been dictated and not written by Mary herself. Although she agreed to allow the commissioners to sentence Mary on 25 October, she still delayed in putting her seal to the death warrant. In spite of the clear threat to her person, her conviction that no one could execute an anointed monarch prevailed. This is not to say that she was sympathetic to Mary – indeed she sent word to Amyas Paulet that he might 'do away with Mary' according to the terms of the Bond of Association – and there were several **precedents for the murder of deposed monarchs** in captivity. However, Paulet would not countenance such a measure.

Precedents of the murder of deposed monarchs

Before the Tudor period a number of English monarchs had been murdered while imprisoned, including Edward II, Richard II (suspected), Henry VI and Edward V.

In the end the Privy Council took the initiative; Burghley had drawn up the death warrant in December 1586 and, in the atmosphere of panic in February when rumours swept the country that the Spanish had invaded, Elizabeth was persuaded to sign it. Although she ordered that it should not yet be sealed, William Davison, secretary to Walsingham, had it sealed and despatched. It was decided that Elizabeth should not be informed until the execution had taken place, which it duly did on 8 February 1587 when Mary went to the block clothed in red as a Catholic martyr. When Elizabeth discovered what had happened she flew into a blind rage. She refused to have any contact with Burghley for a month and had Davison sent to the Tower. Although he was released eighteen months later, he never regained his position. The execution of Mary, Queen of Scots had ridden roughshod over one of Elizabeth's dearest principles. Nevertheless, her Councillors quietly celebrated that the enemy from within was finally destroyed. However, the manner in which Mary was despatched also increased the danger to Elizabeth. Mary had bequeathed her claim to the English throne to Philip II. He now had the justification he required to launch the 'Enterprise of England'.

SKILLS BUILDER

How far did the plots involving Mary, Queen of Scots increase the threat to Elizabeth from Spain?

In order to answer this question you will need to consider:

- the relationship between Mary and Philip II of Spain
- the seriousness of the plots against Elizabeth in which Mary was involved
- the extent to which Walsingham had control over the situation
- the response by Elizabeth's government to the plots
- the consequences of executing Mary for Anglo-Spanish relations.

Triumph: The Spanish Armada and its defeat

Reasons for the 'Enterprise of England'

The execution of Mary, Queen of Scots may well have provided the justification for Philip to launch an attack on England, but it was not the sole reason. The evidence suggests that Philip had been seriously contemplating an armada since 1583 and by December 1585 he began compiling plans and intelligence reports. His struggle with the Ottoman Turks had ended successfully with the defeat of the Ottomans at the Battle of Lepanto in 1571 and prevented the Ottomans from dominating the Mediterranean Sea. Even more significantly, the conclusion of a peace treaty with the Turks in 1585 had freed Philip of his concerns in the south

Why did Philip II launch the Armada against England?

In order to answer this question you will need to review both long- and short-term reasons. What role did the execution of Mary, Queen of Scots play? Was it the key reason or the justification? Explain your answer.

Biography

Marquis of Santa Cruz (1526–1588)

The Marquis of Santa Cruz had already played a vital role in supporting Philip's claims to the throne of Portugal in 1580–81 when the navy under his command drove away the forces of Don Antonio, the 'pretender to the throne'. He recognised the grave threat posed to Spain by England and he established the first plans for the Armada.

and so enabled him to turn the full weight of his attention to the pressing concerns in the north: namely the threats in the Netherlands and the dangerous influence of Elizabeth in that region. The reasons for launching the Armada are therefore more complex than taking revenge on Mary's behalf. The relationship between England and Spain had been a very precarious one from the moment the Church settlement made it clear that Elizabeth intended for England to follow Protestant doctrine. The revolt of the Netherlands further complicated the issue. In spite of Elizabeth's desire not to get involved, increasingly she was drawn into the conflict for strategic reasons of trade and defence, even though she had no sympathy for subjects who rebelled against their anointed lord. Philip became increasingly convinced that Elizabeth was intent upon ousting him from the Netherlands and regarded interference there as an act of war. He was also greatly aggrieved by her support for sea captains Francis Drake and John Hawkins, whose activities in the Caribbean amounted to no more than piracy in his mind. By 1587 preparations for an attack on England were progressing rapidly.

Philip's preparations and support

Philip's preparations included raising the finances, securing support and building the fleet. In late 1586 Pope Sixtus V gave his blessing to the enterprise and promised a million ducats to be paid when Spanish troops landed in England. Missionary priest William Allen, raised to the position of cardinal in 1587, gave his wholehearted backing to the venture, calling upon English Catholics to rise against Elizabeth in his 'Admonition to the Nobility and People of England'. Philip was thus mustering the full might of the Catholic Church against Elizabeth. Meanwhile Philip's naval commander, the **Marquis of Santa Cruz**, was mustering men and ships for the attack that was set for 1587. In the event this was delayed because of the actions of Sir Francis Drake.

Drake's victory at Cadiz, April 1587

Drake postponed the Armada for a year as a result of his pre-emptive strike on the port of Cadiz. Drake destroyed up to 36 Spanish ships (the Spanish claimed it was 24) in the raid on Cadiz harbour. He then moved on to Cape St Vincent, where he claimed to have destroyed 1,600–1,700 barrel staves, which were essential in the manufacture of barrels for storage of supplies on ship. Finally he moved on to the Azores, where he captured a Portuguese merchant ship with a rich cargo of spices and forced Santa Cruz to leave the port to protect the incoming silver fleet. The losses of ships, supplies and time meant that the enterprise had to be set back to 1588. The so-called 'singeing of the King of Spain's beard' was highly significant in the outcome of the attack on England. The additional time allowed England to complete its preparations for attack and the losses sustained by the Spanish weakened the Armada. When the **Duke of Medina Sidonia** replaced Santa Cruz after the latter's death in February 1588, he complained that the supplies and guns were inadequate.

The defeat of the Spanish Armada, July 1588

The plan

It was Philip's intention to co-ordinate the forces of Medina Sidonia and the Duke of Parma. Sidonia was to defeat the English at sea, which would allow Parma to transport his troops – numbering 17,000 – across the Channel and invade England with very little opposition. Six thousand soldiers from the Armada would then reinforce Parma's troops once a foothold had been gained in England. It was an ambitious plan that was fraught with problems. The timing would be crucial since Parma's troops needed to land on the southern coast at high tide because the hulls of his boats were too deep to land in shallow water, and before this could happen Sidonia needed to clear the Channel of any opposition. It took no account of factors out of their control, such as the necessity for good weather, and relied on the establishment of excellent communication channels between Parma and Sidonia, which was difficult to achieve in the sixteenth century. Finally there was great expectation that the Catholic population of England would welcome the invasion and support the Spanish when they landed. The successful invasion of England would create the necessary conditions for Spain to reassert total control over the Netherlands since the rebellious provinces would have lost their main support.

The strength of the Spanish and English forces

The Spanish preparations were reaching fruition by May 1588. Medina Sidonia assembled a fleet of 65 galleons off the coast of Lisbon to be supported by more than 60 smaller vessels. They were manned with 7,000 sailors and 18,000 soldiers. Meanwhile, Parma had mustered a force of over 17,000 men in the ports of Flanders, including crack troops from Spain as well as English Catholic exiles, Italians, Germans and Walloons.

The English force was by no means as strong as that of the Spanish; Elizabeth had 34 well-armed ships and could call upon another 30, if the need arose. However, although the fleet was smaller it was easier to manoeuvre than the Armada, which would be an advantage in the narrow Channel. Most significantly, it boasted a clear superiority in long-range guns, having 153 compared to the 21 on the Armada. The Council also estimated that it could requisition the services of a 135 merchant ships in a crisis. On the other hand, should Parma succeed in invading, Elizabeth would be at a disadvantage; Spain maintained an efficient army that was highly trained and well supplied while Elizabeth would have to rely on the local muster of 'trained bands', and the quality of these troops was often patchy. When the Armada sailed, Elizabeth had 27,000 infantry and 2,500 cavalry stationed on the northern borders and the east and southern coast. An army of 16,500 was assembled at Tilbury and the nobility, bishops and Privy Councillors had called up 16,000 men to act as Elizabeth's personal bodyguard, but again these men were of dubious quality.

Biography

Duke of Medina Sidonia (1550–1615)
Alonso Perez du Guzman was given command of the Armada after the death of Santa Cruz. He threatened death to any captain in the Armada who broke the formation as the ships sailed into the Channel. This order was ignored when the English sent fire ships against them.

The battle

The Armada was first sighted off the Isles of Scilly on 19 July. (The Spanish and the English were using different types of calendar at this time, which is why you will sometimes see later dates in some books.) It failed in its objective to destroy any English shipping it encountered along its route and became trapped off Calais because the long-range English guns prevented the fleet from getting close enough to board the English ships – the favoured tactic in Spanish sea battles. The Spanish fleet was hampered by English tactics that forced it to sail into prevailing winds. Medina Sidonia anchored his fleet off Calais and called for Parma to move his troops across the Channel. However, all attempts at this proved fruitless. Drake scored a significant victory when he launched fire ships at the anchored Spanish fleet. Sidonia mistook them for floating bombs and ordered his fleet to cut their anchors to move out of their way.

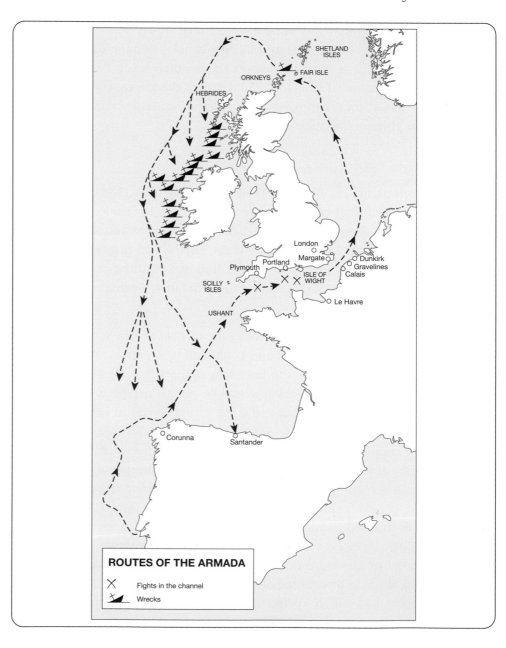

6.5 The route taken by the Spanish Armada

6.6 English ships and the Spanish Armada

A hundred and twenty Spanish ships would have no protection when the high winds arrived. The main battle was fought on 29 July off Gravelines, in Flanders. The English ships outgunned the Spanish fleet and, although Sidonia only lost three ships, he was obliged to pull his fleet out of the thick of the battle. At this point high winds drove the anchorless ships around the north of Scotland and the west of Ireland. Half of the fleet was battered and then sunk in the unfavourable conditions. Thus the English celebrated a glorious victory: 'the Lord blew and they were scattered'.

The significance of the Spanish Armada

The defeat of the Armada did not mark the end of the war with Spain. The Armada was scattered but it was not totally destroyed. In fact, this was just the beginning of a war that lasted for the rest of Elizabeth's reign. Haigh has claimed that the defeat of the Armada solved nothing. Drake and others complained that they had had no chance for plunder from the defeat. Why then is it regarded as so significant in English history? At the time the victory affirmed God's approval for Elizabeth's government and the Protestant Church. Perhaps one of the most important factors in the victory was that it demonstrated the loyalty of the English people to their monarch. It is possible to detect a sense of emerging nationhood. English Catholics ignored William Allen's rallying cry to revolt against the Protestant Queen and chose to support their own monarch rather than an invading Catholic. This also suggests that Elizabeth's Church settlement was largely successful. Catholics were not as alienated as Philip II had presumed. From the point of view of naval history, the battle is famed as the first great naval battle and acclaimed for a victory of superior skills and tactics against a greater force. Elizabeth's own actions enhanced her image and reputation. She is famed for her speech to troops at Tilbury in which she claimed, 'I know I have the body of a weak and feeble woman, but I

Discussion point

Why was the Spanish Armada defeated?

Make a list of reasons from the narrative. Working with a partner, discuss which reason is of greatest significance and why.

6.7 A portrait of Elizabeth I to commemorate victory over the Armada

SKILLS BUILDER

To what extent did Elizabeth achieve her diplomatic aims in her relations with Spain?

In order to address this question you will need to refresh your memory of Elizabeth's aims as outlined in Unit 4. Draw up a list of aims and then compare Elizabeth's achievements against them. On balance, did she succeed or fail?

have the heart and stomach of a king, and a king of England too, and think foul scorn that Parma or Spain or any prince of Europe should dare to invade the borders of my realm. . .' In spite of the many hardships that developed apace in Elizabeth's reign, it has become known as the 'Golden Age' and the defeat of the Armada has contributed significantly to the legend.

Unit summary

What have you learned in this unit?

- Neither England nor Spain was anxious to go to war and significant diplomatic activity took place to try to avoid open conflict.

- Elizabeth sought to avoid being dragged into the religious war in the Netherlands by using her relationship with the Duke of Alençon and employing mercenaries instead of direct intervention. This policy was not successful and played a significant role in Philip's decision to build the Armada.

- The 'interventionists' in the Privy Council persuaded Elizabeth to authorise direct intervention in the Netherlands led by Leicester, but Elizabeth soon regretted the decision and sought to control what resulted in a disastrous campaign.

- The Privy Council became increasingly concerned about the Catholic threat within England after the arrival of seminary priests and Jesuits. This concern was heightened because of Mary, Queen of Scots's presence in England. She was involved in a series of plots, with Spanish backing, until Walsingham finally trapped her in the Babington Plot.

- The execution of Mary, against Elizabeth's wishes, provided the justification for the launching of the Spanish Armada.

- The defeat of the Armada was the result of superior tactics and good fortune and marked the highpoint of Elizabeth's reign.

What skills have you used in this unit?

You have been involved in a number of discussions focusing particularly on causes of events. You have had to identify reasons and explain their significance. You have developed skills in analysing complex issues and weighing up evidence to reach developed judgements.

Exam style question

This is the sort of question you will find appearing on the examination paper as a Section A question:

'Events in the Netherlands were crucial to the decline in relations between England and Spain.'

How far do you agree with this judgement for the years 1573–88?

Exam tips

Refresh your memory on the importance of planning your answer. In order to achieve a fully considered answer to this question, you will need to consider:

- key events in the Netherlands in these years and the reasons why they contributed to a decline in Anglo-Spanish relations
- the roles of key individuals: Elizabeth, Alençon, Leicester, etc. and consider whether their responses increased the conflict and whether alternative strategies could have prevented the developing crisis
- the pivotal role of religion: whether conflict was inevitable even without the rebellion in the Netherlands and the nature of Elizabeth's response
- other factors such as Mary, Queen of Scots: were the plots and the execution of Mary more important in causing conflict?

There is a lot of material to cover here. Drawing up a plan and considering your judgement is essential. In order to reach a decision on the most significant cause for the decline in the relationship, you could consider a counter-factual argument: if one of the causes was removed, what impact would this have had on the relationship? Would the relationship have remained stable? Would war have been avoided?

Now you are ready to write your answer.

RESEARCH TOPIC

How far did the success of Elizabeth's foreign affairs depend upon the resources available to her? Using the Internet and texts from your library, research the following:

- Elizabeth's financial position: what was her income?
- England's trade: how much did it earn and what was the impact of foreign affairs upon it?
- Voyages to the New World: what resources did men like Drake and Hawkins gain? How far did their raids affect Spanish preparations?
- What was the cost of war? How much did Elizabeth spend on equipping the navy and army?

7 Controversy: How significant were the developments in the role and power of Parliament in 1566–88?

What is this unit about?

Unit 1 of this book showed that the Reformation of the 1530s set in motion a number of changes that influenced the development of the Tudor state across the century. Historians agree that the importance of Parliament was greatly increased as a result of the Reformation, but they disagree about how greatly and how quickly this happened. This unit considers the controversy around the role and importance of Parliament during the reign of Elizabeth. You have already considered the first parliament of the reign and the debate surrounding the religious settlement of 1558–59. This unit examines the developments that followed in 1566–88. It begins by considering the context of the debate, using extracts from different historians to summarise the development of Parliament before Elizabeth took the throne and the reasons why historians disagree about its importance thereafter. It then sets the claims of different historians against a summary of what happened in Parliament in these years, so that you can begin to evaluate their opinions and develop a judgement of your own.

In this unit you will:

- analyse what happened in Parliament in 1566–88
- develop an understanding of the issues that cause controversy
- practise the skills required for you to evaluate the views of historians and develop your own judgement.

Key questions

- How important was Parliament within the system of government in 1559?
- What impact did Parliament have on Elizabeth's government in the years 1566–88?
- How far did Elizabeth's Councillors exploit and influence parliamentary attitudes?
- Why has the role and significance of Elizabethan parliaments caused so much controversy among historians?

Timeline

— 1558	**November**	Accession of Elizabeth I; Parliament summoned
— 1559	**January**	Parliament assembled (January); Religious bills introduced (February); *Acts of Supremacy* and *Uniformity* (April); Parliament dissolved (May); Religious Injunctions
— 1560		Geneva Bible published, with Calvinist notes
— 1563		Parliament assembled in January; prorogued in April; Thirty-Nine Articles
— 1566	**March**	Suspension of London clergy leads to Parker's *Advertisements* and the Vestiarian controversy; Parliament assembled in September; dissolved January 1567
— 1568		Arrival of Mary, Queen of Scots in England; Northern Rebellion, defeated in 1569
— 1570		Issue of papal bull excommunicating Elizabeth, declaring her deposed
— 1571	**April**	Parliament assembled, dissolved in May; Ridolfi Plot
— 1572	**January**	Duke of Norfolk tried and sentenced for treason; new Parliament meets (May); Norfolk executed (June); Parliament prorogued (30 June)
— 1576		Parliament in session February/March; Peter Wentworth imprisoned
— 1579–81		Discussions of possible marriage between Elizabeth and Alençon
— 1580		Arrival of Jesuit priests
— 1581	**January**	Parliament reassembled (January); anti-Catholic laws passed; Parliament prorogued (March), dissolved in 1583
— 1583		Throckmorton Conspiracy, leads to Bond of Association
— 1584	**November**	New Parliament meets, called to provide subsidies after the English intervention in the Netherlands
— 1585		English aid sent to the Netherlands (February); Parliament prorogued (March), dissolved in 1586; Philip of Spain orders preparation of Armada (October)
— 1586		Babington Plot; trial of Mary, Queen of Scots; new Parliament, petitioned for Mary's execution (October)
— 1587	**February**	Mary, Queen of Scots executed (February); Parliament dissolved and Drake's expedition to Cadiz (March)
— 1588	**July**	Defeat of the Spanish Armada

Parliamentary development in the sixteenth century

Source A

The precedents established during the 1530s affected the relations between the King and Parliament until the outbreak of the English Civil War and beyond. The monarch had gained the right to determine the nation's religion, but only by enacting legislation through Parliament. Thus, the introduction of Protestantism under Edward VI, the reversion to Catholicism in Mary's reign, and Elizabeth's conciliatory religious settlement . . . were all brought about by acts of Parliament. So long as Parliament was in agreement with, or at least willing to accept, the Crown's religious stance, the involvement of Parliament in religious affairs was to the advantage of the monarch. However, problems developed in Elizabeth's reign when Puritans mounted a campaign in the Commons to overturn the Elizabethan Settlement in favour of a more radical Protestantism . . . The increased importance of Parliament led to more frequent and more vociferous demands in respect of parliamentary privilege . . . that caused conflict in the reigns of Elizabeth, James I . . . and Charles I. When Parliament presented the King with the Grand Remonstrance in December 1641 it had moved beyond demands for the redress of grievances and was demanding a controlling voice in government. How Charles I must have lamented the decision by Henry VIII and Thomas Cromwell to involve Parliament more directly in government by enshrining their religious and political reforms in Parliamentary statute.

From Robert Ellis, *People, Power and Politics,*
published 1993

Source B

For a long time [Tudor Parliaments] were examined in relation to a perceived growth of the House of Commons and a rise in conflict that culminated in the revolution of the mid-seventeenth century. Historians studied Tudor parliamentary history, not in its own right, but in relation to that cataclysmic event . . . [Their] prime concern was the political rise of Parliament and, within it, of the Commons, at the expense of both the monarch and the House of Lords [which] . . . did colour the picture of Parliament that they painted. Politics and political growth, not business and productivity seemed to be both the essence and most important feature of sixteenth-century parliamentary history. Yet Parliament was an institution which carried through many far-reaching changes, and regularly voted additional funds and statutory tools of government at the Crown's request. And it deserves to be studied in terms of its importance within the sixteenth century, not merely with an eye to future conflict. Such a change of approach began in the 1960s [especially in the work of Sir Geoffrey Elton]. Focusing his attention at first on the Henrician Parliaments, but later extending his scrutiny to those of Elizabeth, he demonstrated that they were usually effectively managed, co-operative, and productive. Historians began to focus their attention on previously neglected aspects of the institution: its procedures, membership, bureaucracy, records and, especially, the nature of its business. Thus there emerged what is now described as 'revisionism' . . . a fresh way of looking at Parliament.

From M.A.R. Graves, *Early Tudor Parliaments,
1485–1558*, published 1990

SKILLS BUILDER

Working with a partner, analyse the arguments in Sources A, B and C. What reasons are suggested in these sources for controversy among historians?

How does Source C attempt to reconcile the competing views?

Source C

Revisionist historians, such as Geoffrey Elton, Conrad Russell and John Morrill, have argued that conflict was not inherent in the late Tudor or early Stuart State and suggested that it was in many ways a stable polity. They believe that it is anachronistic to read the 1640s back into earlier decades, and that [assumptions about growing conflict rest] on a perception of events as moving towards a pre-determined goal. Instead, they argue that we need to reconstruct the past on its own terms, to retrieve its political culture as authentically as possible, and not to ascribe significance to those features of the past that appear to prefigure our own world. It is, nevertheless, possible to achieve a balance between different views, which fully acknowledges the important insights of 'revisionism' without losing sight of the fact that the late Tudor and Stuart periods were of immense significance in England's political, constitutional and religious history. Over the past twenty years it has been recognised that Crown and Parliament should not be seen as natural antagonists . . . and that Parliament was an instrument of royal government, not a counterweight to it . . . However, the powers that [the monarch] exercised jointly with Parliament were greater than those which they wielded on their own . . . [and] when working with their Parliaments there was almost nothing that Tudor monarchs could not do . . . Yet there was also the potential for tension and disagreement. What happened if Parliament offered advice that the monarch had not asked for, or did not wish to hear?

From G. Seel and D. Smith, *Crown and Parliaments, 1558–1689*, published 2001

Elizabeth and her Parliaments, 1566–88

Why have relations between Elizabeth and her Parliaments in the years 1566–88 been the subject of controversy?

Sources A–C illustrate some of the disagreements between historians about the role and powers of Parliament in the mid-sixteenth century, but they also demonstrate a significant degree of consensus. The increased power and importance of Parliament between 1529 and 1566 is widely accepted. It is at that point, however, that controversy intensifies, around the role that Parliament sought to play in the reign of Elizabeth, and its relationship with the Queen and her government. Source A refers to a Puritan campaign, a concept that originated with the work of Sir John Neale in the 1950s.

The Neale thesis

The traditional view of Tudor parliaments presented a weak institution, dominated by strong monarchs and used to enhance their power. In 1920, however, A.F. Pollard offered a different interpretation, which was taken up and developed much more fully by Sir John Neale. In *Elizabeth I and her Parliaments*, he argued that the reign of Elizabeth saw significant development of Parliament as an institution, culminating in the emergence of an effective opposition in the Commons, inspired mainly by Puritanism and led by a Puritan 'choir' of around 46 members whom he identified in the Parliament of 1558–59. Their purpose was to strengthen Protestant influence in England by reforming the Elizabethan Church so that it became more like the Calvinist Churches that existed in other parts of Europe.

To achieve this they wanted to ensure that England was ruled by Protestant monarchs, and to root out whatever Catholic sentiment had survived the Reformation and the break with Rome. Because the Church was controlled by bishops, who took their instructions from the Queen, the Puritan clergy were unable to reform the Church from within. The bishops were also a strong force in the House of Lords, as was the direct influence that the Queen could exercise over the lay lords, through favour and patronage. They therefore tried to use the power of their allies in the House of Commons to force the Queen to accept changes, and in so doing encouraged the development of the Commons into an independent unit willing to challenge the monarch's decisions and enforce changes in the constitutional balance of power.

The following passage is taken from the conclusion of Neale's first volume of parliamentary history, which extended to 1581. It defines the key points that made up the Neale thesis.

Source D

The evidence may be speculative, yet it is constant and surely convincing. Planning came from the Marian exiles, an art learnt in exile and prolonged and refined by the organising genius of Calvinism: a 'conspiracy' as the Bishop of London so aptly described it in 1573. The Puritan divines [clergy] who operated through their gentlemen-friends and patrons in the lower house taught their generation and, through them, their Stuart successors, the rudiments of parliamentary politics. The Parliament of 1559 was an astonishing initial experiment [in which they forced a reluctant Queen to go beyond what she intended]. When we reach the Parliaments of 1584–5 and 1586–7 we shall see the striking culmination of all this. The mastery of parliamentary tactics acquired by the unofficial leaders of the Commons, no less in dealing with individual bills than in the great campaigns of 1566 and 1572; their far-reaching definitions of privilege; the extreme sensitiveness of the house whenever it thought its liberties touched – by the Queen, by the Lords or by others; the vigour of debate, straining the narrow limits of the official timetable: all these our story has made sufficiently clear.'

From J.E. Neale, *Elizabeth I and her Parliaments: Vol. 1, 1559–81*, published 1953
(Source taken from paperback version, published 1965)

SKILLS BUILDER

What are the main characteristics that Neale attributes to the 'opposition' group that functioned in Elizabeth's Parliaments?

According to Neale, therefore:

- Elizabeth was faced by an organised opposition in the House of Commons, inspired by religion and directed by clerical leaders. The term 'Puritan choir' was taken from a contemporary description, and implied an organised body, speaking (if not singing) with one voice. Originally led by those who had experienced Calvinist organisation while in exile during the reign of Mary, they were later enhanced by the addition of Presbyterian clergy such as Thomas Cartwright and John Field, who published an alternative to the Bishop's Book and the Prayer Book.

- This opposition was strengthened by changes in the role and composition of the Commons during Elizabeth's reign. The government relied on the support of the Commons for many major bills, while the need for money also strengthened the position of the Commons. Moreover, the Commons grew in number through the enfranchisement of new **boroughs**, rising from 400 to 462 in the course of the reign. A growing number of gentry sat for borough seats, and brought with them the skills learned at the universities and **Inns of Court**, which enhanced both the ability and confidence of MPs in speaking independently on legal, religious and political issues.

- Experience of opposing government policy and resisting royal commands led MPs to develop political tactics and assert their rights and privileges. In particular, Elizabeth's refusal to allow MPs to debate religion, which she claimed as part of her prerogative, encouraged demands for complete freedom of speech. Although she never conceded this, in practice she was unable to prevent the introduction of motions on religious issues, private bills relating to the Church, and debates on the problem of the succession. In addition, MPs were able to obstruct government bills and delay the passing of subsidies until they were able to consider grievances. On certain occasions (some after 1588) the Queen wisely made concessions in order to gain support for areas of greatest priority.

- For all of these reasons the relationship between Elizabeth and her parliaments was characterised by conflict. Most sessions saw some conflict between the Crown, Lords and Commons, and Elizabeth was often unable to pursue her chosen policies. Despite protestations of love, reverence and loyalty towards the Queen herself, the Commons raised serious issues and blunted the effectiveness of her government, forcing her to face confrontation and take extreme measures that she could not always sustain.

In conclusion, Neale argued that the reign of Elizabeth saw the emergence of a powerful House of Commons, able to challenge royal authority and skilled in opposition. The loyalty and reverence afforded Elizabeth enabled her to survive and uphold her key policies, but when less skilled monarchs like James I and Charles I succeeded her, the authority of Parliament enabled opponents to mount a serious, and ultimately successful, attack on royal power.

Revisionist arguments

Neale's thesis inspired further research, and was challenged by a number of historians. Norman Jones investigated the Elizabethan settlement of 1558–59, and demonstrated that the Marian exiles in Elizabeth's first Parliament were neither numerous nor organised enough to influence the settlement. This accorded with Christopher Haigh's claims that a strong Catholic presence, epitomised by the Marian Bishops, meant that Elizabeth's problems in achieving a compromise settlement were caused by conservative resistance rather than any radical Protestant pressure (see Unit 3, pages 68–71). The main challenge to the thesis as a whole came from Geoffrey Elton, whose research into Tudor parliaments during and after the Reformation led him to argue that, far from being characterised by conflict, Elizabeth's parliaments demonstrated extensive co-operation with the government. Elton agreed that the Henrician Reformation had greatly strengthened the role and importance of Parliament – it was, indeed, a key part of his argument that Cromwell had initiated a Tudor revolution – but he emphasised that Parliament was, and continued to be, an instrument of government policy rather than a source of opposition. For Elton, power lay with King-in-Parliament, an institution based on and epitomising the supremacy of law, in which the monarch governed and did so in Parliament for specific purposes. As Michael Graves points out in Source B, revisionism was not a denial of the political conflicts that took place within Elizabethan parliaments, but an alternative view of Parliament in which political conflicts were vastly outweighed by constructive business and political co-operation. Graves himself has demonstrated that much of the business of Parliament did not concern government at all, but focused on innumerable private bills presented by individual MPs and the interests they represented. Source E presents this argument, while Source F develops it further.

SKILLS BUILDER

How far do Sources E and F agree about the relationship between Elizabeth and her Parliaments?

Source E

Parliament's function . . . was to make the government of the realm more effective, and it could also provide the opportunity for an exasperated governing class to use the King's instrument against him. But all talk of the rise of Parliament as an institution, or, worse, the rise of the House of Commons, into political prominence in the reign of Elizabeth is balderdash . . . In the reign of Henry VIII, politics in Parliament achieved their aim because the monarch, proprietor of Parliaments, took the lead. In the reign of Elizabeth, political debates in Parliament, and especially in the Commons, never achieved anything because the monarch was entirely free to ignore them and usually did so. In both reigns politics in Parliament reflected the purpose of non-parliamentary agencies [both within and beyond central government], resorting thither either because laws enforceable in the courts were needed, or because failure had attended action elsewhere.

From G.R. Elton, *The Parliament of England, 1559–1581*, published in 1986

Source F

[Perceptions] of Queen Elizabeth's dealings with Parliament have changed since Sir John Neale wrote his classic account in the 1950s . . . The real conflicts arose when Privy Councillors permitted, or organised Commons agitation to press the Queen to accept policies she disliked – for example over marriage and the succession in 1563 and 1566, over religious reform in 1571, over the execution of Norfolk in 1572, over anti-Catholic laws in 1581, and over the execution of Mary Stuart [Queen of Scots] in 1586. Elizabeth's problem of controlling her Parliament was thus part of her problem of controlling her Council: just as Councillors tried to manipulate information to force policies upon the Queen, so they sought to manipulate Parliament to force policies on her.

From Christopher Haigh, *Elizabeth I*, Second edition, published in 1998

Conclusion: Conflicting interpretations

Revisionist arguments have therefore challenged Neale's view in a number of ways. They do not deny that there was conflict between Elizabeth and her parliaments, but they do suggest that it was insignificant in proportion to the co-operation and support that she received. More importantly, when conflict occurred, it was not orchestrated by a Puritan 'choir', but by members of the Privy Council who sought to utilise their clients in Parliament to pressurise the Queen into accepting their advice. Similarly, relations between the two houses were generally co-operative, and when conflicts arose their members were often to be found on the same side. When the Commons went beyond the actions of the Lords it was often because the smaller numbers in the upper house and their direct dependence on royal favour made it easier for the Queen to apply pressure to individuals and force them to retract. In such cases they were often able to pass the initiative to the lower house. Most importantly of all, there is no evidence that the role and powers of Parliament were in any way advanced by these developments. While experience may well have improved parliamentary tactics on all sides, occasional attempts to extend parliamentary privileges – such as the right to free speech, or to encroach on the royal prerogative by legislating independently on state business – were fiercely and successfully resisted by the Queen. For the most part they were the actions of a small minority, prepared to push the boundaries beyond those accepted by the Privy Councillors and their clients, and they led not only to punishment by the Queen, but also to rejection by the Commons themselves. In general terms, relations between the Crown and Parliament between 1559 and 1588 were harmonious, and where conflicts arose they reflected different perceptions of how to defend a Protestant Queen in a Protestant state.

7.1 Elizabeth and her Parliament

The business of Parliaments, 1566–88

Between 1559 and 1588 Elizabeth summoned five parliaments, which sat for eight sessions, totalling around 22 months in all. The summary below outlines these sessions and the key events and issues that occupied them.

1563–67	Assembled January 1563. Called to ask for subsidies after interventions in Scotland and France, granted without difficulty. Acts passed to regulate apprenticeships, give relief to the poor, protect and maintain the navy. Elizabeth faced with a petition, supported by Commons, Lords and members of Privy Council, asking her to marry and to allow debate on the succession. Also a bill introduced in the Commons, but supported by Lords, for strengthening penalties for refusing Oath of Supremacy – passed both houses, including death penalty for second refusal. Elizabeth dared not veto, so ordered the bishops not to offer the oath a second time. Promised to consider marriage and succession, then prorogued Parliament.
	Re-assembled October 1566. Subsidies granted in peacetime. Issue of succession raised by Duke of Norfolk in Council, followed by concerted campaign in both Lords and Commons, probably organised by Privy Councillors, including Cecil. Attempt made in Commons to delay *Subsidy Bill* until after debate on succession. Queen met a delegation in November and insisted the matter fell within her prerogative. Forbade debate, leading MP Paul Wentworth to raise issue of free speech. Elizabeth defused the crisis by confirming Commons' privileges in general terms, and remitting one third of subsidies as gesture of good will. *Subsidy Bill* passed, but Cecil attempted to attach statement in preamble that Queen had promised to name a successor. Elizabeth forced its removal. Meanwhile, Parliament was considering bills for reform of Church. With time running out, selected as priority a bill to give statutory confirmation to the Thirty-Nine Articles, which would have enabled bishops to weed out conservative/Catholic clergy. Elizabeth forbade further discussion, claiming that it infringed her prerogative right to control religious injunctions. In response, Commons refused to pass 11 government bills awaiting confirmation, and Elizabeth dissolved Parliament in January 1567.
1571	Summoned in the aftermath of the Northern Rebellion and the papal bull excommunicating and deposing Elizabeth. Cecil had wanted to call Parliament a year earlier, but Elizabeth refused, fearing more trouble over marriage and the succession. The fact that this was not raised may reflect Privy Council influence, and/or desire to show loyalty and support for the Queen. Several acts passed to deal with rebels, including renewal of the *Treason Act* of 1534. Also measures against anyone who brought in or published papal bulls, or claimed a right to the throne. Attempt led by Thomas Norton to exclude Mary, Queen of Scots from the succession – softened and side-tracked. Focus shifted to religious measures, and attempt to re-introduce reforms lost in 1566, known as the *Alphabet Bills*. Council and bishops expected to proceed in co-operation with Commons, but William Strickland introduced a motion for reform of Canon Law and then a bill to revise the Prayer Book, both infringements on royal prerogative. Largely based on lectures given at Cambridge in 1570 by Presbyterian, Thomas Cartwright. Strickland arrested, but Peter Wentworth raised issue of Commons' privilege. Strickland released, and punished by Commons, but atmosphere had soured and agreement on other religious bills not secured. Only one passed – to demand that attendance in Church included taking communion (would drive out 'Church-Papists') – vetoed by Elizabeth before dissolving Parliament.

1572–81   New Parliament summoned, assembled in March 1572 in the aftermath of the Ridolfi Plot. Puritan lawyer Robert Bell chosen as Speaker. Focus of Commons, Lords and Privy Council on Norfolk (convicted of treason January 1572; Elizabeth delayed death warrant) and Mary, Queen of Scots. In late March Elizabeth fell ill. If she died, Mary would be Queen. Unified purpose to execute Norfolk and exclude (preferably execute) Mary. Issue managed in the Commons by Bell, Sir Francis Knollys, Sir James Croft and Thomas Norton, Burghley's agent. Attempt by Puritans to introduce a bill stating that the *Act of Uniformity* be enforced only against Catholics, based on John Field's *Admonition to Parliament* (1572) – trying to create freedom for Puritan dissidents. Set aside to avoid conflict with Queen and focus on Mary/Norfolk, but Elizabeth responded by ordering that no more bills on religion should be introduced into Parliament except through consultation with the bishops. Elizabeth refused to allow a bill to have Mary executed as a traitor, but eventually agreed to a bill excluding her from the succession. Accepted Norfolk's execution, but on royal orders, not parliamentary statute. Bill against Mary went to the Queen at end of session (June 1572), laid aside as needing amendment. Parliament prorogued until 1576, and bill lost.

Parliament reassembled 1576. Despite Peter Wentworth, a generally harmonious session. Commons agreed to suggestion by Speaker to let motions be examined in committee before being debated, to speed up business and stop time wasting. Wentworth launched an attack on royal interference, and use of hints and rumours, demanding total freedom of speech. He was stopped and excluded by the Commons, then sent to the Tower by them. Released and restored by the Queen a month later. Meanwhile, Commons granted subsidy and returned to Church reforms, but couched as petition to the Queen and was, therefore, well received. Similarly, petition to the Queen to marry, judiciously phrased, accepted when Parliament prorogued. Both sides were learning management? (NB: background of Grindal and Prophesyings suggest that conflicts over religion and the royal prerogative had not completely disappeared.)

Parliament recalled in January 1581 against background of deteriorating situation abroad and renewed anti-Catholic fears. First examples of Catholic mission to England had appeared (Campion and Parsons), along with an attempt to land papal troops in Ireland. Subsidies were granted. Session focused on anti-Catholic legislation, managed and promoted by Privy Councillors (Knollys, Sir Walter Mildmay and Walsingham) with main differences based on how harsh they should be and how far to protect Puritans from coming within the scope of the legislation. The Queen intervened in the Lords to soften the anti-Catholic legislation, while Norton and Burghley were able to restrict the impact of the *Sedition Bill* on non-Catholic recusants and nonconformists. Committee on religion managed by Mildmay and Walsingham – Puritan measures, but careful conferences with sympathetic bishops avoided conflict and articles handed to the Queen to be implemented by royal prerogative – less got done, but conflict was avoided. Parliament prorogued March 1581, finally dissolved 1583.

1584–85   Parliament assembled November 1584 against background of Catholic threats abroad and religious tensions at home caused by Archbishop Whitgift's campaign to force Puritans into conformity. Main government business was money, and subsidies were granted. Religious problems foreshadowed by a shower of petitions to Parliament against Whitgift's suspensions of Puritan clergy – organised by Puritan lawyers like Robert Beale, Clerk of the Council, in conjunction with clerical leaders, John Field and Walter Travers. Supported by sympathisers on the Privy Council – Knollys, Walsingham, and to some extent Burghley and Leicester, but co-operation broke down when Dr Peter Turner tried to introduce a bill to revise the Prayer Book and substitute Genevan services. The bill was dropped. Commons did draw up a list of reforms that would give greater freedom to the clergy to adapt the Prayer Book, but Elizabeth intervened to prevent legislation. Walsingham arranged a series of conferences with the bishops to mitigate the persecution. Parliament prorogued in March 1585 and dissolved in September 1586.

1586–87 October 1586, new Parliament summoned to address the threat of war abroad and Mary, Queen of Scots at home. Subsidies granted as asked, and Parliament offered more if the Queen agreed to become ruler of the Netherlands. She refused. Puritans still engaged in their campaign to reform the Church, led by Travers and Field, joined by Cartwright, who had returned from exile in Geneva. A 'Book of Discipline' had been drawn up to replace the Prayer Book, and a huge number of petitions to Parliament had been prepared. One, organised by Field and presented to Parliament in 1586, came from 2,537 parishes. However, when Parliament assembled, the revelation of the Babington Plot placed Mary, Queen of Scots at the centre of concerns. She was convicted of treason in October 1586, but Elizabeth delayed signing a death warrant. The concerted effort to overcome her resistance preoccupied the Council until February 1587. At that point a bill to reform the Prayer Book (generally known as Cope's 'Bill and Book') was presented by Anthony Cope, but the Speaker refused to let it be read, citing the Queen's embargo of 1572. Four Puritan MPs challenged the ruling and Peter Wentworth again demanded the right to free speech, but Sir Christopher Hatton prevented a debate and the Queen had the bill confiscated. Wentworth and others were sent to the Tower for private 'plottings' outside Parliament, which were not protected by parliamentary privilege. They remained there when Parliament was dissolved in March 1587.

After the defeat of the Armada a new Parliament was summoned in 1589, to a new political scene. The succession was no longer a problem – Mary was dead and it was tacitly accepted that her Protestant son James would forget any grudges in return for the throne of England. The Puritan leaders were dying – Thomas Norton in 1584, John Field in 1588 and Cartwright two years later – as were the powerful sympathisers on whom any parliamentary influence depended. The Earl of Bedford, patron to many Puritan MPs, died in 1585, Leicester in 1588, Mildmay in 1589 and Walsingham in 1590. Conflict did not disappear from Elizabeth's parliaments, but it did take on a different shape and focus, in which religion and the succession meant very different things.

In addition to those listed above, which are primarily focused on bills sponsored by the government and matters of national significance, Parliament habitually legislated on a range of local and individual concerns.

Source G

The volume of local, sectional and personal bills steadily grew, accompanied by a refinement of the arts of politicking and lobbying . . . The willingness of boroughs and other local and sectional interests to use Parliaments for their own purposes resulted in a spate of private bills. These dealt with a wide range of local concerns, such as security of endowments and property ownership, municipal power to raise money by local levies for public works, and a range of beneficial acts for ports, harbours and havens . . . Most of them began in the Commons, where the knights and burgesses were concerned and often obliged to promote parochial, petty and personal measures for the communities that had returned them.

From M.A.R. Graves, *Elizabethan Parliaments, 1559–1601*, second edition, published 1996

These measures did not always proceed quickly or smoothly. Competition between communities and sectional interests – for example, between Hull and York over navigation of the River Ouse, between London and the outports over the export of wool and cloth – could lead to time-consuming delays. Government bills had to compete for time, especially in the Commons. More numerous, less efficient and less experienced than the Lords, the lower house often contained a large number of novices and had fewer procedures for disciplining members.

Altogether, 433 statutes were enacted in the reign of Elizabeth, but about 930 bills failed. Some were defeated, or vetoed by the Queen, but the vast majority of them simply ran out of time. Alongside the political dramas that tend to occupy centre stage for historians, it must be remembered that Parliament was also a vital part of the administrative, legal and judicial machinery by which both government and people conducted their daily business.

SKILLS BUILDER

What does Source G suggest about the role and importance of Elizabethan Parliaments?

Elizabethan Parliaments: An evaluation

Was there an organised Puritan opposition in the Elizabethan House of Commons?

There were certainly Puritan MPs who were elected to a number of Parliaments and who had contacts among themselves and with Puritan clergy. Peter Wentworth, for example, was a neighbour of Anthony Cope, who presented the Presbyterian bill to reform the Prayer Book in 1586, and an associate of another staunch puritan, Tristram Pistor, MP for Stockbridge in Hampshire. He was also a close friend of Thomas Wilcox, a London clergyman who co-operated with John Field in producing the *Admonition to Parliament* in 1572. Wentworth helped to orchestrate and support William Strickland's attempt to obtain a bill for the reform of Canon Law in 1571, as did another associate, Edward Lewkenor, who had Puritan links in Suffolk. George Carleton, a Northamptonshire gentleman who sat for Poole in Dorset, chose Wentworth as executor of his will, suggesting familiarity and trust. Although Neale's arguments cannot be taken at face value, he did provide clear evidence of such associations, covering up to 30 MPs and a number of Puritan clergy. The terms 'organised' and 'Puritan' can be clearly substantiated although 'opposition' may be a different matter.

This is partly because, as the revisionists have argued, these MPs did not act alone, but in conjunction with members of the Lords and of the Privy Council. Stockbridge, where Pistor was elected, was a small, recently enfranchised borough, under the control of the Duchy of Lancaster and, therefore, of government patronage. Poole was in the gift of the Earl of Bedford, who co-operated with Burghley in managing over 40 constituencies. Undeniably a Puritan and a close associate of Walsingham as well as Burghley, the Earl was also a loyal servant of the Queen. More significantly, Burghley himself, Knollys, Mildmay and Walsingham were all in high office when they helped to orchestrate the campaigns for the Queen to marry, the execution of Norfolk, the exclusion of Mary, Queen of Scots from the succession and for measures to control Catholic influence within the Church and eradicate 'popery' outside it. Any account of Elizabeth's parliaments provides substantial evidence that campaigns in the Commons were often conducted with help from the Privy Council and support from the Lords, and while they were undeniably in opposition to the Queen's wishes, they were not in opposition to the Queen.

Nevertheless contacts and links could work both ways. While many of the issues that caused conflict were essentially political, and likely to be orchestrated from the political centre – the Court and Privy Council – pressures for religious reform came from elsewhere. The concept of a Puritan movement, originating in the clergy and supported by lay sympathisers among the gentry and nobility, was widely accepted at the time in which Neale was writing. Although Strickland's premature attempt to introduce reform in 1571 was a spectacular failure, Puritan pressure from within the Church and among lay patrons continued to gather support and its influence is seen in attempts within Parliament to further reform and to create greater freedom for Puritan dissidents between 1572 and 1581. In many instances these efforts had the support of sympathetic bishops, as well as royal Councillors, and it was only with the appointment of John Whitgift in 1583 that Elizabeth found an Archbishop of Canterbury who relished an attack on Puritan influence. Source H describes the Puritan response to his efforts to enforce clerical conformity.

Source H

The battle was joined. On the Puritan side a semblance of organisation appeared, with John Field in the role of corresponding secretary and business agent. He sent out letters to the provinces urging all the faithful to stand together against subscription . . . Doubtless his busy hand was also behind the shower of petitions that descended throughout the winter on the Archbishop and the Council. They came not only from the clergy but also from the country gentry. Norfolk, Suffolk, Essex, Lincolnshire, Oxfordshire, Cambridgeshire, Kent, Northamptonshire and Rutland were all represented . . . But the day of the country gentleman had not yet dawned. For the time being the attitude of the Councillors was much more important. The Puritan majority on that body did not fail its friends in the emergency. Both their wiles and their power were turned on the Archbishop . . . [They were joined by] the common lawyers . . . who detested the jurisdiction of the Church courts . . . and most troublesome of all, the diplomatist, MP, Clerk of the Council, and brother-in-law of Walsingham, Robert Beale.

From M.M. Knappen, *Tudor Puritanism*, published 1965

SKILLS BUILDER

How far does Source H challenge the revisionist argument that Neale's 'Puritan choir' were simply the clients of Councillors working according to their instructions?

A substantial case, in fact, can be made for the claim that conflict was not created by a Puritan opposition but by the Queen herself. She had good political reasons for refusing to name a successor, or to exclude Mary, and her marriage was not only a private matter that she had every right to protect, it was also a useful diplomatic weapon that she called on until 1581. However, her attitude to religious reform was less soundly based. Her handling of the *Alphabet Bills*, her relations with many of the bishops and her exploitation of Church revenues provoked irritation among moderates as well as the more extreme Protestants. More importantly, her refusal to accept many of the measures put forward, such as the bill to give statutory backing to the Thirty-Nine Articles, was based on a rigid and determined interpretation of her prerogatives. Most contentious of all, her narrow definition of free speech in the Commons – that MPs could only discuss matters of state that were put to them by royal command – was technically correct but politically restrictive and possibly unnecessary.

She was perhaps fortunate that those who were prepared to challenge her on this generally forfeited the sympathy of most MPs by their own extremism and the intemperate terms in which they presented their claims. In 1571, when Elizabeth had Strickland barred from the Commons for introducing religious legislation, the House of Commons demanded and got his restoration. In 1576, when Peter Wentworth launched his attack on the Queen's restrictive interpretation of free speech, his choice of language led the house itself to exclude and imprison him in the Tower.

In conclusion, therefore, Neale's claims that an organised Puritan faction created conflict between the Queen and the Commons cannot be sustained. It is clear that some of the conflicts were in fact extensions of court politics, managed by the Queen's ministers in an attempt to influence her decisions. More importantly, Neale's perception of Puritans as a distinct and well-defined category of Protestant was too simplistic, and recent research has shown that Puritan attitudes were much more varied and fluid than the Presbyterian prototype on which he relied. Mildmay and Walsingham, who worked closely with Puritan MPs, had Puritan attitudes and convictions, but neither was committed to a Presbyterian form of worship in the Church of England, as envisaged by Cartwright, Field and Travers. Source I describes a more subtle development, which survived the appointment of Whitgift to become the backbone of Puritan influence in England.

Source I

Puritan preaching came to be called 'spiritual' in contrast to the 'witty' preaching of the more conservative churchmen. It sprang up at Cambridge about the time of Cartwright's expulsion. It was greatly encouraged by the founding of new colleges such as Emmanuel in 1584 by Sir Walter Mildmay, the Chancellor of the Exchequer, expressly for the purpose of training up a preaching ministry. When Elizabeth quizzed her Chancellor about his erecting a Puritan foundation, Mildmay replied that he would 'never countenance anything contrary to your established laws' but that he had 'set an acorn, which when it becomes an oak, God alone knows what will be the fruit thereof'. From Cambridge, thus fostered, the spiritual preachers issued in steadily increasing numbers to occupy posts that public support found ways of making open to them.

From William Haller, *The Rise of Puritanism*, published 1957

SKILLS BUILDER

Using the evidence of Sources H and I in the context of your wider knowledge, explain the nature and extent of Puritan influence in Parliament in the years 1571–88.

In general, the relationship between Puritan MPs and royal Councillors was characterised by genuine co-operation, often based on shared aims and convictions. Robert Bell, a Puritan lawyer, was selected as Speaker of the Commons in 1572. This hardly indicates hostility or opposition since appointment as Speaker was controlled by the government.

He co-operated with Sir Francis Knollys and Sir James Croft to manage the campaign against Norfolk and Mary, Queen of Scots and remained Speaker until his death forced a replacement to be selected in 1581. His fellow lawyer, Thomas Norton, played a leading role in the campaigns for religious reform, as well as the attempts to pressurise Elizabeth into marriage and the naming of a Protestant successor. He supported Strickland's motion in 1571. He also produced copies of the *Alphabet Bills* that had been lost in 1566 and proposed that they be re-introduced. The bills covered a range of reforms and had been drawn up in conjunction with the bishops.

Norton was the son-in-law of Archbishop Cranmer and was instrumental in the publication by John Foxe – author of the Protestant Book of Martyrs – of Cranmer's revision of Canon Law. He was also employed as a lawyer by William Cecil, and has been identified as Cecil's main agent in the Commons after Cecil became Lord Burghley. It is unlikely that Burghley was directly involved in the religious campaigns undertaken by Norton, but there is no reason to think that he disapproved or took action to restrict them. What united all of these men was the desire to protect a Protestant Queen and a Protestant Church in a hostile Catholic world, by whatever methods and tactics were available. In this work, Presbyterians, Puritans, convinced Protestants, moderate Protestants and anti-Catholics shared a common purpose, and co-operation between government managers and Puritan MPs reflected the wider consensus. Although this might conflict at times with the wishes of the Queen herself, it was not a challenge to her authority. When the more rigid 'Puritans' like Strickland, Wentworth and Cope went further and tried to use Parliament to create a Presbyterian Church, to attack the bishops or challenge the Queen on matters of prerogative, they forfeited the support of the majority and failed.

Discussion point

How far does Neale's evidence suggest that the increase in the number of gentry MPs was a problem for Tudor governments?

Did changes in the composition of the Commons affect its organisation and significance?

Neale argued that the Reformation and the growing importance of the House of Commons led to an 'invasion' of borough seats by non-resident gentry who sought a political platform for their attempts to influence the government. Their greater confidence and better education in comparison to merchants and burgesses contributed to the growing independence of the lower house, and hence to its ability to challenge the Crown and the Lords. Sources J and K summarise his argument.

SKILLS BUILDER

Using the evidence of Sources J, K and L in the context of your wider knowledge, evaluate the political impact of the increase in the number and proportion of gentry MPs.

Source J

It was about this time that there began the great sixteenth-century invasion of parliamentary borough-seats by the country gentry, which in the course of the next half-century was to transform the House of Commons into an assembly mainly of gentlemen, most of whom were there because they ardently desired to be: men of character, education and wealth, who were likely to display independence of mind and exploit the opportunities opened by Henry VIII's indulgent policy. Mary Tudor's brief reign marked a stage in this apprenticeship . . . In elections to her third Parliament the Queen sent circular letters to sheriffs and others in the hope of securing a Catholic assembly and preventing the intrusion of the gentry into borough seats. In 1555, under instructions from King Philip, similar steps were taken – they failed miserably. The Venetian ambassador reported that the House of Commons 'is quite full of gentry and nobility, for the most part suspected in the matter of religion and therefore more daring and licentious than former houses, which consisted of burgesses and plebeians'.

From J.E. Neale, *Elizabeth I and her Parliaments: Vol. 1, 1559–81*, published 1953

Source L

Unlike the shrinking upper house, [the Commons'] membership continued to grow – from 400 to 462. As enfranchisement was the Crown's right it is reasonable to speculate that this process was an attempt to return more royal nominees, or at least loyalists, and to please powerful courtier-patrons, anxious to gratify clients . . . The country gentry were becoming more numerous and more of them were interested in serving a term in the Commons, as a token of their status or as part of their political apprenticeship. Frustrated by the lack of available shire [county] seats, which were increasingly the preserve of the most important county families, lesser gentlemen had to turn elsewhere. This pressure both caused the growth in the number of seats and accelerated the invasion of boroughs by carpet-bagging [non-resident] gentry.

From M.A.R. Graves, *Elizabethan Parliaments, 1559–1601*, second edition, published 1996

Source K

Birth, education, expert knowledge, practical experience and corporate solidarity – all were present in abundant measure in the Elizabethan House of Commons. Flagrant violation of the law and of medieval representative principles [which required borough MPs to reside within the boroughs], resulted in assembling in Parliament the elite of the country – 'the flower and choice of the realm'. The House of Commons reached maturity in Elizabeth's reign.

From J.E. Neale, *The Elizabethan House of Commons*, published 1949

Revisionist historians do not deny the changes in composition, but there is disagreement about its effects. The figures are clear: in 1559 the House of Commons numbered 400 MPs. During her reign Elizabeth created 31 new parliamentary boroughs, raising the numbers to 462. It is also undeniable that the proportion of gentry who sat for borough constituencies was already rising in 1559 and continued to do so, as did their educational standards. In 1563 one third of MPs had attended the Inns of Court or one of the universities (or both), rising to 48 per cent in 1584 and 54 per cent in 1593. The effect on confidence is difficult to measure, but their greater skill in oratory and the drafting of legal measures would undoubtedly prove useful. However, their political impact is more debatable, as Source L suggests.

7.2 William Cecil, Lord Burghley, the chief advisor to Elizabeth for most of her reign

The tendency for borough corporations to elect gentry members reflects the greater desire among the gentry to find places, and the convenience to the borough of having a member who would cover his own costs. It also reflected the wider system of parliamentary management that extended the existing structure of court patronage to parliamentary seats. Many of Elizabeth's new boroughs were in the royal duchies of Cornwall and Lancaster, where royal patronage could control the elections, and three were in the Isle of Wight under the control of her cousin, Sir George Carey. Some were created as a favour to key patrons, and the desire of men like Burghley and Leicester to build up networks of clients within the Commons showed that factional rivalry now included Parliament as a forum, which may also highlight its growing significance. They did not, however, allow this to work to the detriment of government, as Gardiner and Paget had done during the reign of Mary. Between 1559 and 1584 around half of the MPs from boroughs in Cornwall, Devon and Dorset were associates of the Earl of Bedford, who worked in conjunction with Burghley and, indirectly, the government itself. It can, therefore, be suggested that changes in the composition of the house reflected and encouraged wider changes – the increase in the numbers of gentry, improvements in education and literacy, as well as the status of Parliament itself, but that its direct political consequences were limited and even contradictory.

Nor is there any clear evidence that parliamentary tactics were developed to enable MPs to mount a more effective challenge to royal authority. The obvious strategy of attempting to link parliamentary bills or petitions to grants of money and subsidies was used in 1566, and it forced Elizabeth to confirm the Commons' privileges and remit a part of the subsidy in order to speed up its passage. However, it is quite possible that Burghley, then William Cecil and part of the Commons, was involved in planning the Commons' tactics, and he certainly attempted to attach the Queen's promise to name a successor to the preamble of the *Subsidy Bill*. Delays in dealing with government business arose as much from inefficiency as from deliberate intent. Lack of discipline in attendance, in the nature, focus and length of speeches, and the introduction of irrelevant or spoiling motions were endemic problems, as were occasional wrangles between the Commons and the Lords over matters of procedure and precedence. If any progress was made across the Parliaments of 1566–88, it was improved management by the Crown rather than improved opposition tactics. Learning lessons from the dissolution of 1571, Elizabeth allowed the exclusion of Mary from the succession in 1572 to pass Parliament, and then laid the bill aside as needing amendment rather than veto it. It disappeared into obscurity. In 1576 she graciously freed Wentworth from the Tower after the Commons had imprisoned him, attributing his outspokenness to an excess of loyalty. Meanwhile, Speaker Bell had introduced a new procedure by which private motions from MPs, the tactic used by Strickland and others to introduce bills or open unwanted debates, were to be sent to a committee to be scrutinised before being debated, reducing the scope for both irrelevance and delays. For the rest of the period the attempts by the more extreme Puritans to introduce religious bills were contained without major conflict. When Cope's 'Bill and Book' was introduced in 1586 the Speaker would not allow it to be read, and the four Puritan MPs who tried to force a debate were imprisoned by royal command for meetings outside of Parliament, thereby avoiding any problem with parliamentary privilege.

Were relations between Elizabeth and her parliaments dominated and damaged by political and religious conflicts?

On balance Neale's view of the parliamentary opposition, and his contention that parliamentary rights and powers were significantly developed in Elizabeth's reign, cannot be sustained. There is extensive evidence of harmony, and the professions of affection and loyalty that season the rhetoric of both the Queen and MPs in dealing with one another are both numerous and, to a large extent, sincere. Not once in the period did the Commons reject a request for supply, even in peacetime. Historians, such as Graves, have sought to establish a balanced interpretation and rightly point to the business record of Elizabethan Parliaments and the significant achievements embodied in legislation, including the regulation of working hours and conditions and the beginnings of a national system of poor relief. Throughout Elizabeth's reign Parliaments averaged over thirty new laws per session (usually lasting only two or three months) and very few government bills were lost – except those vetoed or set aside by the Queen. It has also been pointed out that the appearance of increasing conflict in comparison to earlier Parliaments may well be the result of more surviving evidence. The Commons journals survive from 1547, but the reign of Elizabeth also saw a number of parliamentary diarists, whose evidence was extensively used by Neale, affording much more detail about the daily workings of the institution.

However, revisionist dismissal of parliamentary conflicts as insignificant, or the result of rivalries and manipulation stemming from the Council [see Sources E and F], also requires some adjustment. Conflict did occur and it cannot be ignored. In a recent textbook, William Simpson examined the controversy and offered a conclusion that accepted many revisionist arguments while challenging some of their claims.

SKILLS BUILDER

How far does Source M challenge the claims made by Elton and Haigh in Sources E and F?

Source M

What was remarkable about the Privy Council [in the years 1566–88] is how united its membership was on the great issues of the day, and how little riven it was by personal or factional quarrels . . . It occupied an intermediate position between a powerful Queen and independent-minded gentry. Neither could be coerced. For most of Elizabeth's reign, however, members of the Privy Council shared the concerns of the gentry, to which many of them belonged . . . While the Puritan choir may have disappeared and there is little evidence of co-ordinated opposition to the Queen, the automatic assent of the House of Commons to royal wishes could not be taken for granted. Fortunately for Elizabeth, she had skilled parliamentary managers in both Houses of Parliament and, on set-piece occasions, her own rhetorical abilities helped her to get her way without arousing unnecessary hostility.

From William Simpson, *The Reign of Elizabeth*, published 2001

The core of the debate lies in understanding what parliamentary conflicts were intended to achieve and hence their implications for political relationships within the Tudor state. If the 'opposition' was determined to change the relationship between monarch and Parliament, and extend Parliament's authority at the expense of the Crown, then conflicts were not only serious and substantial, but also dangerous for a Tudor state built on King-in-Parliament. For the most part there is little evidence of any conscious programme of this kind. However, by the 1580s the Puritan opposition could be seen as moving in this direction, towards an organised challenge to the monarch's power over the Church. If this was the case, the motives were primarily religious, but the outcomes would be politically significant. Cope's 'Bill and Book' was the work of a Presbyterian faction linking academics, clergy and MPs, who were able to mount a campaign within and outside Parliament covering two elections over four years. Their aim was to override the Queen's prerogative and set aside her religious settlement using the power of Parliament. If they succeeded, royal authority would be seriously and publicly damaged. In the event, they failed, and not because of any open royal intervention or heavy-handed exercise of royal authority, but because the majority of MPs did not share their purpose. The 'Bill and Book' was twice rejected within the Commons, and its perpetrators were punished without infringing parliamentary privileges. In effect, events show that this 'opposition' was short-lived and isolated within the political community as a whole.

A more convincing explanation of the conflicts that took place in the years 1566–88 is offered in Source N, which portrays them as arising naturally from the difficult choices that wider religious and political conflicts forced the Queen and Parliament to make.

Source N

Disagreements occurred about the restraints [placed on parliamentary action by Elizabeth, who consistently distinguished] between matters of commonweal and state. The former encompassed not only general social and economic measures, touching the entire community, but also the many sectional, local and personal bills submitted to Parliaments. These could be introduced into Parliament without the Crown's prior consent and freely discussed. In contrast, the two houses could debate only those affairs of state placed before them. Because of Elizabeth's claim that religion was the preserve of her bishops and convocation [and] that her marriage, succession and foreign policy were prerogative matters . . . she was unwilling to allow discussion of them. Yet these were precisely the issues that concerned so many loyal, responsible, Protestant members of the governing class, Privy Councillors amongst them. Indeed, the Queen, not the Commons was the innovator. She [made] royal government a conservative bulwark, the obstinate defender of the status quo, resisting both the dangerous forces of further change and sensible moves to protect the state and the new Church. It should be emphasised that this was a particular problem for the lower house, because bishops and nobles, with their many lines of communication into the court, had other . . . ways of influencing the royal decision-making process. The only practical solution for many politically concerned knights and burgesses was to remove the existing restraints on free speech, both formal and informal, because, without full and frank discussion of urgent matters, they could not be brought to a satisfactory legislative solution.

From M.A.R. Graves, *Elizabethan Parliaments, 1559–1601*, second edition, published 1996

Frustrating as this was for the individuals involved, it did not generate hostility to the Crown or even the Queen herself. It generated conflicts born of intense loyalty and intense fear. In November 1572, as he watched the bill for the exclusion of Mary, Queen of Scots from the succession disappear with Elizabeth's repeated proroguing of Parliament, Burghley wrote to Leicester: 'If her Majesty will continue her delays for providing for her own surety by just means given to her by God, she and we all shall vainly call upon God when the calamity shall fall upon us.' Given the differences between the two men, it was a remarkably honest expression of fear and distress motivated by deep loyalty, and illustrates the essential unity of purpose among the Elizabethan political elite. Elizabeth's parliaments produced a good deal of conflict about the decisions she made and the restraints that she imposed, but it did not dominate proceedings nor cause any lasting damage to Elizabethan government. With a less effective monarch or a less united Council, the outcome might have been different.

Conclusion: The role of Parliament in the late Tudor state

In Unit 1 it was suggested that the Reformation of the 1530s involved a major revision, if not a revolution, in the government of the Tudor state that set the agenda for development across the century. It strengthened the authority and status of the Crown in a way that required its relationship with other institutions to be revised and adjusted, and it also posed problems arising from new or extended powers and responsibilities. Inevitably, these changes created opposition, as vested interests and customary arrangements were affected and as the changes raised conflicts of principle as well as self-interest and self-preservation. The result was protest and rebellion. Responding to the threat, governments took steps to bind the political and social elite more closely to the state. The expanding state offered employment and opportunity, enhanced by seizing the assets of the Church, and the new religion encouraged greater emphasis on individual progress and responsibility, helping to undermine communal loyalties and traditions. The result was a gradual separation of the political elite from its regional context, depriving the lower orders of political leadership. Thereafter, government influence extended beyond the gentry into the ranks of the 'middling sort' through increasing literacy, the spread of Protestant ideas in the south and east, and the growing number of local offices suitable for yeomen and craftsmen to take on. They therefore ceased to provide local leadership for rebellion and protest. Protest did not disappear, but effective leadership was lacking, and any threat to the state diminished as it became increasingly limited and localised.

However, conflicts among the elite remained significant. The most powerful causes were religion and patronage, and the state controlled access to both. Both religious convictions and political ambition drove the factions that struggled for influence over a succession of monarchs, and ambitious clients attached themselves to the leading men at court and in the Council in search of office and in support of genuine convictions.

> **SKILLS BUILDER**
>
> Using the material in this unit and your own wider knowledge of the period, how far do you agree with the view that conflict between Elizabeth and her parliaments in the years 1566–88 was outweighed by co-operation and support for her government?

Discussion point

How far do you think this unit has met the requirement, set out in Source C, to establish a balanced judgement that meets the aims of the revisionists and the need to consider the significance of Elizabethan parliaments in terms of wider political development?

Increasingly, however, these rivalries and conflicts could be played out in Parliament rather than by resort to protest and rebellion. The extension of Parliament's role and powers as a result of the Reformation meant that it became an increasingly important political forum. Its primary function was legislation, but since the monarch required legislation for a number of issues, particularly the settlement of religion, the opportunities for debate and the means of influencing royal policy were greatly increased. Most importantly, it showed that the Tudor state was maturing to a point where political rivalries could be accommodated and managed within the system. By 1549 the gentry had little need to rebel because their conflicts could be worked out within legitimate political channels. In 1554 and in 1568, a defeated faction turned to rebellion as a means of recovering power, precisely because they had failed to achieve their goals through either the Council or Parliament. This served only to demonstrate the futility of such actions and the extent to which political life had changed. The conflicts that troubled Elizabeth's parliaments in 1566–88 were evidence of the enhanced role of Parliament as an institution. They were, in fact, the method by which the elite could pursue their political and religious goals without recourse to rebellion and within the confines of the Tudor state.

Unit summary

What have you learned in this unit?

Elizabethan parliaments played a central role in supporting the work of the government – that is, the Queen, her Privy Council, and other office-holders. They granted subsidies, provided a framework of law to support the administration, allowed other organisations such as boroughs, guilds and merchant companies to manage and protect their interests, and provided an essential link between the monarch and the nation. Within these wider functions, there were periods of conflict, as MPs disagreed with each other, with the upper house, and especially with the Queen about what were the major issues of the day and how they should be dealt with. Differences about issues led to conflicts about the relative rights and powers of the monarch and Parliament, creating the possibility of a power struggle and a threat to the stability of the state. This was avoided because:

- the Queen was relatively skilful in handling relations with Parliament
- her Privy Councillors were loyal and skilful in managing Parliament
- despite individual differences, the Queen, government and political nation represented in Parliament shared common aims and loyalties.

As a result, the role and functions of Parliament did not change significantly during Elizabeth's reign, although there were changes in the composition, procedures and experience of the House of Commons. Its strength and expertise did develop, and by 1588 MPs had a clear sense of their role, rights and powers, which they were willing to defend. In a period of difficulty, such as Elizabeth's last years or during the Thirty Years' War in Europe (1618–48), the experience gained in the parliaments of 1566–88 may have encouraged and enabled Parliament to challenge the power of the Crown. Historians continue to disagree about this issue, but such judgements are beyond the scope of your enquiry.

What skills have you used in this unit?

You have analysed and interpreted different sources to establish and compare the views of historians. You have considered what happened in the parliaments of 1566–88 and interpreted the meaning of events to assess how accurate those views are, and to weigh the strength of the conflicting arguments. In the process, you have used the arguments put forward and your knowledge of the period to develop a judgement of your own. You should now apply these skills to the kind of task that will face you in the Unit 3 exam.

Exam style question

This is the sort of question you will find appearing in the examination paper as a Section B question:

'The political influence of the House of Commons in the years 1566–88 was, and remained, strictly limited.'

How far do you agree with this view? Explain your answer, using the evidence of Sources O, P and Q and your own knowledge of the issues related to this debate.

Source O

Agitation in the Commons alone . . . seems to have done little to change or modify Elizabeth's policies. It usually required sustained pressure from the Lords and at least some of her Council as well to move the Queen, and even then, as on the succession issue in 1566, she sometimes resisted all persuasion. It is hard to avoid the judgement that the political influence of the Commons in Elizabeth's reign was very limited, and this conclusion, reinforced to some extent by the skill with which Elizabeth managed her Parliaments, reminds us that the Commons was not, and did not regard itself as essentially a body of agitators. Its basic role was to co-operate with the Crown and the Lords in passing legislation. The passage of laws demanded, of course, parliamentary management . . . Through the magic of her personality and judicious use of Privy Councillors, the Speaker, the committee system and men of business, she generally managed to get her way.

From A.G.R. Smith, *The Emergence of a Nation State*, second edition, published 1997

Source P

It appears that almost without exception Elizabeth had to be persuaded by her ministers to call Parliament. In 12 out of 13 parliamentary sessions the argument used by her advisers was the need to arrange for the raising and collection of taxation. When in session Parliament was invited to discuss a range of issues such as religious reform and other law-making bills. Debates and discussions were closely controlled by the Speaker and by the Queen's representatives in both houses. The monarch retained the final say on all matters by exercising the royal veto . . . It is clear from the evidence that she regarded Parliaments as a somewhat inconvenient necessity. There is no doubt that the times when Parliament was in session were periods of stress and strain for the Queen, which helps to explain why she was easily irritated and why she sometimes suffered outbursts of ill-temper.

From R. Turvey and N. Heard, *Change and Protest 1536–88*, fourth edition, published 2009

Source Q

Elizabeth did not succeed in imposing her definition of limited free speech on her Parliaments . . . Sometimes her peremptory prohibitions put an end to debate, but she could not prevent the initial airing of political matters. Nor did her imperious demands make the problems go away. In their efforts to free the Commons from the narrow constraints of Elizabeth's control, the Wentworths could be foolhardy, impetuous and politically inept . . . [but they] were not simply mavericks, isolated from the mainstream of parliamentary opinion. Some of the particular causes that Peter pursued, such as the advancement of Presbyterianism, enjoyed scant support, but when he upheld the right to speak freely he was not alone . . . This was not Neale's rising Commons, throwing out challenges to royal authority. Rather, it reflected the response of members to pressing problems, to a restrictive monarch, and to the growing acceptance that Parliament was both the national debating forum and natural counsel to the Queen.

From M.A.R. Graves, *Elizabethan Parliaments*, second edition, published 1996

Exam tips

Success in Part B questions in Unit 3 does not depend on your knowledge of historians and historiography, but on your ability to analyse and cross-reference sources in the context of your knowledge about the period. The sources above offer a range of different points about Elizabeth's relations with Parliament, which can be linked into conflicting arguments. In this way the response is 'source driven', i.e. using the arguments provided by the sources to set up different interpretations and then use your own knowledge to evaluate them against each other and to develop your own judgement from the process. You are **not** required to describe historical debates or the arguments put forward by other historians, and if you choose to make reference to any historians' views beyond those offered in the sources you should keep your points brief and link them into the main arguments that you are developing from the sources and your own knowledge. To address this question:

1 Analyse the question and define the issue clearly in your own mind. This can also provide a useful introduction when you start your answer.
2 Read all three sources and break them down into points for and against the statement in the question. Then link up the points on each side into a coherent argument.
3 Plan your response to develop and explain each of the arguments by taking points from the sources, building on them (and when appropriate, challenging them) with examples from your own knowledge. To do this well you need to begin with the sources, but you also need to go beyond them and use your wider knowledge to develop your arguments fully.
4 Finally, offer your own judgement and support this with evidence from the sources and your own knowledge. Your judgement may be based on a preference for one of the arguments, or it may draw from both of them by showing that the apparent conflicts can be reconciled. Explain this fully in a developed conclusion.

Key advice: Don't start to write your response until you have analysed, cross-referenced and planned it, and know where you are going!

RESEARCH TOPIC

From the first pages of Unit 1 you have been exploring the role of faction and the importance of patronage and client networks in sixteenth-century government, and in this chapter you have considered these relationships in a wider political and social context. To develop your understanding more fully, you could usefully investigate some examples in greater depth. The historians' works from which Sources A–Q have been drawn contain much more detailed information about many individuals and their links with each other and with leading political figures at court and on the Privy Council. You should also remember that criticism of Sir John Neale's interpretations and conclusions does not negate the value of his evidence. His research into the lives of MPs and their associates remains enormously helpful in uncovering the relationships that made politics work. There are also many local records available in published form and in county archives, through which you can develop a local perspective on political networks and parliamentary elections, i.e. who was chosen, what they stood for, and whom they knew. If appropriate, you can work within a group, choosing different areas to investigate, and then pooling your results to evaluate how far the conflicts between Elizabeth I and her parliaments represented a significant political development, and how far they were merely an extension of the traditional politics of the Tudor court.

Bibliography

Haigh, Christopher, *Elizabeth I*, second edition, published in 1998

Smith, A.G.R., *The Emergence of a Nation State*, second edition, published 1997

Graves, M.A.R., *Elizabethan Parliaments, 1559–1601*, second edition 1996

Elton, G.R., *The Parliament of England, 1559–1581*, published 1986

Seel, Graham and Smith, David, *Crown and Parliaments, 1558–1689*, published 2001

Neale, J.E., *Elizabeth I and her Parliaments: Vol. 1, 1559–81*, published 1953

Neale, J.E., *The Elizabethan House of Commons*, published 1949

Graves, M.A.R., *Early Tudor Parliaments, 1485–1558*, published 1990

Knappen, M.M., *Tudor Puritanism*, published 1965

Ellis, Robert, *People, Power and Politics*, published 1993

Haller, William, *The Rise of Puritanism*, published 1957

Simpson, William, *The Reign of Elizabeth*, published 2001

Exam zone

Relax and prepare

Hot tips: what other students have said

From AS to A2 level

- Start reading around the topics studied in class as early as possible. Reading helped me understand how historians present their arguments and use evidence. There is plenty of material about the Tudor period to read.

- A2 level History seems like a big step up at first with more demands made on independent reading and more complex source passages to cope with. However, by the end of the first term I felt as if my written work had improved considerably.

- I do try to find out information from websites. It is sometimes hard to tell which websites might be useful to look at but I have become better at ensuring I know who has produced the site so that I can evaluate its material. Many universities have useful websites.

- The more practice I did on source-based questions, the more confident I became and quite quickly I picked up the necessary style and techniques required for success.

- Don't get flustered or panic. Ask your teacher if you are not sure. History teachers aren't that scary!

What I wish I had known at the start of the year

- I wish I had taken more time reading and noting other material such as the handouts my teacher gave us. Reading around the subject and undertaking independent research would have made my understanding more complete and made the whole topic more interesting.

- I used the textbook a lot during the revision period to learn the key facts. I really wished that I had used it from the beginning of the course in order to consolidate my class notes.

- It helps if you annotate your notes and reading material as you do it. This makes your reading more active and therefore more useful.

- A level History is not just about learning the relevant material but also developing the skills to use it effectively. I wish that I had spent more time throughout the year practising source questions to improve my style and technique.

- I wish I had paid more attention to the advice and comments made by my teacher on the written work I had done. This would have helped me to improve my scores throughout the year.

How to revise

- I started my revision by buying a new folder and some dividers. I put all my revision work into this folder and used the dividers to separate the different topics. I really took pride in my revision notes and made them as thorough and effective as I could manage.

- Before I started the revision process, I found it helpful to plan out my history revision. I used the Edexcel specification given to me by my teacher as a guideline of which topics to revise and I ticked off each one as I covered it.

- I found it useful to revise in short, sharp bursts. I would set myself a target of revising one particular topic in an hour and a half. I would spend one hour taking revision notes and then half an hour testing myself with a short practice question or a facts test.

- Planning answers to key questions is helpful because it saves time later.

- I found it useful to always include some practice work in my revision. If I could get that work to my teacher to mark, all the better, but just attempting questions to time helped me improve my technique.

- Sometimes I found it helpful to revise with a friend. We might spend 45 minutes revising by ourselves and then half an hour testing each other. Often we were able to sort out any problems between us and it was reassuring to see that someone else had the same worries and pressures at that time.

Refresh your memory: Revision checklist

The following provides a useful list for checking the information you need to revise for your exam.

Unit 1: How did the Tudor state develop, 1536–53?

- The Tudor state in 1536

- The development of the Tudor state and the machinery of government, 1536–53
    - The development of the Church, 1536–47
    - Central government: finance and administration, 1536–53
    - The unitary state: the extension of royal authority in the localities, 1536–53

- Evaluation: the significance of developments and the role of Thomas Cromwell

Unit 2: Government and faction, 1539–53

- The role and importance of faction: the fall of Thomas Cromwell and the plots against Cranmer and Catherine Parr

- The extent to which Henry VIII directed policy

- The nature of government under Edward

- Government under Somerset and Northumberland: financial, social and economic policy

- The reasons for Somerset's fall from power

- The succession: Lady Jane Grey and Northumberland's conspiracy

Unit 3: Reformation, conflict and settlement in religion, 1547–66

- Religious policy under Edward: how far did England become a Protestant country?

- Mary Tudor and the restoration of Catholicism

- The Elizabethan Church settlement, 1558–59

- The settlement in action: the extent to which Elizabeth had reconciled her subjects to Protestantism by 1566

Unit 4: Anglo-Spanish relations (1): The era of alliance and diplomacy, 1553–72

- The Spanish marriage and its consequences for foreign affairs

- Elizabeth's aims and the extent to which religion played a role in foreign affairs

- Relations between England and Scotland: the challenge presented by Mary, Queen of Scots

- The pivotal role played by France in Anglo-Spanish relations

- Relationship with the Netherlands and Spain

Unit 5: Controversy: How seriously did the rebellions of 1536–69 threaten the Tudor state?

- State and society: the context of rebellion

- The Pilgrimage of Grace: a community in revolt, 1536–37

- Rebellion of the people, 1549 – the year of commotions
    - The extent of unrest
    - The Western Rebellion
    - Kett's Rebellion

- Rebellion and conspiracy, 1554–69
    - Wyatt's Rebellion, 1554
    - The Northern Rebellion, 1568–69

- The character of the unrest and the threat to the Tudor state

Unit 6: Anglo-Spanish relations (2): Conflict, crisis and triumph, 1573–88

- Relations with France: the use of marriage as a diplomatic tool against Spanish aggression

- Conflict over the Netherlands: the revolt of the Netherlands and the consequences of Spanish and English intervention
- The Catholic threat in England: seminary priests, Jesuits and Mary, Queen of Scots
- The causes of, preparations for and consequences of the Spanish Armada

Unit 7: Controversy: How significant were the developments in the role and power of Parliament in 1566–88?

- The role of Parliaments, 1529–66
- The Neale thesis: religion, marriage and the succession, the Puritan Choir and the privileges of Parliament
- The revisionists: the business of Parliament, changes in composition, the role of the Privy Council.
- The debate: conflict and co-operation
- The role of Parliament and the development of the Tudor state

The controversy lists are very knowledge-based. Don't forget that in Section B of the examination your skills in handling sources will also be tested.

Result

You have spent a lot of time working on plans and constructing answers to the (a) and (b) questions. So you now have a pretty good idea about how to plan an answer and write a response to the question of the examination paper. But what are the examiners looking for? And what marks will you get?

About the exam

As part of your A2 level History course you are required to carry out a study in depth, in this instance *Protest, Crisis and Rebellion in England 1536–88*. You will be required to gain a firm understanding of the chronology of the topic and of the key issues, problems and debates associated with it. You will also be required to explore the nature of challenges and conflict both within the period and relating to the societies and political

systems studied, and will do this by working with secondary sources that provide differing views about historical controversies.

At the end of your A2 course you will take a written exam and you will need to answer two questions. The sources will be supplied with the paper.

- In Section A you will need to reach a substantiated judgement on a historical issue or problem. You will have a choice of two questions, and this question will be worth 30 marks.
- In Section B you will need to compare source material to explore an issue of historical debate, reaching a substantiated judgement using your own knowledge. There will be a choice of two questions and this question will be worth 40 marks.

The exam will last two hours. Make sure you plan your time carefully and allow enough time to answer both questions thoroughly.

Section A

These essay questions, from which you choose one to answer, will have an analytical focus that will require you to reach a substantiated judgement on a historical issue or problem. For example, questions are likely to be worded with the instruction 'how far/to what extent. . .' and to be followed by either a statement or an interpretation that you are asked to weigh up.

Section B

In this section you will be provided with five or six secondary sources that total about 350–400 words. You will then have to answer one question from a choice of two. Each question will ask you to discuss two or three of the sources while exploring an issue of historical debate, and to reach a substantiated judgement based on the sources and your own knowledge.

Questions are likely to be worded with the instruction 'How far do you agree with the view that . . .' You will also be instructed to 'Explain your answer using the sources and your own knowledge of the issues related to this controversy.'

Section A

What will you have to do, and what marks will you get for doing it?

This section tests your ability to recall, select and deploy information and your ability to understand key concepts and features. There are 30 marks available for this section. You will be working at one of five levels. Try to get as high up in the levels as you can.

Level 1

1–6 marks

- **You are able to** produce a series of simple statements.

Knowledge will be generalised with few examples. The answer will not be made relevant to the question.

Level 2

7–12 marks

- **You are able to** produce answers with some development using examples.

The range of examples is likely to be limited. There may be some attempt to link the material to the question but it will not be made explicit.

Level 3

13–18 marks

- **You are able to** produce an answer that shows an understanding of the question and what it is getting at.

The answer will, however, drift into irrelevance at times or be based on material which, although developed in places, is limited in its range.

Level 4

19–24 marks

- **You are able to** produce an analytical answer that shows a clear understanding of the focus of the question.

The answer draws out key points with detailed knowledge used to develop an argument. There may still be some drifting from the specific question or a lack of balance, with some aspects dealt with briefly, but the answer shows some attempt to evaluate the evidence used in the argument.

Level 5

25–30 marks

- **You are able to** produce a sustained analytical answer.

The answer is a well-structured argument that discusses the evidence used to support/reject/modify the statement in the question. The answer evaluates the evidence for the argument.

Now try this question

'The religious changes of the period 1536–66 can be explained by the personal faith of the monarch.'

How far do you agree with this opinion?

As you have worked your way through this book, you have planned many essay responses. This question requires you to trace change over several reigns rather than look in depth at one as you have practised earlier. It is important not to fall into the trap of writing a narrative moving chronologically through each reign. You therefore need to identify a range of factors that you can explore and compare. Look back over your notes to help you develop the following factors.

- The personal religious beliefs of Henry, Edward, Mary and Elizabeth (these can be quite ambiguous as you can demonstrate from your selection of supporting evidence).
- The influence of key officials on religious policy, e.g. Cromwell, Norfolk and Gardiner, Somerset and Northumberland, Cardinal Pole, Cecil and Parker. (Here you can consider whether they played a significant or lesser role in determining the nature of the changes.)

- The importance of the Houses of Parliament. You might note that Parliament worked with Henry VIII, but consider how Mary had to abandon her desire to restore monastic houses because she would not have found support in Parliament and the extent to which Elizabeth had to amend her settlement in order to push it through both houses.

- The role and significance of the clergy. You might consider the extent to which the laity were aware of change. It relied in particular on the co-operation of the parish clergy in implementing change or the extent to which they manipulated the orders to satisfy their religious beliefs. Changes were also applied inconsistently across the country.

GUIDANCE NOTES

Remember that in order to weigh up a statement or interpretation you need to look at the following:

- Explain the statement/interpretation.
- Outline the evidence that could be used to support the statement/interpretation and discuss its validity.
- Outline the evidence that could be used to reject/modify the statement/interpretation and comment on its validity.
- Come to a developed, reasoned judgement that presents your own argument.

The best answers will show that you have thought seriously about the issue or problem and have a well-supported, reasoned argument of your own in relation to the question asked.

This argument will be SUSTAINED, i.e. be present from the introduction to the conclusion. Thus, special care is needed when you write your introduction.

The argument will be based on sustained CRITICAL EVALUATION of the evidence. This will require you to discuss the value of the evidence rather than just provide a list of the evidence itself.

Now use the marking criteria to assess your response.

How did you do?

What could you have done to have achieved higher marks?

The examiners will not be nit-picking their way through your answer, ticking things off as they go. Rather, they will be looking to see which level best fits your response, and you should do the same when assessing your own responses.

Section B

What will you have to do, and what marks will you get for doing it?

This section tests your ability to recall, select and deploy information and to understand key concepts and features. This objective carries 16 marks. You are also being tested for your ability to analyse and evaluate differing interpretations in relation to their historical context. This objective carries 24 marks. Thus, Section B has a total of 40 marks. You will be working at one of five levels. Try to get as high up in the levels as you can. The examiners will be marking your answer twice: once for knowledge and a second time for source evaluation.

This is what the examiners will be looking for as they mark the ways in which you have selected and used your knowledge to answer the question.

Level 1

1–3 marks

- **You are able to** produce a series of simple statements.

Knowledge will be generalised with few examples. The answer will not be made relevant to the question. Links to the sources will be few or indirect.

Level 2

4–6 marks

- **You are able to** produce answers with some development using examples.

The range of examples is likely to be limited and this may be linked to the sources. There may be some attempt to link the material to the question but it will not be made explicit.

Level 3

7–10 marks

- **You are able to** produce an answer that shows an understanding of the question and what it is getting at.

There will be some links between own knowledge and the sources. The answer will, however, drift into irrelevance at times or be based on material which although developed in places is limited in its range.

Level 4

11–13 marks

- **You are able to** produce an analytical answer that shows a clear understanding of the focus of the question.

The answer is drawing out key points with detailed knowledge used to support analysis of the sources. There may still be some drifting from the specific question or a lack of balance, with some aspects dealt with briefly, but the answer shows some attempt to evaluate the evidence used in the argument

Level 5

14–16 marks

- **You are able to** produce a sustained analytical answer.

The answer is a well-structured argument that discusses the evidence used to support/reject/ modify the statement in the question. The answer evaluates the evidence for the argument.

This is what examiners are looking for as they mark your source evaluation skills.

Level 1

1–4 marks

- **You are able to** understand the sources at face value and use them to identify points.

There will be no integration of the sources with each other or with own knowledge – they will be treated singly and separately when coming to a conclusion.

Level 2

5–9 marks

- **You are able to** understand the sources and can use them to develop points relevant to the question.

There will be some linking together of the material from the sources. The answer will reach a judgement based on limited support from the sources.

Level 3

10–14 marks

- **You are able to** interpret the evidence from the sources, drawing out key points from the evidence in the sources.

Develops points that both support and challenge the interpretation under discussion and shows an awareness of the nature of the debate that the interpretation relates to. The answer may well be unbalanced with not all aspects covered, but there is a clear attempt to reach a reasoned answer supported by information and argument from the sources.

Level 4

15–19 marks

- **You are able to** interpret the sources with confidence, showing an understanding of the basis of the arguments offered in the sources.

Answers will relate the interpretations offered by the sources to their wider context by using own knowledge to discuss the arguments presented. Judgements will be reached that integrate the sources and own knowledge to support a well-developed and sustained argument.

Level 5

20–24 marks

- **You are able to** produce a sustained evaluation of the sources to present a fully-reasoned argument.

The interpretations offered by the sources are discussed and evaluated with the validity of the interpretation assessed by reference to own knowledge. Thus, sources and own knowledge are effectively integrated to address the full demands of the question.

Don't forget to take care with your English. The quality of your communication can be used by the examiner to decide which mark to give you within a level. Quality of communication is about more than spelling. It is about whether your answer is well-structured with paragraphs and clear sentences.

Now try this question

How far do you agree with the view that, in the years 1566–88, conflicts between Elizabeth I and the House of Commons were created mainly by her restrictive interpretation of the role and rights of Parliament?

Explain your answer, using the evidence of sources 1, 2 and 3 and your own knowledge of the issues related to this debate.

Source 2

It is true that [Neale's] overview representation of the relations between Elizabeth and her Parliaments as being characterised by conflict and tension is no longer held to be accurate, but some of the specific insights he provided into the Parliamentary politics of the reign are still considered to be of value. There is no doubt that there was, from time to time, considerable discontent among MPs over the queen's actions (or lack of them). It has to be admitted that in the 1560s and 1570s, when the main 'opposition' was over Elizabeth's failure to marry, the succession, the Duke of Norfolk and Mary, Queen of Scots, the agitation was orchestrated by members of the Privy Council, [but] there must have been a large amount of latent discontent . . . for such large-scale storms of verbal protest to be whipped up. In addition, Neale was undoubtedly correct in claiming that, in the 1570s and 1580s at least, a number of MPs worked very hard to persuade their colleagues that the Church of England should be made more Protestant, and that the 'liberties' of Parliament should include the right to discuss whatever MPs wanted whenever they liked and in whatever terms they thought appropriate.

From Keith Randell, *Elizabeth I and the Government of England*, published in 1994

Source 1

Elizabeth . . . took the view that members of Parliament might freely discuss 'matters of commonwealth' . . . but could only debate 'matters of state' when she invited them to do so. She classified as 'matters of state' anything that touched on her person (such as her marriage or the succession) or on her prerogative as supreme governor in things spiritual and temporal (including the settlement of religion, foreign policy, and the granting of monopolies). These were, of course, precisely the subjects that many members most wished to discuss, and the result was a series of disputes over the extent of the Commons' privilege of free speech.

From G. Seel and D. Smith, *Crown and Parliaments, 1558–1689*, published in 2001

Source 3

Much of the activity traditionally regarded as examples of Commons opposition involved the use of Parliament by Councillors to influence the monarch. . . When Councillors wished to change the mind of their obstinate Monarch, they frequently tried to convince her that the political nation demanded the measures they favoured. In particular, most of the activity associated with the so-called Puritan opposition [and the source of so much conflict] was inspired by Councillors who shared their values and concerns.

From John Lotherington (ed.), *The Tudor Years*, published in 1994

GUIDANCE NOTES

These questions can be quite challenging to answer because they require you to integrate the sources with your own knowledge whilst discussing and making a reasoned judgement on an interpretation. The key features of a good answer will be:

- A discussion of the issues raised by the sources that shows a clear understanding of the arguments they present.

- An integration of sources with your own knowledge. Your own knowledge will be used to test the validity of the views expressed in the sources.

- Relevant discussion of all aspects of the controversy raised in the question.

- A developed, reasoned judgement that presents your own argument in relation to the question.

As with answers in Section A, the best answer will contain arguments that are SUSTAINED and include CRITICAL EVALUATION of the interpretation offered in the question.

Now use the marking criteria to assess your response.

How did you do?

What could you have done to have achieved higher marks?

The examiners will not be nit-picking their way through your answer, ticking things off as they go. Rather, they will be looking to see which level best fits your response, and you should do the same when assessing your own responses.

How will I time my responses?

You have 2 hours to answer two questions. Both Section A and Section B give you a choice of questions.

Take some time, about five minutes, to read the paper carefully and think about your choice of questions.

The Section A question carries 30 marks and the Section B one carries 40. You should therefore aim to spend more time on the Section B question, about 1 hour and 10 minutes, compared with about 50 minutes for Section A. Remember that this includes reading and planning time.

Always conclude each answer with your overall judgement so that your answer reads as a coherent response. This is important even if you find you have not got enough time to cover all aspects in the detail you wanted to.

You have now had a lot of practice in planning, writing and assessing your responses to the sort of questions you can expect to find on the examination paper. You are well prepared and you should be able to tackle the examination with confidence.

Good luck!

Research and further reading

In addition to the suggestions made for research projects, students would benefit from wider reading into the period as a whole. An enormous range of publications exists – the suggestions below are intended to indicate the value of particular items in addressing key areas of content and key issues.

Background reading: England in the 1530s – Reformation and Reform

The key developments of 1536–88 cannot be fully understood without reference to the religious and political changes introduced by Henry VIII in the early 1530s. Nor can the conflicting interpretations be understood without awareness of the ongoing debate about the state of the Church in the early sixteenth century and the causes of the Reformation in England. The main points are covered in C. Pendrill, *The English Reformation, 1485–1558* (Heinemann 2000), which summarises the 'revisionist' arguments and offers an extensive bibliography for further research.

Student texts for A Level

The Longman Advanced History series and Hodder's Access to History series both offer volumes that cover the Tudor century and analyse the main issues and debates. R. Lockyer and D. O'Sullivan et al., *Tudor Britain* (Longman 1997) is structured around key issues, while A. Anderson and T. Imperato, *Introduction to Tudor England 1485–1603* (Hodder and Stoughton 2001) maintains a strong narrative spine. More specialised studies include R. Turvey and N. Heard, *Change and Protest 1536–88: Mid-Tudor Crises?* (Hodder Education 1999) and W. Simpson, *Reign of Elizabeth* (Heinemann 2001). The hallmark of all these publications is that they are intended to serve the needs of A Level students in preparing for contemporary examinations. More advanced textbooks include J. Lotherington (ed.), *The Tudor Years* (Hodder and Stoughton 1994).

Further research

For more developed research students should utilise the works of specialist historians. The works of G.R. Elton provide a wealth of information as well as the starting point for many of the major debates. Both David Loades and John Guy have written extensively and in depth about the Tudor period, while A.G.R. Smith, *The Emergence of a Nation State* *1529–1660* (Second Edition, Longman 1997) provides both depth and detail set within a broader developmental context. A similar developmental approach can be found in C.S.L. Davies, *Peace, Print and Protestantism 1450–1558* (Paladin Books 1977), which places political developments within a broader social and cultural context, and L. Stone, *The Causes of the English Revolution, 1529–1642* (ARK paperbacks 1986). Many students find biographical studies accessible, and they are of great value if the central figure is placed within the wider historical context, for example in J. J. Scarisbrick, *Henry VIII* (Eyre and Spottiswoode 1968) and E.W. Ives, *Anne Boleyn* (Blackwell 1986).

Controversy source material

Protest and rebellion (Unit 5): the key text is A. Fletcher, *Tudor Rebellions*, first published in 1968 and extensively revised by D. MacCulloch for re-issue in 2008 (Longman). It offers detailed coverage of all the rebellions of the period and useful analysis of recent research. A. Wood, *Riot, Rebellion and Popular Politics in Early Modern England* (Macmillan 2001) focuses on popular movements and brings sociological as well historical perspectives to the subject. T. Imperato, *Protest and Rebellion in Tudor England 1489–1601* (Heinemann 2008) analyses the nature and impact of protest across the period, and offers useful guidance on how to evaluate the conflicting claims made by historians and reconcile their different interpretations into a balanced judgement. D. Loades, *Henry VIII: Court, Church and Conflict* (National Archives 2009) has a wider focus on political affairs, but offers key insights into the impact of the Pilgrimage of Grace and Henry's response to opposition.

Development of Parliament (Unit 7): the work of Michael Graves offers a thoughtful and balanced evaluation of Neale and his critics. As a resource for teachers, R. Ellis, *People, Power and Politics: Political Change Through Time* (Nelson Thornes 1995) provides a developmental account of Tudor government across the period, useful methodology for analysing change and development, and an excellent range of historical sources that can be used in developing the skills required.

Finally, any student who wishes to learn how to write fluently and convincingly should spend a little time reading William Haller.

Glossary

Anabaptist A Protestant who believed in the primacy of the Bible, baptism only for adult believers not infants, and the complete separation of Church and state.

Anathema The most serious form of excommunication – anyone under its sentence was damned to hell with the devil.

Aragonese faction Officers and courtiers who sympathised with Catherine of Aragon and opposed Henry's plans for divorce, marriage to Anne Boleyn and the religious changes enacted by Henry and Thomas Cromwell.

Armada The Spanish word for navy.

Auld Alliance A series of treaties between France and Scotland, first made in 1295–96, directed against England. If England went to war with France, she risked the possibility of a Scottish invasion from the north.

Authoritarian Form of government that emphasises the authority of the head of government, to which individuals must submit.

Autocratic Having unlimited power – a term often applied to hereditary rulers.

Azores A group of nine volcanic islands in the north Atlantic Ocean that were colonised by the Portuguese in the fifteenth century.

Boroughs Towns (and sometimes villages) run by a local council or corporation that had the right to choose two members of Parliament. With a small number of electors, they could be easily influenced to choose a candidate favoured by the Crown, or by local nobility.

Calvinist Follower of the doctrines taught by John Calvin in Switzerland: the sovereignty of God, the authority of the scriptures and predestination (the belief that God chose that certain souls were to be saved).

Catholic League An extremist group established by Duke Henry of Guise, whose main purpose was to destroy the French Huguenots. After 1584 it was subsidised by Philip II as the means of stopping the spread of Protestantism in the Netherlands.

Chantry A small religious house that supported one or more priests. It was established by an endowment for the purpose of singing masses for the souls of the dead founders.

Church papists A disparaging term for those English Catholics who outwardly conformed to the established Protestant Church and yet inwardly remained Roman Catholics.

Cleves A duchy in the Holy Roman Empire, located on the northern Rhineland.

Codicil A document that amends a will.

Communion in both kinds Receiving both the bread and the wine – in Catholic services the laity only received the bread; in Protestant services the laity received both.

Comptroller An ancient spelling of controller that refers to a position in the royal household.

Council of Trent One of the most important councils of the Catholic Church, which met for three sessions in the period 1545–63, during which it condemned Protestant heresies and defined Catholic doctrine.

Customary rights Rights based on custom, or long usage, rather than written law.

Debasement Extracting gold and silver from coins and replacing it with base metal.

Diplomacy The conduct of negotiations and other relations between nations. In the sixteenth century this term would be used to refer to foreign policy.

Disputation A formalised method of debate that was designed to uncover truths in theology. It had developed from the scholastic tradition of the Middle Ages.

Dry stamp A copy of Henry's signature that was stamped onto documents and inked in to provide a perfect 'signature'.

Elevation of the Host The Catholic ritual of raising the consecrated bread and wine during the celebration of the Eucharist in the Mass, indicating that transubstantiation has taken place.

Enclosure Refers to the enlargement and fencing of fields by individual owners, necessary to improve agriculture. If communal land and wastes were included, the poorest people lost grazing and gathering rights.

Engrossing Gathering more land to expand an individual's holding, often implemented using enclosure.

Episcopacy The body of bishops that presided over the dioceses of the Anglican Church.

Escheator A royal official with the power to execute wills and deal with property issues where estates were reverting to the Crown. There were significant opportunities for corruption and for making large profits from the role.

Excommunication The censure pronounced by the Pope on an individual who has committed an act that requires him or her to be separated from the Church and to be forbidden to take any of the sacraments. It is necessary that other Catholics should not associate with the excommunicated person.

Faction A like-minded group who work together to advance a cause. Traditionally factions were defined by personal links and political ambition, but in this period they were also shaped by religious conflict.

Garrisoning Stationing troops in a place.

Hapsburg–Valois conflict The series of wars between the imperial house of Charles V (Hapsburg) and the royal house of Francis I (Valois) between 1521 and 1559.

Homily A sermon, usually a reflection upon scripture or doctrine.

Huguenots Members of the Protestant Church in France who believed in Calvinist doctrine.

Hundreds Areas of administration.

Iconoclasm The practise of destroying religious images associated with the Catholic Church and believed by Protestants to encourage superstition and false worship.

Inns of Court Residential colleges in the City of London, where legal training was offered to both prospective lawyers and the sons of gentry in preparation for managing their estates and for their role in local government.

King-in-Parliament The supreme law-making body created after it was clearly established in the fifteenth century that laws required the assent of the king and both Houses of Parliament.

Laity All those people who are not in the clergy.

Lay Of the laity, not the clergy.

Letters of patent A legal instrument taking the form of an open letter by the monarch granting certain rights or privileges to an individual or company.

Liberties and Franchises Special privileges granted by monarchs to allow individuals or institutions to control the legal system in an area. Originally they helped control difficult areas, but they also acted as a barrier to royal authority and consistent application of the law.

Lord Chamberlain The officer in charge of the royal household, responsible for its management and for the public appearances of the king.

Lord Lieutenants Members of the county nobility who deputised for the King in his military role, and took responsibility for organising local defence against both internal and external threats.

Lord Privy Seal He could deal with private correspondence on behalf of the king, sealing it with the king's private seal, which, like the formal 'Great Seal' of state, showed the validity of a document.

Marian exiles The English Calvinist Protestants who fled to the continent during Mary's reign.

'New man' A man of modest origins whose position in government was entirely dependent on the king. This contrasted with the older nobility who regarded their position in government as a birthright.

Papal bull A particular type of letter or charter issued by the Pope. A bull is the seal used at the end of the letter to give it authenticity.

Patronage The granting of help by a patron. Royal patronage included granting land and income, positions at Court or in other powerful roles.

Pilgrimage of Grace A serious rebellion that began in Lincolnshire in October 1536 and spread across the north. It reflected widespread hostility to changes in the Church and the increasing authority exercised by central government over local government, customs and traditions and was probably the most serious challenge to his authority ever faced by Henry VIII. Although the revolt was suppressed in 1537, and the ringleaders executed, there were signs of simmering discontent in the north for some years.

Popular In the sixteenth century this meant 'of the people', that is, outside of the elite who normally made political decisions.

Predestination The doctrine that everything has been foreordained by God, especially that certain people have been chosen for salvation (entry to heaven).

Presbyterian The Presbyterian Church is a Christian Church that has no hierarchy but instead has a structure in which power is vested in ministers and lay elders.

Its doctrine is based largely on the sovereignty of God and the authority of the Bible. It was the model used by John Calvin in Geneva.

Primate The position held by the Archbishop of Canterbury as the superior bishop in England, including holding authority over the Archbishop of York.

Primer An introductory textbook.

Privateer A person or a ship that was given written permission by the government to attack enemy vessels in a time of war. It was cheaper than retaining a navy to carry out the task.

Privy Chamber The King's immediate, private household, staffed by friends and chosen companions.

Prorogue To suspend a parliamentary session or to discontinue it without formally ending the session.

Purgatory The Catholic Church taught that the souls of the dead went to purgatory to atone for sins committed during life. When their time had been served, the souls were released into heaven. Families of the dead could speed their journey by making offerings to monks and priests to pray for them. This doctrine was rejected by Protestants as having no biblical foundation.

Puritanism The beliefs and practices of more extreme Protestants who were influenced by John Calvin. Puritans aspired to introduce some key features into the Church of England: an emphasis on preaching and private prayer rather than ceremonies and rituals; the removal of all traces of Catholic practice; and the reduction of central control exercised by the Crown and the bishops.

Quasi-royal Having the power but not the rank or title of a king.

Rabbit warrens Enclosed and artificial creations like deer parks, which ensured that the hunting and eating of rabbits was confined mainly to the upper levels of society.

Realpolitik Politics and diplomacy that is based on practical considerations and not on ideology or religion.

Sacramentarian Christians who denied the real presence of Christ in the Eucharist.

Sacraments Rituals given a particularly important place in Catholic practice because they were regarded as capable, in themselves, of contributing to the salvation of all those who were present.

Sea beggars Pirates who made a living capturing shipping in the North Sea; they are associated with the struggle for Dutch independence.

Seminary A theological college primarily aimed at educating for priesthood.

Society of Jesus (Jesuits) St Ignatius Loyola founded the Society of Jesus in 1534, originally to do missionary work in Jerusalem but the Jesuits were soon directed to focus on stopping the spread of Protestantism in Europe.

Sola fide The Protestant doctrine of justification by faith alone, first taught by Martin Luther, and which contradicted orthodox Catholic teaching that it was necessary to perform good works in order to achieve salvation.

Statute of Uses A Use was a legal arrangement used by the gentry and nobility to give property to their heirs without paying feudal dues. In 1536 Cromwell enacted a law against them which landowners resented; it was repealed in 1540.

Sterling English currency that took its name from the sterling silver content.

Surplice A white gown that reached down to the ground, with wide sleeves.

Tercios A mixed infantry formation of 3,000 professional soldiers (pikemen and musketeers).

The 'assembled commons' Mainly farmers, labourers and tradesmen, but joined by members of the local clergy as well as monks from the threatened abbeys.

Vagabond A wanderer who has no fixed home, usually because he is driven from place to place looking for work.

Veneration A special act often associated with the honouring of a saint in the Catholic Church.

Vernacular The native language.

Wakefield plot In 1541 a small group of conservative gentry and clergy in the Wakefield area planned to murder Archbishop Holgate, the President of the Council of the North, and seize Pontefract Castle. However, the conspirators failed to gain popular support and were quickly rounded up. About 15 of them were executed and about 50 others fined or imprisoned. Thereafter the north remained quiet until 1568.

Walloon Refers to region in the south of what is now Belgium; also the language spoken by many in that region.

Yeomen A class of prosperous peasants who worked their land themselves so were not gentleman. They often took on parish offices and had some education.

Index